PRIME
TIME

WHO NEEDS THIS BOOK?

Answer: *Any adult woman* who is interested in preventing illness and maintaining the highest level of health possible through practical self-help and a personalized, health-oriented medical program.

HAVE YOU EVER ASKED YOURSELF . . .

What really makes up a healthy diet? Do I need extra vitamin and mineral supplements?

What is osteoporosis? Should I be concerned even if I am young and healthy?

Why do I have so much trouble losing weight at this point in my life? Is there a diet that will really work?

How can I eat out and have fun while maintaining a healthful diet program?

Is exercise really necessary at my age? How do I start a program if this is new to me, and which exercises are the best?

Why should I have an annual medical exam? What should I expect in a good, health-oriented medical exam?

How often do I need Pap smears and mammograms? Is there any potential harm in having a mammogram?

What can I expect when I go through menopause, and what help is available?

Would hormone therapy be helpful for me? Are there any side effects?

How can I reduce my chances of getting breast cancer and other forms of cancer?

What should I know about skin care, sunscreens, and plastic surgery?

How can I know if I am having a mid-life crisis? What are the signs and symptoms of depression and anxiety? Where can I get help?

How do I deal with all the changes going on in my life?

In this book you will find the answers to these questions and much, much more. By putting into practice the advice given here, by taking action through self-help and proper medical care, you may very well find that you function more effectively in almost every area of your life.

A Complete
Health Guide
for Women
35 to 65

PRIME TIME

Dr. Sharon Sneed
Dr. David Sneed

WORD PUBLISHING
Dallas · London · Sydney · Singapore

PRIME TIME: A COMPLETE HEALTH GUIDE FOR WOMEN 35 TO 65

Library of Congress Cataloging-in-Publication Data

Sneed, Sharon, 1953–
    Prime time : a complete health guide for women 35 to 65 / Sharon
Sneed and David Sneed.
      p. cm.
    Bibliography: p.
    Includes index.
    ISBN 0-8499-0716-0
    1. Middle aged women—Health and hygiene.   I. Sneed, David, 1953–
    II. Title.
RA778.S633   1989
613'.04244—dc19   89-5463
                                            CIP

Printed in the United States of America

9 8 0 1 2 3 9 MP 9 8 7 6 5 4 3 2 1

To our mothers
Frances Ann Sneed
and
Ernestine Berry Meadows
for their unfailing love and understanding

ABOUT THE AUTHORS

Drs. David and Sharon Sneed are experts in preventive health issues and place special emphasis on achieving a healthy lifestyle within the family unit. Sharon, as a Ph.D. nutritionist, and David, as a family physician with a busy clinic in Austin, Texas, combine their expertise to provide factual, up-to-date, and practical health advice for their readers. Married for fourteen years and parents of three children, Sharon and David can relate to and understand the health problems facing you and your family.

Sharon Sneed is a practicing nutrition consultant in Austin, Texas. She has earned two postgraduate degrees in nutrition, including a Ph.D. from Texas Woman's University in 1979. Following her graduate school work, she was accepted as a *National Institute of Health Postdoctoral Fellow* at the University of California at Berkeley. She has taught at several universities, including the *Medical University of South Carolina*. Since 1983, Dr. Sneed has been involved primarily with private practice nutrition and dietetics. She has helped thousands of patients with various health problems associated with improper diet. She is a registered dietitian (R.D.) with the American Dietetic Association, as well as a licensed dietitian (L.D.) in the state of Texas.

Dr. Sharon Sneed has more than a dozen lay and professional publications to her credit. Most recently, she has co-authored the book *PMS: What It Is and What You Can Do About It* (Baker Book House, 1988) with Joe McIlhaney, Jr., M.D. She continues to be a popular radio and television talk-show guest throughout the country, as well as a seminar speaker in the fields of women's health, nutrition, and the preventive concept of health care.

David Sneed is a family physician with a large medical practice in Austin, Texas. After graduating from the Texas College of Osteopathic Medicine in 1979, he completed a three-year family practice residency in Charleston, South Carolina. David is a *Fellow of the American Academy of Family Physicians (AAFP)* and a *Diplomate of the American Board of Family Practice*. He is an active member of his local medical society, the Texas Academy of Family Physicians, as well as state and national medical organizations.

CONTENTS

Section IV: Disease Prevention

Are You Satisfied with Life?
Do You Have Problems with Self-Esteem?
Some Answers
Summary

Section VI: Summing It Up

LIST OF TABLES

ACKNOWLEDGMENTS

This book was possible because of the understanding and support of many fine people. Our first acknowledgment goes to our wonderful children, Shannon, Lauren, and Jonathan, who had to "make their own fun" for several months while we were working on the manuscript.

Professionally, we would like to thank our editor, Beverly Phillips, who is a true master of her trade. Her thoughtful input into this book has been invaluable. We would also like to thank Pat Cavalier of Austin, Texas, for reading the manuscript and for providing insightful information about its content and organization. We deeply thank Jim Kreisle Jr., M.D., a psychiatrist in Austin, for his professional evaluation and suggestions in the content of Section V (Your Inner Self). We would also like to thank our special friends for their support, including Dr. Greg and Carolyn Marchand, Dr. Joe McIlhaney, and Ann Rinehart.

SECTION I

An Introduction

CHAPTER 1

35 and Counting— What's Happening to Me?

Have you ever wondered whether life really does go by faster as we get older? A week seems almost interminable to a child. And, yet, sometimes it seems that we have just gotten the Christmas decorations put away when we find ourselves unwrapping them again and reading the crumpled pieces of last year's newspapers. Another year has gone by, another birthday has passed, and we are another year older in what seems to be the flash of an eye. Wow! Who stepped on the accelerator?

For most of you, the past 10 to 30 years have been spent taking care of others—pregnancies, raising the children, working on a career, managing your home, planning other people's schedules, cooking meals, and trying to have some time of your own.

As the biological clock relentlessly ticks, you may be finding that you just can't continue to take your body and health for granted anymore. Things are happening differently now. There may be some new aches and pains. Those winter colds seem to last longer. Your eyesight may be changing, and you may be asking yourself, "When did I get this new wrinkle?" You are feeling the need to take action, and that is what this book is all about. *We provide the information; you provide the action.*

This book is designed to be a self-help tool that will enable you to achieve your own best level of health and fitness.

THE PERFECT AGE

When should a woman begin a serious health program geared at disease prevention? The simple answer is that *it is never too early or too late to take good care of yourself.* However, 35 to 40 is the absolute

3

optimum age to begin since the body is in the early phases of certain physiological changes which can be forestalled with appropriate preventive measures. But, if you are currently in your 40s, 50s, 60s, or beyond, it is also a great time to begin healthier habits. Never say "it's too late for me" or "I'm young and don't have to worry about those things yet." The fact is—this program is for all adult women who want to look and feel their very best. Whatever age you are right now, it is the right time to begin your own personal, health-oriented medical program.

IT TAKES LESS TIME THAN YOU THINK

Once you have the right information for your new, healthier lifestyle, you must then carve time out of what may be a very busy schedule to accomplish these new goals. And if you think that you don't have time for this new program, consider this question. When was the last time you watched a two-hour television program? In slightly more time than this, spread out over the entire week, you could have completed your entire exercise program and had time left over to prepare a few healthy snacks and to do some meal planning. *Good health habits do not have to monopolize your time or your money.* In fact, they will increase your time, through increased energy levels and productivity, and will eventually save you money by lessened expenditures on medical bills and time lost from work.

We talk to hundreds of new patients each year who must make significant changes in their health habits. And we know for a fact that in order to accomplish this goal, you must prioritize your activities, and your commitment to improved health and wellness must be somewhere near the top of the list from now on. There are a million excuses not to practice the health tips in this book if they are not a top priority. But, remember this, you will be rewarded for that effort and commitment many times over with good health and increased energy.

IT'S HIGH TIME FOR PRIME TIME

Prime time means the best time. And life after 35 can indeed be your best time if you combine the maturity of adulthood with the good health of youth. In order to achieve these results, you must put forth a little effort to prevent disease from occurring. This book helps you to do just that.

One hundred years ago, women didn't have to worry about their health past age 35 to 40; many of them did not even live that long.

Today age 40 is a mere milestone on the way to 80 and beyond. And, consider this. Most of you will live one-third to one-half of your life after menopause. And here's the good news—you can make these years the best part of your entire life.

We are not suggesting that all disease can be prevented. Sometimes, things just happen, even if you are making all the right choices. Good health should certainly be thought of as a blessing rather than a guarantee. But as practicing health professionals, we have seen clear evidence that for those persons who are willing to invest a relatively small amount of time and energy in the preventive-medicine concept for health care, the returns are great in terms of good health, vitality, and new zest for living.

PREVENTIVE HEALTH CARE

What is the preventive health-care concept? Quite simply, the preventive-medicine concept in health care means that through methods such as those presented in this book and outlined below, you will improve your ability to forestall or even avoid illness, giving you many more years of enjoyable health than you might have had otherwise. The basic components of preventive health care include:

1. Using self-help methods (improved diet, exercise and fitness).

2. Obtaining regular medical checkups oriented toward disease prevention (i.e., go see your doctor on a prescribed schedule, not just when you are acutely ill).

3. Following recommended advice (i.e., use of sunscreens, seatbelts, certain vitamin/mineral supplements, etc.).

4. Avoiding unhealthy habits (tobacco, drug and alcohol abuse).

5. Promoting good mental health (get help when you need it).

LET'S GET REAL

One week before this manuscript was finished, a 56-year-old woman was referred to our office for a diabetic consultation. From the moment she sat down, her manner was defensive, skeptical, reluctant, and uncooperative. Frankly, we wondered why she had come in at all.

During the consultation session, it became obvious that on several previous occasions this patient had been through a sub-standard, diabetic-diet hospital lecture—one of those sessions in which you are expected to change your whole way of life based on a one-hour presentation. In her own words, ". . . then an 18-year-old came in and proceeded to tell me how I could make special requests of the chef at a Denny's restaurant when I'm out shopping. She had no concept of what she was really asking me to do and whether or not it would fit my own way of life. It was ridiculous to try to change my life with such superficial and unrealistic information."

Certainly not all hospital diabetic instructions are this brief or rudimentary. However, the moral of this story is: *If any health program does not meet your needs in real-life situations, it simply will not work.*

In this book, we pride ourselves on the fact that most of the information is practical and has a direct bearing on how you should plan your own health-care program. We talk about everything from the best fast food choices to which sunscreen might best meet your needs.

TOO LITTLE, TOO MUCH

The American lifestyle has changed dramatically over the last fifty years and has had a tremendous impact on our health status as a nation. By-in-large, the thing we once had a lot of, physical exercise and activity, we now get too little of. We used to walk everywhere and nothing was automatic. Now there is a machine for everything and our index fingers are in great shape from pushing all the buttons. Just imagine how many calories you would expend filling a washtub with water, hand scrubbing the clothes, wringing and hanging out the clothes, and then emptying that heavy tub full of dirty water.

And, what about our food supply? *What used to be the horn of plenty is now the barrel of excess.* Our foods are cheap, accessible, convenient, and tempting—apparently contributing factors to why over 60 percent of American women want to lose weight.

Nonetheless, our life expectancy rate has continued to climb. However, whereas we once died from lack of antibiotics and surgical/medical techniques, we now die more frequently of cancer and heart disease. *Did you know that 1 out of every 2 Americans die of heart disease and that the percentage of people acquiring cancer is on the rise?* Let's pull ourselves together and adjust our attitudes and lifestyles so that the many abundances and opportunities for good health in our communities are a real plus.

HOW TO USE THIS BOOK

This book is designed to be a health guide for the rest of your life. For that reason it is not necessarily meant to be read straight through.

Various sections may be more meaningful at particular times of your life. You may place special emphasis on different aspects of wellness, based on your current health status or personal genetic tendencies.

For example, if your genetic tendency is toward heart disease, then the section on diet and exercise may be of paramount importance for you personally. However, you will find additional, relevant information in the section discussing hormone replacement therapy. On the other hand, if depression runs in your family and you are fearful that this is becoming a problem for you, then you may first want to read Section V, Your Inner Self, rather than begin with all the facts about estrogen, fitness, and so forth. After this, you can come back to the first three sections and catch up on the physiological aspects of preventive health care, especially since most psychiatrists now recommend a total health program for their patients. So read what interests you most, then the rest. There is something for each of you in every chapter.

Remember—steady, progressive change is more likely to achieve the long-term results you are looking for. Persistent effort and small changes each day add up to major changes at the end of a year, which is about how long you can expect it to take for these healthy alternatives to become a permanent part of your life. The tortoise really does win the race in this case. And, remember this, *your goal should be not to merely live longer, but to live better.*

SECTION II

Strictly Female

CHAPTER 2

What to Expect at Menopause

Menopause is a word of tremendous impact to most women. Sometimes feared and resented as a tangible expression of the aging process, sometimes eagerly anticipated as relief from the possibility of pregnancy and monthly menstruation, menopause is of great interest to most women over 40. Understanding the physical changes that occur at this life stage and having an increased awareness of the potential health problems and their solutions will greatly aid you in this time of physical transition.

You must first understand that *menopause is a life event, not a disease*. It is marked by a woman's last menstrual period, but this cannot be confirmed as being the last period or menopausal period until 12 months after that last period (Barbo, 1987). This "change of life," or the *climacteric*, as it is often called, does not occur suddenly in most cases, but slowly over several years and with a variety of symptoms (see Table 2.1). Bodily changes may be extremely subtle, and up to 10 percent of women will experience no menopausal symptoms other than the cessation of their periods (Barbo, 1987). However, 75 to 80 percent will become aware of these changes and 50 to 65 percent will require some form of therapy (Barbo, 1987). With the trend toward a longer lifespan, most of you reading this book can expect to spend one-third to one-half of your life postmenopausally. And, you will certainly not be alone —by the year 2000, 12 percent of the world's population will be women age 45 and over. For hundreds of years the average age at menopause has not varied, occurring at about age 50, give or take one to two years (Mishell, 1987). What has changed are the large numbers of women who are now affected by menopausal symptoms due to their extended life expectancy. One-third of all females in the Western world

11

Table 2.1. Estrogen Deficiency Timetable

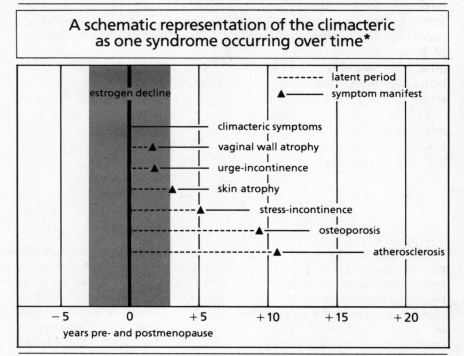

*Reprinted by permission from Wyeth Laboratories information, 1988. Original research from W. Utian, *Menopause in Modern Perspective* (New York: Appleton-Century-Crofts 1980), p. 108.

are between the ages of 44 and 55 years of age (Mishell, 1987). Understanding the changes which are taking place within you and learning ways of preventing health complications associated with these changes will be one of the most important decisions you will ever make.

EVENTS LEADING TO MENOPAUSE

At approximately age 40, the frequency of ovulation begins to decrease, and this is accompanied by a decline in the production of estrogen and other hormones by the ovaries. This decrease in function varies with the individual and is not always in a steady digression, but it does lead to a sequential loss of function in a predictable manner.

Throughout your young adult life, your ovaries have managed a series of complex hormone and bodily functions designed to optimize the development and fertilization of an ovum, implantation of the fertilized egg, and the support of an early pregnancy. The years before menopause span this transition period of diminishing ovarian function. The *perimenopause*, as this time is called between the ages of 40 and 50, is usually from 2 to 8 years in length and is marked by great hormonal and menstrual variability. Finally and inevitably, the hormone levels subside to a point at which you no longer have menstrual periods.

Life does not end at menopause, and for some it is a time of great awakening. With another 30 to 40 years of prime time ahead of you, it is to your greatest advantage to adopt healthy lifestyle practices which will help you enjoy this time to its fullest measure.

PREMATURE MENOPAUSE

Premature menopause is the loss of menstrual function before age 40 (Barbo, 1987). This is an unusual situation occurring in less than one percent of women. Although the exact cause is usually unknown, early menopause can signal certain serious medical conditions and needs to be carefully evaluated.

Any woman under 40 with the symptoms of menopause (no menses for 12 months and symptoms of estrogen loss) needs a thorough medical examination. This would include a complete history and physical and tests of certain hormone levels. Elevated levels of follicle-stimulating hormone (FSH) and lutenizing hormone (LH) along with low levels of estradiol (your body's main estrogen) are diagnostic in this situation.

Aggressive hormone replacement therapy is indicated in most cases of premature menopause and in young women who undergo surgical removal of their ovaries. This will help control the symptoms of sudden estrogen loss and prevent premature aging processes, including osteoporosis and coronary heart disease.

THE EFFECTS OF MENOPAUSE

The effects of menopause can be summarized in just one word— *change*. For three or more decades your body has probably been running smoothly with very little alteration in the regular rhythm of your monthly cycle. Now, either gradually or quite suddenly, it seems as if everything is different.

Estrogen, like most hormones, has a very specific function within the body and acts on specific target tissues. Consequently, these estrogen-sensitive tissues can be the first casualties related to the hormonal changes of menopause. An overview of the symptoms commonly seen and related to the loss of estrogen include:

1. alterations in the menstrual cycle
2. hot flushes and sweating
3. breakdown of tissue strength
4. emotional symptoms
5. other nonspecific complaints

Menstrual Changes

Variation in the menstrual cycle is usually the first evidence of the hormone changes taking place prior to menopause. While this can occur in the mid 30s, usually this does not happen until after age 45. As estrogen levels decline, your cycle develops an irregularity and unpredictability that can be worrisome after all those years of regular menstrual periods. Eventually a period or two is skipped, and ultimately the periods disappear completely.

The extent to which your hormone levels will fall and to what degree you will experience symptoms are highly variable within individuals. We have all known women who upon entering menopause just stopped having periods and really never looked back. However, the majority of women (50 to 60 percent) do need help at this time, and statistically, you may be one of them if you have not already been through menopause.

It is important to remember that ovulation can still occur even though your periods become irregular. Therefore, if you want to prevent pregnancy, *birth control is still required*. For more extensive information about contraception after 40 see pp. 47–50. It suffices to say that unless you use some permanent means of birth control, such as a vasectomy for your husband or a tubal ligation for yourself, then pregnancy remains a very real possibility until after menopause. Other preferred contraceptive possibilities after age 40 include the barrier methods (i.e., diaphragm, foam and condoms, sponge).

If you are older than 45 and have not had a period for one year, then there is a greater than 90 percent probability that you have experienced menopause already (S. Rubin, 1987). This is important to note because any vaginal bleeding after this time is considered abnormal and needs to be evaluated by your physician. About 10 percent of women will have postmenopausal bleeding and, more importantly, of those women, about 20 percent will have a malignancy as the reason for their bleeding (S. Rubin, 1987). As you get older, the risk of malignancy increases; therefore, the further away from menopause you get, the more seriously any vaginal bleeding should be considered.

The Hot Flush

This is the most common problem experienced by women in the perimenopausal years. Sometimes called a *hot flash*, this uncomfortable sensation is usually sudden, repetitive, often irritating, but not dangerous or life-threatening. About 75 percent of postmenopausal women will have hot flushes. For most of them, these annoying sensations will begin to decline four to six years after menopause (Odom and Carr, 1987).

The flushes are extremely unpredictable, occurring with varying frequency, intensity, and duration. They are usually described as a sudden, uncomfortable feeling of intense warmth in the face, neck, and chest. This is accompanied by varying degrees of perspiration, from moist palms to profuse sweating that may necessitate a change of clothing (Barbo, 1987).

Hot flushes most commonly occur at night and may be accompanied by several other symptoms, including heart palpitations, headache, nausea, anxiety, irritability, and sleep disturbances. Nighttime hot flushes may not always cause a person to awake but frequently cause significant changes in the sleep pattern, which, in turn, may lead to irritability and fatigue. This is probably one of the major reasons that estrogen therapy improves psychological well-being in many women.

The cause of hot flushes is clear—a reduction in the circulating levels of estrogen and an increase in the levels of lutenizing hormone (LH). Exactly why these changes cause the flushes is much less clear. During these episodes, in which as many as 50 percent of women will have visible flushing, there is a definite increase in skin temperature, heart rate, and oxygen consumption (Barbo, 1987). Ambient temperature also seems to play a role in the frequency and severity of the flushes. Women are more likely to experience hot flushes in the summer or in a warmer climate than in cooler climates.

Regardless of the exact physiologic mechanism involved in hot flushes, symptomatic relief is readily obtainable. Estrogen therapy has proven to be the most effective means of controlling these uncomfortable sensations. The exact effective dose of estrogen varies from woman to woman and may change as she proceeds through her menopausal years.

Breast Changes

The breast for many women represents the most obvious evidence of their feminine form. As an estrogen-sensitive tissue, your breasts will react to reduced hormone levels. These changes consist of loss of glandular breast tissue and increasing amounts of fibrous tissue. There may be some loss of turgor, form, and fullness occurring gradually after menopause.

Some problems you may have experienced prior to menopause may now disappear. With reduced hormone levels, premenstrual breast discomfort may now subside. Fibrocystic breast changes frequently regress, and for many women, these unpleasant problems completely resolve at menopause.

Estrogen replacement therapy does affect the breasts. Excessive doses may cause discomfort and fullness. However, estrogen therapy may also delay the tissue changes which occur in the breasts at menopause. A careful examination of the breasts prior to any hormone therapy is essential, and regular exams by your physician should continue throughout your life.

A careful breast examination program is important because 80 percent of breast cancers occur after age 40. This program includes regular exams by your doctor, careful self-breast examination, and appropriate use of screening mammograms to detect early disease. Although controversial at one time, numerous careful studies have shown that *estrogen therapy does not cause breast cancer*. This is indeed good news in light of the many beneficial effects that estrogen can have on the health and well-being of the menopausal woman. In fact, a large study by the Center for Disease Control reported a reduction of breast cancer in women who took birth-control pills. We will discuss breast cancer at length in a separate chapter.

The Reproductive Organs

The female reproductive organs are certainly affected by the declining levels of estrogen in the postmenopausal period. Specifically the vulva, vagina, cervix, uterus, fallopian tubes, and ovaries are all to one degree or another affected by menopause. Proper treatment of estrogen loss can reduce or prevent symptoms of itching, dryness, painful sexual intercourse, and actual shrinkage of these reproductive organs.

The *vulva* begins to change as hormone levels fall. This tissue, which is around and just outside the vagina, will decrease in size, the pubic hair will decrease, and the skin will become thinner. Thinning of the skin makes it more susceptible to trauma. Intense itching is common, especially in fair-skinned women (Barbo, 1987). Unfortunately, the vulva does not respond well to estrogen therapy, either oral supplement or topical ointment. However, the dryness and itching can be significantly reduced with topical testosterone ointment.

Annual inspection of the vulva and vagina is still important, even in women who have had a hysterectomy. Any abnormal skin lesions can be easily biopsied in your doctor's office. Cancers of the vulva and vagina can be much more easily treated if diagnosed at an early stage.

The *vagina* differs significantly from the vulva in that it is highly responsive to estrogen stimulation. At menopause the lining of the vagina begins to thin and the acid content of the vaginal secretions begins to change, allowing bacterial organisms not usually found in the vagina to multiply. Without hormonal supplementation, these changes can lead to an inflammation of the vagina with symptoms of dryness, burning, itching, abnormal discharge, painful sex, and bleeding. If this is the case, symptoms can be so severe that normal sexual relations cannot be maintained.

For women with very mild symptoms, the use of a vaginal lubricant may be all that is needed. More severe symptoms require estrogen therapy. Estrogen causes the vagina to become more like it was before menopause. With estrogen, the blood supply to the vagina increases by about 50 percent, and the vaginal secretions become more normal in content and volume. With 50 percent of women over 50 years of age and 60 percent of women over 60 having problems with vaginal lubrication, estrogen therapy to correct this problem and avoid sexual dysfunction after menopause is very important. Don't be afraid or reluctant to tell your doctor about painful sexual relations. Otherwise, he or she may wrongly assume by your silence that everything is as it should be. This would be unfortunate, perhaps even tragic, in light of the excellent results which can be achieved with estrogen therapy.

Another major problem occurring during menopause involves the loss of tissue support in the pelvis. Vaginal relaxation and even prolapse (falling out) of the genital tract can sometimes occur. This problem is due primarily to the number of children a woman has had and the difficulty of the deliveries. Estrogen therapy will not improve the pelvic floor tone, and in severe cases surgical correction may be the only treatment available.

The *cervix* and *uterus* also undergo tissue change after menopause. The cervix regresses somewhat in size, and the cervical opening becomes smaller. The uterus becomes much smaller in size, and fibroid tumors of the uterus also shrink, though they will not entirely disappear. Any growth of the uterus or a fibroid should be investigated for possible malignant change. Likewise, any abnormal or postmenopausal bleeding should prompt an investigation for possible cancer.

The ovaries and fallopian tubes. Even before menopause, the production of estrogen by the *ovaries* begins to decline. Eventually, this estrogen production ceases and the ovary itself decreases in size. After menopause, your doctor should not be able to feel your ovary when he does a pelvic exam. Annual pelvic exams are important to check for enlargement of the ovaries, which could be a sign of malignant change. A gradual reduction in size of the *fallopian tubes* also takes place at menopause.

The Urinary Tract

The urinary tract undergoes major changes in the postmenopausal years, a process which results in a decreased ability to control the urine and may eventually lead to urinary incontinence. Incontinence is an all too common occurrence in women (12 to 40 percent) and can be a frustrating problem to deal with (Karafin and Coll, 1987). One of the main reasons for incontinence is that the lower urinary tract (urethra) and the reproductive tract (vagina/vulva) are very similar types of body tissue. For this reason the urethra, the tube which drains the bladder, is affected just like the vagina during menopause. The urethra is extremely estrogen-sensitive and with hormone decline will undergo atrophy of its mucosal lining. Along with these urethral changes are symptoms of painful urination, urinary frequency, and urgency to void. These complaints are known as the *urethral syndrome* (Barbo, 1987).

With development of the urethral syndrome, a woman loses one-third of her ability to maintain urine control (Mishell, 1987). Estrogen therapy, either topical or oral, can be effective in alleviating the urethral syndrome and its accompanying adverse effect on bladder control.

Loss of tissue support for the pelvic organs occurs frequently after menopause due to a variety of factors. The development of a *dropped bladder* or *cystocoel* results in another major reason for decreased bladder control. As the area of the bladder that connects to the urethra drops down, it loses the beneficial intra-abdominal pressure which helps maintain bladder control. This is not under estrogen control, but as we mentioned earlier, it is due to multiple factors in a woman's life and can be corrected surgically if severe.

The third factor involved in urinary incontinence is the relaxation of muscle around the urethra itself. This is also related to the generalized pelvic relaxation which occurs primarily in menopausal women who have had several children (Barbo, 1987). A surgical procedure is available to tighten these muscles and help regain bladder control.

In light of these facts, it is little wonder that many menopausal women have problems to some degree with urinary incontinence. Estrogen replacement therapy can improve urethral function by 30 percent and may significantly help with this embarrassing and troublesome problem.

The Skin and Hair

One of the largest organs of the body, the skin, is the focus of attention for millions of women attempting to maintain their youthful appearance. After menopause, the skin is subject to increasing dryness, wrinkles, sagging, pigmentation changes, thinning of scalp hair, and increased amounts of facial hair. These effects are not just due to "aging," but are related to the hormonal changes of menopause. However, the rest of the health-oriented program presented in this book will help you to slow the effects of aging and make correction of the hormone problems even easier.

Healthier appearing skin is almost always possible to achieve and usually within a short period of time on estrogen therapy (Mishell, 1987). The reason for this is that the skin has numerous estrogen receptors, mostly in the face, with lower concentrations in the skin of the breast and thighs (Barbo, 1987). As estrogen decreases, the skin becomes thinner, more easily traumatized, and impaired microcirculation develops, resulting in decreased blood flow to the skin.

The skin is richly supplied with blood vessels and depends on good circulation for healthy function. With age the skin capillaries decrease and the result is thinning of the skin, loss of tissue strength, and decreased turgor. Deterioration of the skin's elastic network also occurs, allowing sagging and wrinkling. Estrogen enhances the skin's blood supply by increasing the number of capillaries and improving the skin's strength by increasing the collagen fibers in the skin itself. Smoking, on the other hand, is highly destructive to the microcirculation of the skin both directly and indirectly, first by reducing estrogen levels and second by hastening the onset of menopause.

In the skin, collagen accounts for 97.5 percent of the fibrous protein present. After menopause, skin collagen decreases about 2.1 percent per year, with most of the decline occurring in the first 10 to 15 postmenopausal years (Mishell, 1987). Studies have shown that *estrogen therapy can stabilize collagen loss and even increase skin collagen levels.* In one group of postmenopausal women, skin collagen levels were restored to the same levels as that of premenopausal women after only six months of therapy. All the collagen-enriched make-up in the world can't do that for you! The skin "aging" effects of estrogen loss are increased by excessive exposure to the harmful ultraviolet rays of the sun. These harmful effects can be substantially reduced by avoiding sunburn, using hats and loose clothing to cover up with, and by using sunscreen preparations (PABA 15 or greater).

SKIN CARE RECOMMENDATIONS

- Proper nutrition—eat a proper diet as described elsewhere in this book.
- Use moisturizing lotions liberally to prevent dryness.
- Avoid excessive exposure to sunlight and use sunscreens.
- Avoid smoking.
- Begin estrogen replacement therapy after menopause.

- Have a careful annual inspection of the skin for disease.

- Exercise regularly to improve your circulation.

- Get an adequate amount of rest.

Along with changes in the skin come changes in the hair. Thinning of the scalp and pubic hair may occur after menopause. There is a great deal of excitement about the use of a newly released medication to help control or even restore hair loss. Used mainly by balding men, *minoxidil* (or *Rogaine* as it is marketed) is a prescription medication which is applied to the scalp to slow or stop hair loss. In some cases it actually increases the numbers of scalp hair. This medication appears to be helpful in women with excessive hair loss as well. Since this is a prescription medication, you will need to ask your physician for more information.

Hirsutism, or excessive hair growth, is a problem for some post-menopausal women who note an abnormal increase in the amount of facial hair. This development is a result of the change in ovarian function. The ovary produces female (estrogen) and male (testosterone) hormones. Around menopause, as the estrogen production decreases, the testosterone effects become more pronounced. This problem could be a normal functional response by the ovary, but can sometimes indicate a pathologic problem of the ovary or adrenal gland. In most cases, treatment of hirsutism is not necessary, but your physician should first rule out an underlying pathologic condition and then decide whether or not to treat the problem.

If treatment of excessive hair growth is desired, then efforts should be directed at the source of the problem. The ovary is the major source of increased testosterone in hirsute women (Speroff et al., 1983). Adrenal gland problems are very uncommon and can be checked with a few laboratory tests. Suppression of the ovary for most women over 40 is best accomplished with progesterone, either taken daily by mouth or injected once every three months. Unfortunately, the response to treatment is slow, requiring six to twelve months of continuous therapy before decreased hair growth is noted. Shaving, waxing, depilatories, and pulling out the hair with tweezers do not alter the hair growth significantly. Only electrolysis, which destroys the root of the hair, results in permanent removal of unwanted hair. The optimum treatment for hirsutism is the combined use of ovary-suppressing medication with electrolysis six months after starting therapy (Speroff et al., 1983). Severe hirsutism which is unresponsive to the usual treatment methods is a very reasonable indication for hysterectomy and bilateral removal of the tubes and ovaries.

CHAPTER 3

Hormone Therapy in Menopause

Every woman over the age of 40 should have a plan for the kind of treatment she will receive during menopause. Menopause is a reality that all women will eventually experience. To be unprepared or ill-informed of its consequences and potential treatment could significantly diminish the quality of as much as one-third of your life and possibly even shorten your life. Hopefully, you are having annual exams with your doctor; these are ideal opportunities to formulate objectives for your health care beyond menopause and discuss plans for hormone therapy. At a recent conference we attended on women's health issues, the importance of estrogen replacement after menopause was emphasized. Unless you have definite reasons not to take estrogen, *all postmenopausal women should receive estrogen replacement.* If your present physician doesn't agree, seek a second opinion.

In the past, the use of estrogen replacement in menopause has been controversial. This earlier controversy may explain why some women and even some physicians are still reluctant to use estrogen therapy. Estrogen was initially hailed as a panacea for all the ills of the post-menopausal woman. What could be simpler? If a woman lacks estrogen, just give her some. Unfortunately, it's not quite that easy, and we have now learned who should and who should not receive estrogen replacement. In the mid 1970s the use of estrogen was challenged as reports of increased uterine cancer in women taking estrogen were brought to light. These reports and other concerns initially created confusion and skepticism regarding postmenopause hormone therapy.

Numerous studies have now clearly documented the advantages of hormone replacement. Equally important, there is now a much better understanding of the potential risks associated with hormone therapy

21

and how to minimize the risks and potential complications. Most of you will live one-third of your life after menopause, and 75 percent of you will experience symptoms related to menopause (Huppert, 1987). A complete and careful understanding of hormone replacement therapy will allow you and your physician to make sound choices regarding your health care.

THE BENEFICIAL EFFECTS OF HORMONE THERAPY

Control of Hot Flushes

Of all the symptoms associated with the menopause syndrome, the hot flush is the one most frequently mentioned by women. Perhaps this is because so many women experience this uncomfortable sensation. As many as 82 percent of women report hot flush symptoms lasting intermittently for longer than one year, and 25 to 85 percent continue to have hot flushes for more than five years before these symptoms finally fade away (Huppert, 1987).

Estrogen is the most specific and effective treatment for control of hot flush symptoms. Almost all women can experience relief with therapy. Clinical experience has shown that a dose of .625 to 2.5 mg of Premarin daily is necessary to relieve hot flushes in most women (Mishell, 1987). This is a higher dose of estrogen than is needed to relieve the symptoms of vaginal tissue change and bone loss.

If you cannot take estrogen, then progesterone therapy may provide some relief from the hot flushes. While not quite as effective as estrogen therapy, progesterone has been shown to result in a 60 to 75 percent reduction of hot flush episodes (Mishell, 1987). The recommended doses of progesterone for the treatment of hot flushes is 100 to 150 mg of DepoProvera injected monthly or 10 mg of Provera taken orally every day (Mishell, 1987). Unfortunately, progesterone therapy without estrogen is associated with 25 to 50 percent incidence of abnormal bleeding. This problem makes its use more attractive to women who have had a hysterectomy or who have specific contraindications to estrogen therapy. In most cases we recommend that estrogen therapy also include progesterone for at least part of the month. Although it is not proven, it seems probable that this combination of progesterone and estrogen has an additive effect in relieving hot flushes.

There are other medications which have proven useful in reducing the incidence and severity of hot flushes. *Clonidine*, also known as *Catapres*, is an anti-hypertensive medication which has proven valuable in treating hot flushes. However, in women beginning this medication with normal blood pressure, there can be a high incidence of bothersome side effects, especially dizziness. Perhaps if a woman had hypertension, which is a relative contraindication to the use of estrogen, then clonidine could be used to control both blood pressure and the hot flushes. *Bellergal* is a combination medication which has proven effective in reducing hot flushes. This twice-a-day medication appears to be the least effective of the treatments and has the greatest potential for unwanted side effects.

Relief of hot flushes is apparently not the only benefit of treating the vasomotor symptoms of menopause. *Women being treated for hot flushes with estrogen therapy show significant decreases in insomnia, anxiety, irritability, and show improvement of memory as well.* It is believed that the relief of hot flushes during sleep improves the quality of sleep and prevents the adverse effects of chronic sleep disturbance. Estrogen therapy has been found to help women fall asleep faster and also increases rapid eye movement (REM) sleep (Mishell, 1987). This treatment really makes more sense than most sedatives and sleeping pills which are used to treat insomnia. The sleeping pills can be addictive and provide no other health benefits.

Prevention and Treatment of Genitourinary Atrophy

One of the major effects of menopausal estrogen loss is atrophy (wasting away) of the estrogen-sensitive tissues of the genitourinary tract. Specifically, the vagina and urethra are primarily affected by this hormonal decline. Symptoms include vaginal dryness, itching, and burning. Abnormal discharge and abnormal bleeding may occur. These symptoms can lead to a problem of painful intercourse if left untreated. Urinary urgency, frequency of urination, pain, and incontinence also can result from estrogen loss (Huppert, 1987).

The consequences of genitourinary atrophy when interfering with sexual performance may lead to a decreased sexual desire, anxiety, and poor self-esteem (Mishell, 1987). Ultimately this problem can adversely affect the sexual performance of your husband and lead to even further dysfunction within your relationship. These symptoms can be successfully treated in most cases with estrogen therapy, and if treatment is begun soon after menopause, they can often be avoided entirely.

Low doses of estrogen can effectively prevent and treat problems associated with tissue atrophy. Oral doses of .3 to .625 mg daily of Premarin will usually resolve all vaginal symptoms (Mishell, 1987). The use of estrogen creams applied in the vagina is also effective, but there is really no additional benefit in using a vaginal medication instead of oral estrogen (Huppert, 1987). The vaginal estrogen is absorbed into the circulatory system in a manner similar to oral estrogen and has the same potential side effects as the oral form. The only additional benefit that a vaginal cream has is that it may act as a lubricant as well. If only symptoms of vaginal atrophy are being treated, relief can be expected after two to twelve weeks of daily estrogen therapy. Once these symptoms are controlled, the dosage of medication can be reduced by one-half or to only two to three times per week for maintenance therapy (Mishell, 1987).

Estrogen therapy is also highly effective in treating postmenopausal stress urinary incontinence (leaking urine when you laugh or sneeze) and the urethral syndrome. Within six weeks of therapy, improvement can be noted in urinary incontinence (Mishell, 1987). The estrogen dosage and length of treatment is a little greater than that for purely vaginal symptoms. Daily doses of 1.25 mg Premarin or 2 grams (half an applicator full) of vaginal Premarin cream should be used for two to three months and then reduced by half thereafter (Mishell, 1987). *More than 50 percent of women with the annoying symptoms of stress urinary incontinence respond favorably to estrogen therapy.*

The urethral syndrome is a combination of symptoms including urgency, frequency, and painful urination in the absence of a urinary tract infection (Mishell, 1987). After an infection has been ruled out, daily treatment with 1.25 mg Premarin or one half applicator of vaginal Premarin cream for two to three weeks will be effective. When the symptoms have resolved, the dosage can usually be reduced by half, but the estrogen must be used indefinitely. If estrogen therapy alone is unsuccessful, periodic urethral dilation may be needed in addition to the estrogen.

Prevention of Osteoporosis

From the standpoint of potential disability and even death, prevention of osteoporosis is certainly one of the most significant indications for estrogen therapy in postmenopausal women. With over 200,000 hip fractures annually and 15 to 20 percent of those directly leading to an individual's death, osteoporosis is of major concern. *Estrogen loss is the most significant cause of the decrease in bone mass.* When estrogen therapy is used for the prevention of osteoporosis, it does not take weeks or months, but years of treatment.

Although the precise mechanism by which estrogen therapy prevents bone loss is unclear, it is obvious that estrogen therapy does prevent bone loss and subsequent fractures (Huppert, 1987). The sooner therapy is begun after menopause, the better, as over 50 percent of the total bone mass may be lost in the first seven years of menopause (Odom and Carr, 1987).

It has been established that .625 mg of Premarin is the ideal daily dosage to prevent bone loss in all women (Mishell, 1987). The addition

of progesterone for at least 10 to 14 days of the month appears to enhance the effects of estrogen therapy in preventing bone loss (Huppert,
1987). *With estrogen, proper diet and exercise, the optimum regimen for
prevention of osteoporosis can be achieved.*

In light of the fact that all women are at some risk for the development of osteoporosis and the evidence of numerous other beneficial
effects of estrogen therapy, *we recommend that all menopausal women
receive estrogen unless there is a major contraindication.* (See p. 29–30
for more on contraindications.) The recommended therapy would be
a minimum of .625 mg Premarin daily and 10 mg Provera for 14 days
each month. Ideally, this plan should be accompanied by a diet with
sufficient calcium as well as adequate physical exercise. *Treatment
should be started within three years of menopause and continued, if
possible, for life.* The prevention of osteoporosis is discussed in greater
detail in chapter 17.

Improved Well-Being

Menopause is an important milestone in the life of most women. It
is important to remember that *change for most people creates stress.* For
many women, menopause is not only a time of numerous physical
changes, but it is often a time when significant social changes are
occurring as well. It is now clear that changing levels of hormones
may contribute significantly to feelings of depression, irritability, frustration, anxiety, mood swings, sexual dysfunction, and physical complaints such as headache and insomnia (Mishell, 1987).

*Carefully controlled studies have shown that estrogen therapy has bene-
ficial effects on psychological and sexual function.* Women receiving estrogen are reported to have improved memory, decreased irritability,
and a significant reduction in anxiety (Ettinger, 1987). Other studies
have shown estrogen therapy to be successful in improving sexual satisfaction with increased sexual desire, enjoyment, and vaginal lubrication.

Evaluation of psychological symptoms during menopause needs to
begin with a careful history and an effort to distinguish more complicated and serious psychological disorders from the problems associated
with menopause. A history of individual sensitivity to hormones characterized by mood symptoms while taking birth-control pills, postpar-
tum depression, and premenstrual syndrome may indicate a woman
who will be more likely to have menopausal emotional difficulties
(Mishell, 1987). Blood tests of follicle-stimulating hormone (FSH) and
estrogen levels may be helpful, especially in women with psychological
and sexual complaints, but no other evidence of menopause.

Therapy for psychological and sexual difficulties during menopause
is multifaceted. Careful understanding of the nature of the problem

and reassurance that you are not going "crazy" is extremely helpful. Estrogen replacement is the cornerstone of therapy and very likely will improve your overall well-being. *As much as one month of treatment may be needed before changes can be noticed.* For some women who have lost interest in sex, especially those who have had their ovaries removed, the addition of testosterone may be helpful. Both individual and couple counseling can certainly help you develop skills needed to cope with the stresses in your life. Counseling is frequently needed in cases of sexual dysfunction, especially if the problem is a longstanding one. Women's support groups can also play an important role in helping you adjust to the changes which occur at this time in your life.

It is not normal to feel depressed, anxious, and irritable most of the time. Discussion of these problems with your doctor is the first step in getting the help you need. Don't let emotional problems which can be prevented or treated during menopause rob you and those you love of personal happiness and satisfaction.

Prevention of Cardiovascular Disease

Ischemic heart disease is the number one cause of death in the United States. What if estrogen therapy, which is needed by so many women anyway, could also significantly reduce your risk of having a heart attack? Increasing numbers of case studies indicate just that. Estrogen therapy appears to reduce the risk of cardiovascular disease by as much as 50 percent (Ettinger, 1987).

As is the case with many important issues in medicine, this area has not been without controversy. In fact, one issue of the *New England Journal of Medicine* published several articles discussing the use of estrogen and its effects on heart disease. One particular article showed a decreased risk of severe heart disease among estrogen users and another showed exactly the opposite. Now, however, Dr. Leon Speroff, a leading gynecologist, states that *the evidence that estrogen protects postmenopausal women against heart disease is overwhelming.* Perhaps we can help clear up some of the confusion by looking at how estrogen affects various cardiac risk factors.

One of the main benefits of estrogen is its effect on the lipid profile. *Estrogen reduces total cholesterol and LDL (low-density lipoprotein) cholesterol and increases HDL (high-density lipoprotein) cholesterol by as much as 10 percent* (Huppert, 1987). Remember that LDL cholesterol increases and HDL cholesterol decreases your risk of coronary artery disease. A 10 percent reduction may not sound like much, but if your cholesterol is 250 mg/dl and it is reduced by 25 points, then your risk of heart disease should decrease by 50 percent.

Unlike women who take birth-control pills, which contain much greater amounts of hormone, women on estrogen replacement have no apparent increased risk of blood clots and stroke. Likewise, blood pressure seems to be as much as 6 to 7 percent lower in postmenopausal hormone users versus non-users (Mishell, 1987).

Overall, studies have indicated annual death rates three times less in women on estrogen and as much as seven to eight times less if the woman placed on estrogen had previously undergone removal of her ovaries (Bush et al., 1983). From this and other studies, it seems safe to say that at the very least *estrogen replacement therapy probably does not increase your risk of stroke or heart disease and more likely reduces your risk of developing coronary artery disease.* Certain types of progesterone given with estrogen seems to block estrogen's favorable effect on the blood lipids. For this reason we continue to recommend estrogen replacement with medroxy progesterone (Provera), which has no effect on blood lipids, for women with a uterus and estrogen alone for women who have had a hysterectomy.

Protection against cardiovascular disease is the most important benefit of estrogen therapy and adds further weight to the importance of long-term, possibly lifelong, estrogen therapy for women.

THE POTENTIAL RISKS OF ESTROGEN THERAPY

Concern has been raised from time to time regarding the safety of prolonged estrogen therapy. This has been a controversial area—one which continues to merit evaluation by major research centers. Potential adverse effects of estrogen therapy include:

- Endometrial hyperplasia and cancer
- Breast disease
- Gallbladder disease
- Hypertension and vascular disease
- Diabetes mellitus

Endometrial Carcinoma

Development of endometrial hyperplasia and carcinoma is the most significant health risk for women on estrogen therapy (Odom and Carr, 1987). The endometrium is the lining of the uterus, and there appears to be a progression of abnormal growth from adenomatous hyperplasia to early cancer with unopposed estrogen therapy. Unopposed estrogen therapy occurs when estrogen is taken by a woman who still has her uterus and is not also on progesterone (Provera) therapy. Adenomatous hyperplasia, an abnormal buildup of the lining of the uterus, precedes carcinoma in 25 to 30 percent of cases (Speroff et al., 1983). This risk needs to be put into perspective, however, as women not on estrogen have only a risk of endometrial cancer of about one in 1000 women. With unopposed estrogen therapy, this risk may increase two to four times, with the risk in estrogen-treated women being only 4 per 1000 (Mishell, 1987).

It is now clear that the risk of endometrial cancer is related to dose and duration of estrogen therapy and to the use of progesterone to combat the unopposed estrogen effects. Progesterone interferes with the replenishment of estrogen receptors and increases the activity of an enzyme which breaks down estrogen (Huppert, 1987). By these methods, the addition of Provera to the monthly cycle of estrogen can reduce the risk of adenomatous hyperplasia and subsequent endometrial carcinoma to almost zero (Huppert, 1987). In women who do develop endometrial cancer while on estrogen, the disease appears to be much less invasive than in women who have never taken estrogen (Odom and Carr, 1987).

Combining progesterone with estrogen in hormone replacement therapy virtually eliminates the threat of endometrial cancer for postmenopausal women.

Breast Cancer

The effect of estrogen therapy on the development of breast cancer remains controversial. Some studies have shown no association at all, while others indicate a small increased risk after prolonged therapy (Huppert, 1987). Progesterone in combination with estrogen has been suggested as a way to reduce this possible risk in a similar way as it is recommended to prevent endometrial cancer. This protective effect of progesterone has never been conclusively proven, however, and some studies suggest that progesterone itself may increase the risk of breast disease (Mishell, 1987).

In light of the continuing controversy, we continue to recommend estrogen-progesterone therapy in menopausal women with their uterus intact and estrogen alone in those who have had a hysterectomy. *If benign or malignant breast disease develops, then estrogen should be discontinued.* Careful attention to breast cancer screening procedures is always advisable in light of the frequency (1 out of 11 women) and the high death rate (37,000 per year) from breast cancer.

Hypertension and Vascular Disease

As we have already noted, the risk of blood clots and stroke are primarily in women on birth-control pills, especially those who smoke.

Postmenopausal estrogen doses are much lower and not associated with increased risk of blood clot or stroke. Likewise, the risk of significant hypertension in women on estrogen replacement is also very low (Huppert, 1987).

Gallbladder Disease

Estrogen therapy increases the risk of *cholelithiasis* or *gallstones*. Women age 45 to 49 have an overall risk of 87 per 100,000 women to develop gallstones. With estrogen use, this risk increases to 218 per 100,000 women (Huppert, 1987). This is still a fairly low probability of developing gallstones. A low-fat diet helps reduce the incidence of gallbladder disease.

CONTRAINDICATIONS AND POTENTIAL SIDE EFFECTS

Contraindications are reasons not to do something, and in this case, reasons to consider not taking replacement hormones. There are *absolute contraindications*, which are circumstances in which you should never take a medication. And then there are *relative contraindications*, the circumstances in which the individual may suggest that the benefits of therapy outweigh the potential risks.

Absolute contraindications to estrogen replacement therapy are:

- Pregnancy
- Undiagnosed abnormal genital bleeding
- Previously diagnosed or suspected breast or uterine cancer
- Active thrombophlebitis or thromboembolic disease (blood clots)
- Acute liver disease

Relative contraindications to estrogen replacement therapy are:

- Chronic liver disease
- Obesity
- Preexisting uterine fibroids
- Endometriosis
- History of thrombophlebitis or thromboembolism

- Hypertension
- Migraine headaches
- Smoking

The most serious side effect of estrogen replacement therapy is unexpected breakthrough bleeding. This requires prompt and complete investigation to rule out cancer. Other potential side effects include enlarged and painful breasts, nausea, weight gain, increased facial pigmentation, edema, headache, and heartburn.

The addition of progesterone creates its own side effects. The major complaint will be the resumption or continuance of short menstrual periods. Other potential side effects include breast tenderness, edema, and depression. While we list these potential side effects to be informative, you need also to know that not all women will experience these symptoms.

ESTROGEN REPLACEMENT:
MANAGEMENT AND THERAPY

In 1983, an estimated 2.9 million women took more than 749 million conjugated estrogen tablets (Kennedy, Baum, and Forbes, 1985). Because of this high usage, drug manufacturers have made many different types of estrogens and progesterones available. The proper selection of hormone, dose, and delivery method can make a difference in your health, well-being, and comfort.

First, the reasons you are taking hormones need to be established. If relief of hot flushes or tissue atrophy is your only goal, then the lowest effective dose for the shortest period of time is advised. Control of hot flushes will require higher doses than tissue maintenance alone. If prevention of osteoporosis and heart disease is the aim of therapy, then you will need to take hormones indefinitely. A clear definition of goals and an adequate understanding of the risks and benefits of hormone therapy needs to be discussed with your physician prior to beginning treatment.

Your annual health-oriented screening exam, including a physical evaluation, blood pressure check, thorough breast and pelvic exam, and Pap smear should be completed before hormones are prescribed. Some physicians feel that an endometrial biopsy which checks the lining of the uterus for abnormal tissue prior to hormone therapy is a prudent idea. But this is a debatable point. We believe the decision to biopsy before therapy should be based on the individual's medical history and previous menstrual bleeding patterns. Lastly, a screening mammogram, if not recently done, should be obtained. This is a *must!*

Estrogens

Ideally, estrogen replacement would simply replace the same estrogen your ovaries have stopped making. Unfortunately, this is not possible, and we must give a substitute estrogen. Synthetic estrogens, although much more potent than natural estrogens, are associated with increased levels of triglycerides. And triglycerides can increase your risk of heart disease. They also have an effect on the liver which could, in turn, increase blood pressure and the risk of developing a blood clot (Mishell, 1987). Natural estrogens are not associated with these problems and are our choice for replacement therapy. In Table 3.1 we have listed the natural estrogen supplements available in today's market.

The natural estrogens available are all equally effective in treating and preventing the consequences of estrogen loss after menopause. Estrogen is usually prescribed in the oral form, but vaginal application and the newly introduced transdermal-estrogen skin patch are also highly effective. Once oral estrogens are absorbed, they are metabolized in the liver. Unlike synthetic estrogens used in birth-control pills, natural estrogens have a minimal effect on the liver and there is no increased risk of blood clots reported with their use postmenopausally (Mishell, 1987).

Whether you use oral, vaginal, or transdermal estrogen, it should be taken in a cyclic manner. We recommend giving the estrogen

Table 3.1. Natural Estrogens

Generic Name	Brand Name	Dose Available (mg)
Oral		
Conjugated equine estrogens	Premarin, Estrocon	.3, .625, .9, 1.25, and 2.5
Piperazine estrone sulfate	Ogen, Hormonin	.3, .625, 1.25, 2.5, and 5
Micronized estradiol	Estrace	1 and 2
Topical-vaginal		
Conjugated equine estrogen	Premarin	.625 mg/gram
Estropipate	Ogen	1.5 mg/gram
Topical-transdermal		
17-B Estradiol	Estraderm	.05 mg/day and .1 mg/day

beginning on the first day of the month and continuing through the twenty-fifth day. The cycle is then repeated at the first of each month. For most women, this method is effective and easy to remember. For women with their uterus intact, we recommend adding 10 mg of Provera daily along with at least the last 10 days and preferably the last 14 days of estrogen therapy. The transdermal patch is applied to the skin every three to four days according to the same schedule, with Provera added the last 14 days of the cycle. Table 3.2 is a calender showing our suggested dosing regimen.

Progesterone

As we have already discussed, adding progesterone to estrogen therapy has a protective effect on the endometrial lining of the uterus. When given for 10 to 14 days of the month, the maximal protective effect is experienced, and the incidence of endometrial hyperplasia falls to zero (Mishell, 1987). The risk of endometrial carcinoma is not only decreased but is actually lower in estrogen-progesterone treated women than in those women not on any hormone therapy (Mishell, 1987).

There are several effective progesterones which provide endometrial protection. Unfortunately, some of these produce increased unpleasant side effects or counter the beneficial effects of estrogen therapy, particularly with regards to cholesterol levels. We recommend medroxyprogesterone acetate (Provera) 10 mg because it has minimal effect on the blood lipids, does not oppose the beneficial effects of estrogen on bone, and prevents endometrial carcinoma (Mishell, 1987).

Table 3.2.   Recommended Monthly Dosing Regimen

1	2	3	4	5	6	7
8	9	10	11	12	13	14
15	16	17	18	19	20	21
22	23	24	25	26	27	28
29	30					

Estrogen   Estrogen   Drug-free
                  with   Interval
                  Progesterone

Adapted from information supplied by Wyeth Ayerst Laboratories, 1988.

Vaginal Bleeding

Despite the numerous benefits of hormone therapy and the convincing evidence of the need for combined estrogen-progesterone therapy in women with a uterus, many women are skeptical of their own personal need for hormone treatment. The major stumbling block to beginning hormones seems to be the possibility that menstrual bleeding will continue or may restart. A majority of women whom we advise to begin hormones are not at all excited about the prospects of prolonging their menstrual periods when they were really looking forward to not having periods anymore. Hopefully, we can provide some encouragement to those of you who recognize the need for hormone therapy but hate to think about continued menstrual periods.

Most menopausal women taking estrogen and progesterone will have withdrawal bleeding. At a dosage of 1.25 mg Premarin per day, 92 percent will have bleeding; at a dose of .625 mg per day, about 80 percent will have withdrawal bleeding (Whitehead and Fraser, 1987). Even without progesterone, breakthrough bleeding occurs from 24 to 32 percent of the time, depending on the dose of estrogen (Whitehead and Fraser, 1987).

Because it is the withdrawal of the hormones which induces menstrual bleeding, some have suggested giving estrogen with a small dose of progesterone every day of the month so there would be no withdrawal bleeding. This procedure was tried in four different studies, but too many patients developed light, irregular, and unscheduled bleeding for this to be recommended routinely (Whitehead and Fraser, 1987). Estrogen can be given safely on a daily basis, especially in those women who experience hot flushes. However, the progesterone probably should be given in a cyclic manner so that withdrawal bleeding will be predictable.

As long as a menopausal woman's menstrual bleeding occurs when expected in conjunction with estrogen-progesterone therapy, there is no reason for routine endometrial biopsy unless abnormal breakthrough bleeding occurs. For women taking only estrogen, endometrial biopsy should be done at least yearly and as needed to evaluate any other abnormal bleeding (Odom and Carr, 1987).

Hormone Treatment Recommendations

All menopausal women should be considered for hormone replacement therapy as soon as menopause occurs. Taking into consideration the significant protective benefits against osteoporosis and heart disease, even women without the uncomfortable effects of menopause such as hot flushes should be placed on estrogen. When you consider all the

potential benefits of estrogen therapy against the potential risks of hormonal therapy, *the current evidence clearly favors hormone replacement
for all postmenopausal women who have no contraindications to estrogen.*
For those women who are more than ten years past menopause and
have not taken hormone replacement therapy, the decision to begin
hormones will have to be considered on an individual basis. Your doctor should be able to present reasons for and against your beginning
hormones at this time.

Our specific recommendations for hormone replacement are as
follows:

Menopausal women *with* a uterus who can take estrogen
     Premarin (or its equivalent) .625 mg daily
     Provera 10 mg daily
     Dosing schedule: Premarin 1st through 25th of month
                                    Provera 12th through 25th

Menopausal women *without* a uterus who can take estrogen
     Premarin .625 mg every day of the month

Menopausal women who cannot take estrogen
     Provera 10 to 20 mg daily
     Depo-Provera 150 mg injected every three months

Women more than ten years past menopause and not on
hormone replacement
     Same recommendations as above

If symptoms of estrogen deficiency such as hot flushes persist, the
Premarin may be increased to 1.25 mg. If the hot flushes persist on
the days while off therapy, the Premarin can be given every day of the
month. If symptoms of excess progesterone occur, the dose of Provera
may be safely reduced to 5 mg daily.

Any of the oral or transdermal natural estrogens previously mentioned may be used instead of Premarin. Due to variability of absorption, the vaginal estrogens are not recommended for daily therapy.
Injectable estrogen is available but has no particular advantage over
the other forms. There are some drawbacks with the injectable form,
not the least of which is a painful monthly injection.

Youthful Plus . . .

It has been said that "youth is wasted on the young." Certainly most
of us who experienced good health during our teens and twenties did
not fully appreciate the gift of good health. Your life ahead, leading into

the menopause transition and beyond, can be some of your most productive and satisfying years, or as we like to say, "Prime Time." The wisdom, security, and confidence which come with years of life experience are *now paying off.* And this time can be so much more satisfying if you really feel good.

"Youthful plus" means having the health and vitality of youth coupled with the wisdom of maturity. What could be better? You can feel this way too. For most women, estrogen replacement therapy is essential in maximizing this goal. The health benefits of hormone therapy after menopause are indeed substantial and include:

- Decreased risk of coronary heart disease
- Prevention of osteoporosis
- Elimination of hot flushes
- Prevention of genitourinary atrophy
- Psychological and sexual improvement

What a deal!

CHAPTER 4

PMS and You

Premenstrual Syndrome (PMS) is an amazing and perplexing part of womanhood. It is misunderstood, overdiagnosed, and underdiagnosed all at the same time due to a general lack of accurate information. Some doctors claim that it does not exist while others use it for a catch-all of "what ails you." In this chapter we will attempt to condense some of the information now available on PMS to give you an overview of this important women's issue. For more detailed information on this subject, we recommend the book *PMS: What It Is and What You Can Do About It* (Baker Book House, 1988) by Sharon Sneed, Ph.D., and Joe McIlhaney, M.D.

WHAT IS PMS?

Premenstrual syndrome is a group of recurring physical and emotional symptoms which occur at approximately the same time each month in relation to a woman's monthly menstrual cycle. The symptoms can range from simple things like water retention or breast tenderness to more serious problems including suicidal feelings. Table 4.1 is an abbreviated list of premenstrual symptoms.

NOTE: *Different women can have different symptoms and yet they can all have PMS. Also, the severity of monthly symptoms varies each month in the same woman and differs greatly among women. That is, some women experience very mild PMS while others can be totally debilitated at this time.*

Table 4.1. An Abbreviated List of Premenstrual Symptoms

Abdominal bloating
Generalized swelling of the body
Tingling of fingers and arms (parasthesias)
Carpal tunnel syndrome (Numbness of the hands related to swelling
   in the wrists)
Breast tenderness
Backache
Headaches
Acne
Sinus congestion (due to increased fluid production from the sinuses)
Pain in the arms and legs, especially the joints
Tiredness and fatigue
Lack of coordination
Clumsiness (dropping things more than usual)
Poorly-fitting dentures
Increased problems with hypoglycemia
Ulcerations in the mouth
Tension
Irritability
Anxiety
Mood swings
Outbursts of temper
Shouting
Forgetfulness
Desire to withdraw from people
Suicidal feelings
Compulsive activity
Change in sexual interest
Insomnia
Inability to initiate activities or accomplish work at the usual pace
Marital conflict
Food cravings
Increased appetite

INCIDENCE OF PMS

As many as 90 percent of all women are affected to some degree by PMS (Johnson, 1987). With this overwhelmingly large percentage of women involved, it seems clear that PMS is as normal a part of womanhood as having a baby (many of the same hormones are involved). However, some women go beyond the realm of normal and experience severe PMS symptoms. As many as 10 to 20 percent of all women have PMS so severely that they seek medical help. If you are one of them, it is comforting to know that you are not alone.

Premenstrual syndrome seemingly has its heyday in the 20s and 30s age groups, but for some women the symptoms continue or even increase after age 40. Eventually, PMS symptoms subside and disappear completely with menopause. Each woman's experience varies greatly on this issue. It has recently been suggested that PMS may be caused by a shortage of estrogen in the body. If this is the case, it stands to reason that PMS would worsen as menopause approaches. However, for many women, PMS is not a significant problem after age 40. Many questions still exist.

There is very little clear-cut information concerning the relationship of PMS and the woman approaching menopause. The actual distinction between the symptoms of menopause and those of PMS are quite clear, however. For example, *common menopausal complaints such as hot flushes, vaginal dryness, and the like are unrelated to PMS and are not cyclical in nature.*

Our experience in working with PMS patients is that PMS can be a significant problem in the 40s, but is usually tapering off at this time.

CAUSES OF PMS

As stated earlier, PMS may be a normal, if somewhat uncomfortable, experience for many women. For those whose body chemistries have somehow gone awry, disease patterns are at work. The actual cause of PMS is unknown. Below are the best educated guesses for the cause(s) of PMS in current research literature.

1. Progesterone deficiency

2. Estrogen deficiency

3. Subclinical thyroid deficiency

4. Altered carbohydrate tolerance

5. Endogenous opiate withdrawal (All people have opiate-like hormones present in their bodies. During the premenstrual phase, these levels have been found to decrease. PMS could be caused by withdrawal of these natural opiates. Since aerobic exercise increases the opiates, this may be the reason that regular exercise is of great importance during this time of the month.)

DIAGNOSIS OF PMS

Diagnosing PMS may start with you but should be confirmed by your physician. (Make sure you choose a physician for this problem who truly understands PMS.) To begin the documentation of your symptoms, you must have a way to record them accurately. On the next page, we have provided a PMS calendar (Table 4.2). We recommend that you make a few photocopies of this before beginning.

This calendar revolves around your monthly menstrual cycle. *Your record responses must be accurate and as objective as possible.* Instructions for filling out this chart are as follows:

1. Determine from the list of possible symptoms (Table 4.1) which problems seem to bother you most when you are premenstrual. Circle or highlight these and assign coded abbreviations for them, such as "T" for tension or "A" for anxiety.

2. Record these codes on the PMS calendar beginning at the end of your next menstrual period. *Always record your symptoms as they occur—don't try to remember what happened the next day* (see Table 4.2).

3. Mark your menstrual flow days with a circled "M."

4. Keep this record for three consecutive menstrual cycles.

5. To evaluate your calendar, you must compare it with the sample calendar shown in Table 4.3. If the symptoms are spread out over the entire menstrual month, then your problems are not caused by PMS, and you should seek medical help to determine the cause. However, if most of the symptoms are clustered around the week to ten days prior to your period starting and perhaps three to five days after your period starts, then you may have PMS.

NOTE: *If you seek further medical help for PMS, take your completed calendar with you; your doctor will want to see it.*

TREATMENT AND PREVENTION OF PMS

As with most illnesses, everything is better when you are at a higher level of fitness, and this includes PMS. In fact, many of the treatment programs recommended for PMS are similar to the ones presented in this book for general fitness. If your level of fitness, nutrition, and weight control is at its best, you may even prevent symptoms of PMS from ever occurring.

Treatment can usually be divided into two phases—that which you can promote yourself and that which requires the help of a

Table 4.2. The 3-month PMS Calendar

Use this type of calendar to record your *five worst symptoms*. Two sample months are shown in Table 4.3.

Examples of coding: **A**—Anxiety **AB**—Abdominal Bloating
BT—Breast Tenderness **H**—Headache **M**—Menstruation

	Month 1	Month 2	Month 3
1			
2			
3			
4			
5			
6			
7			
8			
9			
10			
11			
12			
13			
14			
15			
16			
17			
18			
19			
20			
21			
22			
23			
24			
25			
26			
27			
28			
29			
30			
31			
32			
33			
34			
35			

Table 4.3. The PMS Sample Calendar

In Chart "A" the woman is diagnosed as having PMS. In Chart "B" the timing of symptoms does not have a clear relationship to the menstrual cycle; this woman's symptoms may have another cause that should be investigated.

	Chart A	Chart B
1		
2		a
3	h	A
4		
5		a
6		
7		
8		H
9		
10		
11		
12		
13		
14	A	
15	HA 6t	H
16	a	a
17	a	
18	A	A
19	A h	
20	Ha AB	
21	HAB	
22	HAB (M)	(H)
23	AB (M)	
24	(M)	(M)
25	(M)	(M)
26	(M)	(M)
27		(M)
28		(M) h
29		h
30		
31	H	A
32		
33		
34		
35		

41

physician. We will briefly outline the treatment of PMS as it relates to this division:

1. *Education and reassurance.* Read other books on PMS. Reassure yourself that this is normal and know that if your symptoms are severe you can seek a physician's help. You should be aware that most women deal with this condition to a certain extent. Know that this condition is treatable and that you do not have to let it hold you prisoner.

2. *Pursue a regular exercise program.* This will improve PMS symptoms immensely. Four aerobic workouts per week are recommended.

3. *Maintain correct bodyweight (or something close to it).* If you are more than 15 pounds over your ideal weight, consider a reasonable weight loss diet such as the ones presented in this book.

4. *During the PMS days avoid* caffeine, sugar, meal-skipping, and other irregularities in your eating patterns, such as over- or under-eating. Maintain a healthful diet which contains a little more protein than on your usual days.

5. *Talk with family and friends when appropriate.* Place a kitchen magnet on your refrigerator door to tell your spouse discreetly that this may be a difficult few days for you.

6. *Control sources of stress.* Don't volunteer for more than you can comfortably do during these days.

7. *See a physician for a correct diagnosis.* Choose one who has treated PMS before. We recommend OB/GYN doctors or family practitioners. Call their office first to determine whether or not this is something they deal with. Another resource may be a large hospital in a metropolitan area—many now have PMS clinics.

8. *Use prescription medications as recommended by your physician.* If your doctor deems it appropriate that you should take a certain prescription or even hormone therapy a few days out of each month, we believe you should do so (assuming this physician is an expert in PMS).

9. *Try a few supplements.* Specifically, vitamin B-6 and magnesium have been shown to be somewhat effective in the treatment of PMS symptoms. For vitamin B-6, use no more than 100 mg/day, to be taken all month long. If this does not help you, discontinue after a three-month trial. For magnesium, take no more than 250 mg/day. This is best obtained through a general vitamin/mineral supplement. Do not take more than these amounts. See the PMS book (Sneed and McIlhaney, 1988) for details.

CHAPTER 5

Sexuality and Aging

Sexual feelings play a major role in our life experience. *Human sexuality is normally an experience which may change in nature and expression, but remains with us throughout our lifetime.* Most mature individuals will readily recognize the importance of their own sexual nature and appreciate the impact that the effects of emotions, physical health, personal beliefs, and attitudes of society have on their own sexuality.

The misconception that sex and passion belong only to the young is rapidly being rejected by the millions of people over 40 who are totally unwilling to accept the concept that their sex life is over or declining just because they are not having more children. There is no solid evidence that hormone changes cause direct changes in sexual response. In fact, social factors play a much stronger role in determining sexual behavior (Iddenden, 1987).

The stereotype of the typical postmenopausal woman regarding her sexuality has not been particularly kind or accurate. Women do not become asexual beings without need for intimate love, affection, and companionship just because they stop menstruating. Acknowledging your needs and rejecting this unfair stereotype which has been placed upon you can be a first step toward liberation.

Most women find it uncomfortable and embarrassing to discuss sexual difficulties either with friends or with their doctor. Many physicians are equally uncomfortable with this subject and are often reluctant to ask specific questions about a patient's sex life. Fortunately, more and more doctors *are* understanding the need to address the issue of sexuality along with other important issues of health-oriented medicine.

There is no standard of sexuality by which to measure yourself, nor should there be. The sexual experience is probably as varied and different as each individual. There are, however, some questions which may provide clues to sexual dysfunction and suggest the need for intervention before unfavorable permanent changes in your sexual life occur. The following questions could be used as points of discussion with your doctor:

1. Are you sexually active? If not, why?

2. Has there been a change in the level of your sexual desire?

3. Is intercourse enjoyable? If not, why?

4. Do you have any discomfort during intercourse?

5. Have you had a change in vaginal lubrication?

6. Do you reach orgasm satisfactorily?

7. Does your partner have any sexual problems?

One report on women's health stated that interviews with women aged 40 to 60 showed that 44 percent had never discussed menopause with their doctor. And you can bet that an even smaller percentage had ever discussed sexual issues. Yet, most women have a keen interest in their bodies and their sexuality and read page after page in lay publications regarding health. Some of this information is accurate, but the rest simply compounds the myths of menopause and adds confusion to the complicated personal issues of aging and sexuality. Let's carefully examine the issues of sexuality during menopause.

PHYSICAL CHANGES AND SEXUALITY

As you know by now, the effects of menopause and estrogen loss can be profound, especially on the estrogen-sensitive tissues of the genital tract. With prolonged loss of estrogen, the vagina and vulva will eventually undergo atrophic (tissue wasting) changes which certainly can affect intercourse.

Painful intercourse, medically known as dyspareunia, is a frequent complaint of menopausal women. Thinning of the vaginal wall and decreased vaginal lubrication, both caused by estrogen loss, usually respond quite well to estrogen replacement therapy. Without treatment, the problem of vaginal thinning and dryness can lead to pain and inflammation during intercourse. This unfortunate situation can begin a vicious cycle of pain, deteriorating sexual response, loss of sexual desire, and ultimately, frustration and disappointment for both sexual partners.

The hot flushes of the perimenopausal years with their profound effects on sleep, well-being, and mood change can also contribute to a lack of sexual desire and activity. Prompt treatment, simple counseling, and understanding between a couple can often solve or prevent many difficulties of a sexual nature after menopause.

SURGICAL CHANGES AND SEXUALITY

As many as 50 percent of you may have the need for a hysterectomy by age 45. One of the first things most women want to know when faced with this surgery is what happens after the abdominal and vaginal soreness resolves—"What will my sex life be like after surgery?" There is no evidence to suggest that women have a decreased sexual drive or orgasmic potential after a hysterectomy whether the ovaries are removed as well or not (Mishell, 1987). *Fear, doubt, and concern with loss of femininity are the major reasons for any alteration in a woman's sexual response.*

Breast surgery is another serious threat to self-image and a woman's emotions. Not only is there the potential harm of breast cancer itself, but also fears of rejection by one's mate can promote self-doubt, anxiety, and alteration of sexual attitudes. The health problems which result in the need for surgical intervention are unfortunate, but sensitive counseling before and after surgery can help alleviate unfounded fears and improve a couple's attitude regarding sex after breast surgery. Excellent reconstructive surgery is now a real possibility and can provide substantial improvement in a woman's self-image. More about this in chapter 8 when we discuss cosmetic surgery.

EMOTIONAL CHANGES AND SEXUALITY

Few people will dispute that emotional factors influence human sexuality. *Emotional and psychological issues are the basis of the female sexual response.* The first phase of this response is the desire phase, and without it, the excitement phase and finally the orgasm phase will never occur. The level of desire is known as *libido.* Desire or libido is a result of a complex interplay of emotions involving love, physical attractiveness, self-esteem, physical health, moral and cultural expectations, and environmental factors.

Someone has said, "You are who you think you are." This statement is particularly true regarding sexuality. As a woman facing menopause or one who has passed this event, you are faced daily with societal pressures to remain "young and beautiful." These messages, some subtle and some not so subtle, may damage your self-esteem and the positive body image you have of yourself, causing emotional wounds which can alter your sexual feelings.

Our advice is simple—*don't fall for these negative messages.* Being beautiful at any age revolves around your inner being and self-concept. By following the health-oriented recommendations in this book, you can achieve your optimal physical and emotional well-being.

The menopausal woman can be sexually active and vigorous. You can enjoy orgasm and especially physical intimacy as much or possibly more than ever. Sex can and should be emotional and communicative as opposed to just physical. The mature couple often can enjoy love-making without actual intercourse, concentrating instead on sensual touch, quiet talk, and the joy of being held. Don't repress or deny these natural feelings and emotional needs. If you do, it can often lead to frustration and bitterness of spirit.

SEXUAL CHANGES IN THE MALE

The sexuality of a person is often determined by the sexuality of his or her partner. Through death or separation, many women may be faced with the loss of their spouse. Others, due to the sexual dysfunction of their partner, may repress their own sexuality and ultimately become apathetic and dysfunctional themselves. A woman's understanding of the sexual problems of aging men may be helpful in preventing long-term difficulties and anxieties in the sexual relationship with her spouse.

As with menopausal women who may require a longer period of time for vaginal lubrication to occur, men in their 50s take longer to achieve a satisfactory erection. The erection may not last as long and the time between ejaculations, the refractory period, is usually longer for older men. This situation varies from person to person and should not be interpreted as the man having lost interest in you or finding you less desirable. Men who are unaware of their own physical changes and become disturbed by them may unfortunately avoid sexual relations. *Without good communication, a couple can soon find themselves consumed with unspoken resentment, guilt, and loss of self-esteem. Self-centered feelings of personal inadequacy by either partner can only lead to more problems.*

In addition to problems of aging, *a man's sexual performance is greatly affected by his own health.* Problems such as diabetes, thyroid disorders, excessive use of alcohol, kidney and liver disease, and cardiopulmonary problems can often adversely affect a man's sexuality. Sometimes the medications used to treat such disorders are as much to

blame as the illness itself. Antihypertensive medication, antidepressants, and tranquilizers frequently cause problems with male impotence.

Every effort should be made to evaluate and treat male impotence whenever possible. Effective treatment of male sexual dysfunction usually depends on the cause. All too often, denial of the problem, lack of communication, and suppression of personal feelings are major barriers to successful resolution of a couple's sexual dysfunction.

CONTRACEPTIVE ISSUES FOR THE MATURE WOMAN

Although increasing numbers of women are considering pregnancy later in life, they are usually the exception after age 40. At this point, most women have completed their families and are now looking forward to a new phase of their lives. Fear of unwanted pregnancy, especially with the associated increased health risks of late-life childbearing, can create sexual problems for a couple.

Serious consideration should be given to permanent contraception or sterilization (for the man or the woman) by any woman over age 35 who has completed her family and is absolutely sure she does not want more children. Over one million men and women per year undergo sterilization procedures (Hatcher and Guest et al. 1986), including tubal ligation for women and vasectomy for men.

Vasectomy is a simple sterilization procedure for men which blocks the vas deferens and prevents the passage of sperm. A safe operation with a low incidence of complications (bleeding, the most common complication, occurs in about 1.6 percent), the vasectomy can be done in a doctor's office with a minimal amount of time lost from a person's job.

Some controversy regarding possible long-term side effects of this procedure suggested a potential increased risk of heart disease after vasectomy. This possibility, however, was found only in a study involving animals. Subsequently, four major studies have shown no increased risk of heart disease in men, and a single large study showed an actual decrease in cardiac risk after vasectomy (Hatcher and Guest et al. 1986). Reversal of a vasectomy is possible, but is successful only 18 to 60 percent of the time. For this reason, vasectomy should be considered a permanent decision.

Tubal ligation is the sterilization procedure for women which blocks the fallopian tubes and prevents the egg and sperm from ever meeting. The procedure is generally safe and sure, with a failure rate of less than 4 per 100,000 women. The greatest risk involved in the procedure is that of undergoing general anesthesia for which deaths can occur (1 to 10 per 100,000). Still, the one-time risk of *a tubal ligation is far less threatening to the life of a healthy 40-plus woman than birth control pills or pregnancy itself after age 40* (Hatcher and Guest et al. 1986).

Like the vasectomy, a tubal ligation is potentially reversible with delicate microsurgery techniques. Potential reversal rates of 50 to 70 percent have been reported, but you should still view your decision for a tubal ligation as a permanent one. Complications occur less than 1 percent of the time, and most women now undergo tubal ligation in day surgery centers, followed by two days of rest at home and no heavy lifting for a week (Hatcher and Guest et al. 1986).

Barrier contraceptives such as the diaphragm, condom, foam, and sponge have been considered the optimal means of contraception for women older than 35 who do not want permanent sterilization. There are numerous choices among barrier contraceptives; individual choice depends on a variety of factors and personal preference.

Safety and effectiveness certainly rank high on any list of selection criteria for contraceptive means. Barrier methods are in general quite safe, with little or no adverse side effects. Table 5.1 demonstrates the first-year failure rates of various birth control methods. Barrier methods have the additional benefit of lowering your risk of acquiring a sexually transmitted disease. Cost, ease of use, and acceptance by both spouses should all be considered in your choice of contraception.

Table 5.1. First-Year Failure Rates among Contraceptive Methods

Method	Lowest Observed Failure Rate (%)	Failure Rate in Typical Users (%)
Tubal ligation	0.4	0.4
Vasectomy	0.4	0.4
Birth control pill	0.5	2
IUD	1.5	5
Condom	2	10
Diaphragm	2	19
Sponge	9–11	10–20
Cervical cap	2	13
Foam, cream, jelly	3–5	18
Coitus interruptus	16	23
Rhythm, mucous test	2–20	24
Douche	—	40
Chance	90	90

Adapted from R. Hatcher and F. Guest et al. *Contraceptive Technology* 13th ed. (New York: Irvington, 1986).

The *intrauterine device (IUD)* has been the choice of many women for birth control. While having a fairly low failure rate (1.5–5 percent), the IUD has significant risk associated with increased risk of sexually transmitted diseases, pelvic inflammatory disease (PID), infertility, and ectopic (tubal) pregnancy (Hatcher and Guest et al. 1986). Because of these potential problems, many physicians are reluctant to prescribe or replace an IUD for most women.

Oral contraceptives, more commonly known as birth-control pills, are used by more than 10 million women in the United States. As they get older, many of these women would like to continue this means of contraception, but their doctors have been concerned about the increased health risks associated with oral contraceptives after age 35. The main concern is the increased risk of cardiovascular problems. This increased risk is noted primarily in women who smoke. Thus, birth-control pills should never be taken by women over 35 who continue to smoke. However, new medical studies now support the safe use of birth-control pills until the age of 45 in women who *do not* smoke (Hatcher and Guest et al. 1986). With the lowest failure rate of all non-surgical contraceptives, birth-control pills are now considered to be a safe and highly effective contraception for many nonsmoking women after age 35.

Table 5.2. **Perspective on Voluntary Risk**

Risk	Chance of Death in a Year
Smoking	1 in 200
Automobile driving	1 in 6000
Power boating	1 in 6000
Playing football	1 in 25,000
Using tampons (toxic shock)	1 in 350,000
Oral contraception nonsmoker	1 in 63,000
Oral contraception smoker	1 in 16,000
Using IUD	1 in 100,000
Barrier methods	none
Natural methods	none
Tubal ligation	1 in 20,000
Hysterectomy	1 in 1600
Vasectomy	none
Term pregnancy	1 in 10,000
Abortion 9–12 weeks	1 in 100,000
Abortion 13–16 weeks	1 in 25,000

Adapted from R. Hatcher and F. Guest et al. *Contraceptive Technology* 13th ed. (New York: Irvington, 1986).

Contraception is a voluntary decision for women and not entirely free from risk in all cases. This increased risk should, however, be put in perspective. Table 5.2 compares the risk of death among various voluntary activities. Hopefully, this will help you understand more accurately the degree of risk involved in contraceptive choices. Decisions regarding birth control ultimately rest with you and your partner. However, before making that decision you need to consult your physician on the safest and most effective means of contraception for your own personal use.

We are all sexual beings and have deep inner needs for closeness and intimacy. Couples, as they grow older, may sometimes take these feelings and each other for granted. Suppression of your emotional feelings and lack of meaningful interaction can only lead to frustration and an increasing sense of isolation. We believe that sensitive communication of needs and selfless consideration of the other person's desires can help sustain a healthy, vibrant relationship between two loving people.

CHAPTER 6

How Safe Is Sex?

In the early 1980s, AIDS infections were virtually unknown. Today, it is estimated that 1.5 million Americans are infected with the AIDS virus. This statistic is only slightly less than the number of Americans who have diabetes. AIDS and other sexually transmitted diseases such as herpes, chlamydia, and human papillomavirus (HPV) are extremely common now and dramatically increase each year.

ACQUIRED IMMUNE DEFICIENCY SYNDROME (AIDS)

AIDS, as much as any other disease today, causes fear and anxiety among most people. No doubt this is due to there being no cure as yet for AIDS, along with the fact that increasing numbers of heterosexual individuals are acquiring the disease. There is cause for alarm and concern since most AIDS patients die within two years of contracting the illness. The costs of treating these people are rising rapidly. Currently, the annual cost of hospitalization for AIDS patients almost equals the annual cost of hospital care for all patients with lung cancer, or about 1.4 billion dollars.

AIDS is caused by a virus called Human T-cell Lymphotrophic virus, type III. This virus causes changes in the body's immune system, allowing a wide variety of serious infections and malignancies to occur. Virus infections do not respond to traditional antibiotics.

The fact that a cure for AIDS has not yet been found is only one of the disturbing problems of this disease. Another is that someone infected with the AIDS virus can carry the illness for years before any symptoms become apparent. Even without symptoms of the

51

Table 6.1.   High-Risk Potential for AIDS

1. Homosexuals (primarily male)
2. Intravenous drug users
3. Women with AIDS-infected sexual partners
4. Hemophiliacs (recipients of large amounts of blood)
5. Immigrants from Haiti or Central Africa

disease, infected individuals can give the infection to others. For this reason, all high-risk individuals (see Tables 6.1 and 6.2) should be tested for the AIDS virus.

The way you get AIDS is primarily through sexual contact, intravenous drug abuse, contaminated blood transfusions, or transmission to a newborn baby by an infected mother. Today, all blood is carefully screened before transfusion to insure safety. Recipients of blood transfusions from January 1, 1979, to June 1, 1985, may be at increased risk because the transfusions were not being tested at that time; prior to 1979, AIDS was very rare.

For women who do not use intravenous drugs, the real risk of AIDS is by way of sexual contact. In fact, sexual contact is by far the most common way the infection is spread. *Truly "safe sex" occurs only in a strictly monogamous (single-partner) relationship where neither partner is infected.* Premarital AIDS testing would be advised for any person who had engaged in high-risk activities such as homosexual sex or IV drug use in the previous 10-year period. Premarital testing is also advised for anyone who has not had strictly monogamous or single-partner sex.

Just as important as knowing the different ways that AIDS can be spread is knowing the ways it is *not* spread. There has been much fear and anxiety surrounding the issue of AIDS in our communities as the disease has become more common. It is becoming increasingly likely

Table 6.2.   Women Who Should Be Tested for AIDS

1. Sexual contacts of men with AIDS.
2. Sexual contacts of men in high-risk groups.
3. Women with multiple sexual partners in areas with a high incidence of AIDS.
4. Intravenous drug users.
5. Recipients of blood or blood products between January 1, 1979, and June 1, 1985.
6. Recipients of artificial insemination from donor sources between January 1, 1979, and June 1, 1985.

that someone you know, work with, or even live with may someday contract the AIDS virus.

You cannot get AIDS from normal daily activities. AIDS is not spread by shaking hands, sitting with infected individuals, or being together in the workplace or school. Careful studies have shown that AIDS is not spread by coughing, sneezing, toilet seats, or even superficial kissing. No AIDS infections have been found to come from mosquitoes or other insects.

The most important information you can have about AIDS is to have sex only with a partner who is at low risk of carrying AIDS. Don't have sex with anyone who has tested positive for AIDS or anyone in a high-risk group who has not stopped all high-risk activity for at least six months and then tested negative for AIDS.

CHLAMYDIA

Chlamydia infection caused by the organism *Chlamydia trachomatis* is *the most common venereal or sexually transmitted disease today.* More than 4 million infections are caused by chlamydia each year, and these infections are a major cause of pelvic inflammatory disease, infertility, and infections among newborn babies. It is estimated that the cost of treating chlamydia will reach 2.18 billion dollars a year by 1990 (Washington, Johnson, and Sanders, 1987).

Typical symptoms of this disease can be an abnormal vaginal discharge and slight bleeding or pain with intercourse. Chlamydia may be present in both men and women, and both sexes can be carriers without any symptoms of the disease. Treatment with antibiotics is effective, but both partners must be treated. Effective prevention of this disease is achieved by using barrier contraceptives such as condoms and limiting your sexual activity to a monogamous relationship with a noninfected partner.

GENITAL HERPES

Genital herpes is another sexually transmitted viral infection caused by *Herpes simplex* virus type 1 and 2. Initial or primary herpes infections occur in 200,000 people annually, but recurrences are much more common, with up to 20 million episodes each year (Hatcher and Guest et al. 1986).

Symptoms of this disease are small, painful blisters on the genitalia which rupture and then form shallow ulcers. Recurrences last about four to five days, and the person is infective primarily while these blisters or ulcers are present. *Some viral shedding can occur even when the individual seems normal, so the absence of any ulcers does not entirely guarantee safety.*

There is no cure available, but your doctor can prescribe a medication which may shorten the duration of the symptoms. Problems related to herpes can range from minor to severe, and recurrences are variable. Severe complications can occur if an infected mother transmits herpes to her newborn child.

Once again, effective prevention involves limiting sexual contact to a one-partner relationship with a noninfected person and using barrier contraceptives, preferably condoms.

HUMAN PAPILLOMAVIRUS

Human papillomavirus (HPV) is a rapidly increasing problem because it is often present without symptoms, is recurrent, and has a long dormant period after the initial infection occurs. This infection is particularly serious because *there is a definite link between HPV and the development of cancer of the cervix.* In fact, 95 percent of all cervical cancers contain the human papillomavirus.

Obvious symptoms of HPV infection include the development of genital warts. Treatment of HPV-caused warts is done with freezing, laser, and chemical methods. Because of the increased risk of cervical cancer, it is important to treat both the woman and her partner. Up to 50 percent of sexual partners of women who have cervical warts will also contract genital warts themselves.

Women with HPV genital warts or HPV abnormalities on their Pap smear should be aggressively treated and screened yearly with a Pap smear. Women who have had cervical dysplasia due to HPV should probably continue to use condoms during sexual activity even after treatment. Prevention of the disease is the same as for chlamydia.

Prevention Strategy. The following strategies are recommended for prevention of sexually transmitted diseases:

AIDS—	Monogamous sexual relations.
	Do not engage in high-risk activities such as homosexual sex, IV drug use, sex with men in high-risk groups, and sex with multiple partners.
Chlamydia—	Monogamous sexual relations.
	Barrier contraceptives.

Herpes—	Monogamous sexual relations.
	Use a condom even if your partner does not have an active recurrence.
HPV—	Monogamous sexual relations.
	Barrier contraceptives.
Screening strategy—	AIDS testing should be done on any potential sexual partner who has engaged in activities considered high risk for the AIDS infection in the preceding 10 years, including having multiple sexual partners. *You should be tested if you have been involved in high-risk activities or have had sex with men who are considered at high risk.*

CHAPTER 7

Saving Face (or Preventing Skin Damage)

Skin care products make up the vast majority of the enormous cosmetics industry. The goal is to preserve, protect, and restore our most visible physical attribute, our skin. In fact, this is such a personal and emotional issue that Madison Avenue marketeers are able to talk us into all sorts of skin care products that don't effectively work on anything but our egos. Don't feel bad if you have fallen into this trap. We all do on occasion. However, with reliable information and acceptance of the fact that skin does age, we can escape this trap more often than not and have the freedom to choose the items we really need. And even more important than the cosmetics issue is the fact that skin cancer is on the rise. The ozone layer, an atmospheric protective coat that surrounds the earth, is decreasing, and we are receiving more ultraviolet, cancer-causing radiation than ever before. In chapter 16, we will discuss the prevention of skin cancer. In this chapter, we have presented information to help you slow the aging process of your skin and choose cosmetics wisely. You will be amazed to find that prevention of skin cancer and good skin care habits go hand-in-hand.

THE AGING PROCESS

Skin will inevitably change with time, but we *can* lessen the effects and slow the progression of this process. The aging process causes a generalized thinning of the skin, a decrease in sweat and oil gland activity, and a weakening of the skin's supporting structure of collagen and elastin. Also, the same gravity which keeps our feet on the ground slowly and incessantly pulls at our skin, further contributing to skin

56

changes. Finally, the fat layer underneath the skin in the facial area becomes thinner with age; thus, the skin is not as taut as it once was when the underlying fat layer was thicker. These factors work together to cause sagging and wrinkling in our skin no matter what precautionary measures we take.

AVOID THE SUN AND TANNING STUDIOS

There is no more important advice for good skin care than proper protection from the damaging effects of the sun. In essence, *too much sunlight causes wrinkles!* The American Cancer Society's slogan "Fry Now, Pay Later" is absolutely true. Excessive sun exposure causes skin cancer, age spots, freckles, generalized aging of the skin, and problems with the eyes. A recent study at Johns Hopkins found that regular heavy sun exposure makes a person three times as likely to develop cataracts. Fortunately, the use of hats with a brim and sunglasses can greatly reduce this harmful effect.

Ultraviolet (UV) radiation from the sun is the culprit behind all this trouble. UV light is made of ultraviolet A (UVA), the tanning rays, and ultraviolet B (UVB), the burning rays. UVB causes immediate damage in the form of sunburn. However, UVA can penetrate the skin and weaken the collagen and elastin tissues. Thus, none of it is good for you, contrary to what tanning studios advertise.

Our body has no way of warning us of an overdose of UV rays until it is too late and the damage has already been done. Too much sun can happen quickly, often without pain and even on a cloudy day. Reflected sunlight from sand, water, snow, or even concrete can increase your overall exposure. The effects of UV light speed the aging process by thinning the skin, decreasing the protective pigment, and encouraging skin changes which can lead to cancer.

Much has been said in the news recently about the decline in the ozone layer. Ozone in our atmosphere shields the earth from harmful UV radiation. It is estimated that *for every 2 percent the ozone layer declines, the incidence of skin cancer will rise by 1 percent.* This topic will undoubtedly gain increasing worldwide attention as we come to grips with our past ecological mismanagement.

Of major concern now are the growing numbers of commercial tanning studios and home tanning beds and lamps. These tanning beds produce almost pure UVA and tout themselves as the safe way to tan without burning. This sounds great because UVB are the rays which cause burning. Unfortunately, there is a catch. Clear evidence now points to the harmful effects of UVA on the supporting structures of the skin, namely the collagen, elastin, fibers, and blood vessels. The results will be not only a tan today (which will fade), but long-term problems of premature wrinkling and sagging of the skin. Don't fall for the pitch. And, remember—"tan today, sag tomorrow."

AVOID MECHANICAL STRETCHING

Don't panic—we are *not* talking about those great laugh lines. Keep on smiling! We simply want to encourage you to *avoid needless stretching of your face*. This may include squinting (whether you need sunglasses or prescription lenses), sleeping facedown, nervous habits of any kind which stretch the facial skin in some way, pursing your lips, and even scrubbing your face with a towel or facecloth, to name a few. Repetitive stretching such as this can weaken the underlying collagen layers. But there's no need to be paranoid about moving or touching your face—simply avoid unnecessary stretching movements.

CLEANSE AND MOISTURIZE

One hundred and one questions arise when you walk up to that cosmetics counter. Everyone wants to convince you that their product is better, more exclusive, will make you look younger, and will noticeably improve your skin. Whom should you believe? Let us tell you a little more about some of these products to help you make decisions.

All moisturizers are made from water, oil, wax, and emulsifiers in different blends and combinations. *The so-called "miracle ingredients" such as collagen, elastin, vitamin A, placenta, and vegetable extracts are added for show and marketing potential.* They have never been found to be effective in reliable, controlled studies conducted by real scientists. That is *not* to say that moisturizers are useless. Quite the contrary, moisturizers are essential in helping your skin retain its own water content. They do not actually add moisture to the skin, but they do prevent water loss by evaporation. The question we raise is why pay extra for a collagen product which won't be any more effective than a cheaper moisturizer without the collagen? *The additive that is worth paying for is sunscreen.* So try to find a moisturizer that not only makes your face feel dewy instead of greasy but one that also contains a sunscreen, at least an SPF 15.

When looking for a cleanser, try to find a water-soluble lotion or cream which fits your face-type. Again, all the fancy ones may be no better than the grocery store variety. Paula Begoun, in her book *Blue Eyeshadow Should Still Be Illegal* (Beginning Press, 1988), recommends a cleanser called Cetaphil Lotion by Owen Laboratories. This is available at most pharmacies and supermarkets. At any rate, proper cleansing without mechanical stretching (try splashing your face repetitively instead of using a washcloth or a tugging motion) is very important and will improve the turnover time of the cells on the surface of your skin.

RETIN-A: THE NEW FOUNTAIN OF YOUTH ?

If you spent all your summers at the pool trying to get that perfect tan as a teenager or live in the Southwest as we do, help for damaged skin is now available. Start more effective sun protection procedures now and consider using Retin-A to decrease the existing effects of pho-toaging on your skin.

A recent research study published in the *Journal of the American Medical Association* reports that a prescription medication called retinoic acid (Retin-A) *reduces wrinkles, improves skin texture, and increases pinkness in sun-damaged skin. This cream, which has been normally used in the treatment of acne, improved skin appearance in all the subjects tested after just two weeks of use.*

Younger people with prematurely aged skin from excessive skin exposure are most likely to benefit from the use of Retin-A. It works by speeding up the skin's cell production and removing dead cells at a faster rate. Collagen production is actually increased and the skin becomes thicker. Retin-A also increases the skin's blood supply, thereby improving color and skin health. *Even age spots will fade somewhat with continued use.* Retin-A is the closest thing to a miracle in skin care that we have available.

RETIN-A: DIRECTIONS FOR USE

Retin-A must be used properly to achieve the greatest benefit. You should start with the lowest strength possible, which at this writing is the .025 percent cream from Johnson and Johnson Laboratories. Do not use the alcohol or gel based Retin-A since this could be drying to your skin. In most cases, a pea-sized drop will cover the entire face. While being treated, your skin will actually be more sensitive to sunburn and you should use a sunscreen with at least SPF 15 or even greater. Also, during the first few weeks, you should avoid any facial irritants such as abrasive face scrubs, astringents, or products with an alcohol base. Few serious side effects have been reported; of these, a transient irritation of the skin is the most common. While some people will notice results in a few weeks, most Retin-A users will not see significant improvement until eight to twelve weeks. Remember, Retin-A is used in addition to other good skin-care techniques and does not replace the need for careful avoidance of prolonged sun exposure and the use of sunscreens.

Retinoic acid is not a new phenomenon. Dr. Albert Kligman of the University of Pennsylvania has used Retin-A as an acne treatment for over 20 years. Some of his patients noticed other improvements in their skin, and out of that came other carefully monitored studies to assess its effectiveness on decreasing wrinkles.

In summary, Retin-A is best started at age 35 or over and may be continued, according to Dr. Kligman, "for the rest of your life." Once you have developed a tolerance for the cream, the red, irritated look will subside in most people. Maintenance levels of Retin-A are something on the order of two to three applications per week as opposed to the initial daily applications. The results will be fewer wrinkles and smoother texture to the skin. Unfortunately, tissue sagging will not be improved with this treatment. Retin-A is a prescription medication obtainable only from your physician. *Cosmetics touting a vitamin A content or something similar to Retin-A are unrelated and will not give you results (no matter what the salesperson says).*

SKIN CARE SUMMARY

- Avoid excessive sun exposure.
- Use sunscreen with at least SPF 15.
- Stay out of tanning studios.
- Avoid unnecessary squinting and other skin-stretching habits.
- Keep your face cleansed and moisturized.
- Consider using Retin-A.

CHAPTER 8

Cosmetic Surgery—
Is It for You?

Each year, more and more women consider and actually undergo cosmetic surgery. Whether to appear younger or change a physical attribute they have always thought to be a flaw, this field of medicine is expanding in geometric proportions. Part of this increase can be attributed to the fact that new out-patient procedures have made certain cosmetic surgeries more affordable and successful while being less intimidating. Cosmetic surgery is no longer just for movie stars—it has indeed come to the masses.

The decision to undergo cosmetic surgery is a personal one. We readily acknowledge that some of these physical changes may satisfy many needs and often will provide an extra measure of self-confidence which otherwise might have been unattainable. Certainly in cases of accident, disease, or congenital deformities, cosmetic surgery is not only welcomed but considered a blessing.

What of the 55-year-old woman who wants to look 40 once again? Can this really be done? Of course, the main quality which will help this person look younger is to be healthy, at her correct bodyweight, in good physical condition, and at peace with herself. Beyond that, a face-lift or any other cosmetic surgical procedure is merely icing on the cake, and as such, is an option.

This sums up our view on physical beauty—*no amount of make-up or cosmetic surgery can cover up a body that is in poor health and suffering from neglect.* Thus, good health comes first—cosmetics and surgery should come second. If you are taking good care of yourself and have some physical attribute which you feel could be improved, then by all means learn about the alternatives available to you.

The purpose of this chapter is to present you with an overview of some of the procedures which are now available. The ones outlined here are not experimental but have been performed thousands of times and have produced dependable results when performed by an experienced surgeon.

GENERAL CONSIDERATIONS FOR
COSMETIC SURGERY

1. Complete removal of scar tissue is impossible, as this is the body's natural response in the healing process. It will take at least six months for surgical scars to fade and often as long as twelve months. However, a skilled surgeon can purposefully place scars where they can hardly be detected. Results can be amazing.

2. You must be prepared to play a role in your own recuperative care. It may involve taking medicines, caring for stitches, or any number of other details. Proper postop care can often determine the success of the entire surgery.

3. You will have a much greater chance for success if you are in good health and are at your correct bodyweight. Some surgeons will not even perform a face-lift if you are not within fifteen pounds of your correct weight, as any weight loss after this time can cause further sagging of the skin.

THE FACE-LIFT

The face-lift (or rhytidectomy) is performed to remove excess, loose or sagging skin from the face and neck areas. The extent of this surgery depends on your particular desires. It is hard to determine "how much younger" one would look after this procedure, and most surgeons realistically admit that it simply makes you look "good for your age."

During youth, the skin has very few lines and wrinkles; the soft tissues seem to fit firmly over the underlying layers of muscle, bone, and fat. As we age, though, the firm fatty lining just under the skin, which fills out the various tissue contours, actually shrinks, causing the skin to fit more loosely. A similar process takes place when loss of weight causes the overlying skin to sag. (NOTE: A slow rate of weight loss is much better for helping your skin regain elasticity. The weight-gain-weight-loss roller coaster is very harmful to your skin.) The greatest changes appear to be under the chin and upper neck, at the outermost portion of the eyebrows, and at the skin folds near the corner of the mouth. Sagging also takes place rather prominently along the border of the lower jaw line. Most of these skin folds become more distinct as a result of the downward pull of gravity and also as a result of muscular action in these areas.

Classically, the surgery is designed to lift, stretch, and remove the sagging skin while supporting the underlying facial musculature. In most cases an incision is started inside the hairline at the temples, continues downward in a natural line around the back of the earlobe and extends into the scalp or nape of the neck. Occasionally, an incision may extend inside the front of the ear. A small incision is frequently necessary under the chin to provide access to excess neck skin.

Surgical treatment of facial sagging will result in limited benefit where very fine skin wrinkles are the most prominent complaint. Other methods to be discussed later may be more effective with this particular problem.

The optimal age to have a face-lift has changed along with new and improved surgical techniques. There is no longer any need to wait until hanging folds or almost irreversible changes have taken place. Although face-lifts are still recommended for persons in their 60s or 70s, overstretched muscles with lack of tone, particularly in the eyelid region, become more difficult to repair. In fact, preference for this surgery has shifted to the early 40s, or perhaps even earlier under some circumstances, when small corrections can be made and enjoyed for a lifetime.

The face-lift operation may now be performed in your doctor's office on an outpatient basis. Or, if you prefer, you may be admitted to a hospital. This surgery is now possible under a local anesthetic which numbs just the area to be treated. In such cases, you are usually given a sedative first and should remain comfortable throughout the surgery. General anesthetics may also be used in certain cases. The cost of this surgery varies, but usually ranges from $3000 to $5000 dollars.

THE CHEMICAL PEEL

The chemical peel (or chemosurgery) is a technique used to restore wrinkled, scarred, or blemished facial skin. *It is primarily effective to eliminate or reduce fine vertical lines* near the upper and lower lips, "crow's feet" around the outer edges of the eyes, and, to some extent, the wrinkles on the forehead and cheeks. The chemical peel is not a substitute for a face-lift; it is not effective in removal of sagging skin. *In fact, the face-lift and the chemical peel are complimentary procedures and are often completed in the same surgery.* One removes the sags, and the other minimizes wrinkles. The chemical peel may also be used to minimize scars from acne or chicken pox.

The chemical-peel procedure is typically performed in your doctor's office or in an out-patient setting under a local anesthetic. The procedure consists of the application of a prepared "phenol" solution which will eventually cause the upper layers of the skin to crust over and peel off. This is essentially no different from the process which occurs after a limited second degree burn. A crust or scab develops which can eventually be removed with ointments, creams and moisturizers. When the new skin has been completely regenerated after several weeks, it will be permanently a bit lighter in color than it was before. The skin will usually feel tighter and smoother after this procedure. The cost of this surgery ranges from $500 to $1500.

DERMABRASION

Dermabrasion or sanding is a procedure used to minimize pits, scars, or other irregularities on the skin's surface. It is performed by the surgeon using a rapidly rotating wire brush over the affected area to smooth out sharp scar edges that can cast unfavorable shadows when viewed in overhead lighting. *Dermabrasion does not remove the scar; it merely improves the appearance by making the total surface structure more uniform.* Costs depend on the size of the affected areas.

EYELID SURGERY

Eyelid surgery (blepharoplasty) is an operation designed to remove excess skin and fatty tissue on the upper and lower eyelids. This procedure is done to eliminate wrinkles, bags around the eyes (which are really pouches of fat), and sagging eyelids.

Fatty pouches around the eyes are actually an inheritable trait which can sometimes lead to visual impairments. When the condition of the skin has progressed to the point where the muscular fibers around the eyelids have become overstretched, repair becomes more difficult. Fortunately, the results of early treatment can be highly successful. There may be more wrinkling or fullness in the skin as years go by; however, *once fatty tissue "bags" are removed, they generally do not return.*

Eyelid surgery may be performed under a local anesthetic which numbs the area to be treated, or a general anesthetic may be used. The cost of this operation ranges from $2000 to $3000 and may be completed in an out-patient setting.

THE TUMMY TUCK

Abdominoplasty is one form of body contouring which has become popular over the last several years. It is basically an operation performed to remove fatty tissue and skin folds in the mid- and lower-abdominal region. These fatty tissues most often accompany the stretching of all the abdominal structures due to pregnancies or obesity. It is essential that the first steps toward removal of this abdominal fatty tissue be through diet and exercise. However, these two steps may not be enough to provide total correction for some of these problems since the changes stem from underlying structural modifications. It is very important to note that *surgical procedures of this kind are not intended for weight reduction*, which is still a dietary and activity-related problem. Surgeons also caution that minor degrees of abdominal wrinkling or looseness should not be treated surgically.

The surgical advantages of any type of body contouring procedure must be weighed against the anticipated risk of surgery and long-lasting surgical scars. In the case of abdominoplasty, there may be more risks involved than for any of the procedures which we have discussed thus far. The common term *tummy tuck* seems to minimize the fact that this operation constitutes major surgery that is performed in a hospital under a general anesthetic. Also, there will be a rather lengthy scar along the bikini line running from hip to hip. Nonetheless, it is a welcomed therapy by those really needing this kind of help, and the scars do fade with time. The cost of this operation ranges from $2000 to $6000, depending on the complexity of the case.

LIPOSUCTION

We have had many patients on weight-loss programs who wanted to seek out this procedure and tell the administering doctor to "turn on that suction machine and don't stop 'til I'm a size ten." Wouldn't that be easy! In reality, *liposuction is intended for use on people of normal weight who have fat stores in disproportionate quantities* around the hips, buttocks, thighs, abdomen, under the chin, and in other areas.

Suction-assisted lipectomy may be performed under a local anesthetic which numbs the area to be treated or under a general anesthetic for hospitalized patients. Surgery begins with incisions of about one-half inch in length in the area where the suction will be performed. A blunt-ended tubular instrument with an opening near the end is passed through the incisions. A suction unit is then attached to the other end of the tube, and the surgeon will then carefully place the tube in the fat tissue area to be removed.

Surgeons warn that you should not expect perfection with this procedure. There is the possibility that skin over the treated area will have a rippled or uneven effect. If surface imperfections such as dimpling (often called cellulite) are present before surgery, they will probably still be there after surgery. The cost of liposuction ranges from $1000 to $5000.

THE BREAST-LIFT

The breast-lift, or mastoplexy, is a surgical procedure designed to raise and contour sagging or loose breasts that have lost volume and elasticity after childbearing. It can also reduce the size of the areola, the dark pink skin surrounding the nipple. Women with large, pendulous breasts which may cause back pain and other problems may benefit from a reduction in the size of their breasts as well as a lift at the same time. This procedure may be done in your surgeon's office, in an out-patient facility, or in a hospital. Though it is usually performed while the patient is under a general anesthetic, local anesthesia to numb the area around the breasts may be used.

In this operation, the surgeon will essentially draw the entire breast up into the top half of the skin by eliminating the skin on the under-side of the breast and suturing it together. In most cases, the nipple must be moved, making breast-feeding no longer possible. In patients with only minimal sagging, a modified procedure may be used to ex-cise only skin from the large areola area immediately surrounding the nipple. The cost of this surgery ranges from $1000 to $4000.

BREAST AUGMENTATION

Breast augmentation is performed to enlarge small, underdeveloped breasts that have decreased in size or atrophied after childbearing. It is also done to balance asymmetry that may result from post-mastectomy reconstruction. It is usually performed under a general anesthetic, requiring brief hospitalization.

Typically, the surgeon makes small incisions on the underside of the breast through which he will place a breast implant or prosthesis. The cost of this surgery is from $2000 to $3000.

POST-MASTECTOMY RECONSTRUCTION

Post-mastectomy reconstruction is reconstructive plastic surgery to restore the form and appearance of a breast following total or partial removal. This procedure can improve your appearance and help restore self-confidence if you keep in mind that the desired result should be improvement and not perfection.

Post-mastectomy reconstruction is a hospital procedure and requires general anesthesia. It is often insurance reimbursable, as it is related to the initial breast cancer operation. We will not discuss this procedure in detail since there are many variations and each case is individual. If you have had a mastectomy, you may want to consider this option and talk with some plastic surgeons in your area about your own case. Cost for this procedure varies widely.

RISK OF SURGERY

While we have not addressed the many potential risks and complications which must be considered before undergoing any elective surgery, they do exist. Make sure you understand the "what ifs" before choosing any of these procedures.

In all cases of cosmetic surgery, your emotions and personal feelings must be considered. Sometimes when under stress, people seek quick solutions to longstanding problems of insecurity and self-doubt. Those stressful and pressure-filled times are not the best time to consider this type of surgery. On the other hand, careful consideration and realistic expectations coupled with a skilled and thoughtful surgeon can often achieve the desired results. Just remember that a "new" face does not guarantee a new life nor will shaping your body with liposuction reshape or necessarily change your life.

If You Want the Job Done Right— Do It Yourself

CHAPTER 9

The Basics of Healthy Eating

Lasagne, hamburgers, coq au vin, chip and dip, quiche, chili, banana and oat-bran muffins, pasta, fruit smoothies, Chicken Parmesan, Moo Goo Gai Pan, stuffed baked potatoes, pancakes, broccoli au gratin, New England pot roast, and strawberry shortcake. These are but a few of the wonderful meal prospects which await you following proper cooking and grocery shopping instruction. (*And you thought this was going to be more of the same old, boring "diet food."*) After we tell our patients what is in store for them in this healthful and carefully planned diet, they usually ask, "Where do I sign up?" We hope you will feel the same way after reading the next few chapters. We will not only discuss what to eat and not to eat, but we will also include some *important tips on healthy food preparation*. In the appendix of this book you will even find a few of our healthy-version recipes. With a little effort and an open mind to new methods of cooking, we think you will enjoy food as much or even more than ever before.

Now that we have captured your attention with promises of good things to come, let's get down to some basic nutrition information that is a must for every adult woman. It is not our intention to discuss *all* necessary nutrients, just the ones that have a direct bearing on the types and quantities of foods you should choose for your own personal diet plan.

NUTRITION ISSUES FOR THE ADULT WOMAN

In professional, nutrition-research literature, women's nutritional requirements are grouped according to age: 19 to 22, 23 to 50, and over 50 (NAS-NRC, 1980). The actual nutrient requirements as established by the Food and Nutrition Board of the National Academy of Sciences–National Research Council are listed in Table 9.1. Now let's look at specific nutrients which merit special attention.

Cutting the Calories

As a rule of thumb, *adults must consume fewer calories as they age in order to maintain their weight.* One of the primary reasons for this is that after age 20, the basal metabolic rate (i.e., the rate at which your body burns calories) decreases by 2 percent every decade. Thus, you would require calorie decreases at each subsequent decade of life, assuming you maintained your weight with an intake of 2000 calories per day at age 20. (See Table 9.2.)

These changes may not seem very significant to you since the calorie difference between what you need at age 20 and at age 40 accounts for

Table 9.1.   Recommended Dietary Allowances (RDA) for Women, Revised 1980

Nutrient		Age Range		
		19–22	23–50	51+
Vitamin A	(IU)	5000	5000	5000
Vitamin D	(IU)	300	200	200
Vitamin E	(IU)	30	30	30
Vitamin C	(mg)	60	60	60
Thiamin	(mg)	1.1	1.0	1.0
Riboflavin	(mg)	1.3	1.2	1.2
Niacin	(mg)	14	13	13
Vitamin B6	(mg)	14	13	13
Folacin	(ug)	400	400	400
Vitamin B12	(ug)	3.0	3.0	3.0
Calcium	(mg)	800	800 *	800 *
Phosphorus	(mg)	800	800	800
Magnesium	(mg)	300	300	300
Iron	(mg)	18	18	10
Zinc	(mg)	15	15	15
Iodine	(ug)	150	150	150

From the Recommended Dietary Allowances, Revised 1980, Food and Nutrition Board, National Academy of Sciences—National Research Council.

*In other portions of this book, we have stated reasons as to why the calcium recommendation in this table may not be high enough to prevent osteoporosis. See chapter 17 for details.

Table 9.2.   Calorie Requirements
with Progressing Age

Decade of life	Calories Needed to Maintain Weight
20 years	2000 calories
30 years	1960 calories
40 years	1920 calories
50 years	1882 calories
60 years	1844 calories
70 years	1807 calories

no more than the calorie equivalent of one large slice of bread. However, this does seem to be one of the main reasons that bodyweight increases with age. So one would do well to keep in mind the nutrition axiom: *It takes only 100 calories/day of extra food eaten and stored as fat to gain ten pounds in one year.* Based on this, it is easy to see how those extra pounds accumulate even when you are eating the same amount of food (or less) than you always have.

There is much speculation as to why this metabolism decrease occurs with increasing age. It is probably related to the fact that we tend to engage in less physical activity after age 20. Also, the percentage of our body which is composed of fat increases with age even if our weight remains the same. This is what we all refer to politely as "mid-life redistribution," more commonly known as the "middle-age spread." Since fat cells burn far fewer calories than do muscle cells or other functional cells, your body burns less calories overall as the percentage of bodyfat increases and the percentage of lean body mass (muscle, bone, non-fat body components) decreases. More plainly, *fat cells are little fuel storage tanks that just sit there conserving energy until they are needed, whereas muscle cells are small fuel-burning engines which use a certain amount of energy even when idling.* Your personal health goal should include a plan for decreasing the fuel storage tanks (fat) and increasing the number of operating engines in your body (muscles). This is one of the only ways you can effectively increase your metabolic rate. Exact calorie requirements for your own body type will be discussed in chapter 12, as you learn to design a diet that meets your own specific needs.

Be Prudent with Protein

Protein is that part of our diet which provides the necessary building blocks for muscles, blood proteins, and other essential elements of life.

The smaller structural units from which protein itself is made are called *amino acids*. Of the twenty or more amino acids known to man, only eight are essential amino acids. This scientific designation refers to the fact that they are dietarily essential and cannot be produced within the human body. The essential amino acids include isoleucine, leucine, lysine, methionine, phenylalanine, threonine, tryptophan, and valine.

In general, most women require 40 to 60 grams of protein per day to meet their nutritional needs (Alford and Bogle, 1982). However, many Americans consume much more than this amount. *It seems that culturally we have some deep-seated need to consume more protein than is required.* Some people even feel that protein is the best possible food choice and that without large amounts of it, they would either take ill or wither away altogether.

However, just the opposite may be true. A noted study has revealed that dietary restriction of protein just short of malnutrition reduced the rate of aging in rats (Haynes and Feinleib, 1980). The rats in this study that lived the longest, remained the healthiest, and had the fewest cancers were also the ones that had a low protein diet, but one high enough to prevent protein malnutrition.

To ensure that you are not consuming too much or too little protein, we will be very specific in our recommendation of how much protein you need at your current weight and age. In Table 9.3, you will find a chart of suggested protein intakes for all women age 19 and over. This chart is based on the Recommended Dietary Allowances (RDA), which indicates that adult women need 0.8 grams of protein per kilogram of bodyweight or 0.364 grams per pound of bodyweight. To see how this works as you plan your daily menu let's look at the following example.

Table 9.3. **Protein Requirements for Women Age 19 and Over**

Bodyweight (in pounds)	Grams of Protein Needed Per Day	Suggested Ounces of Meat Per Day*
100–110	37–40 ⎫	
110–120	40–44 ⎭	3
120–130	44–47 ⎫	
130–140	47–51 ⎬	4
140-150	51–55 ⎭	
150–160	55–58 ⎫	
160–170	58–62 ⎭	5

*Based on a well-balanced diet with other protein sources such as milk, breads, cereals, and vegetables included regularly.

Assuming you eat a well-balanced diet with at least two servings of milk (or the equivalent) per day plus a few breads and cereals and so forth, *you need to consume only three to five ounces of lean meat, fish, or poultry (or meat substitute) per day, depending on your current bodyweight.*

There are certain factors which increase your need for protein. They include illness or disease, fever, trauma or general destruction of body tissue, severe burns, surgery, and wound healing. In these cases, you should usually increase your protein intake by a third and then return to a normal intake when you are well (Alford and Bogle, 1982).

In conclusion, protein is an essential part of life. The amino acid building blocks of protein are needed in the maintenance, replenishing, and repair of all soft tissues. However, after adulthood has been reached, we simply do not need large amounts anymore. In fact, *large amounts of protein may serve as a detriment to our overall health after maturity has been reached.*

Just Say No—to Dietary Fats

Dietary fat may be the most controversial aspect of the American diet. There is conflicting advice from different authorities. Some health professionals seem confused about what kinds of fat should be used. And, our patients want solid answers to complicated questions such as why peanut butter is restricted on a low-cholesterol diet even though the label states, "Contains No Cholesterol." For now, let's take a look at some basic information about what fat really is.

Dietary fat can generally be classified in two ways—it is either saturated or unsaturated. *Saturated fats* tend to raise the blood cholesterol level and therefore must be restricted in the diet for those who have elevated cholesterol levels. Saturated fats are usually fats of animal origin including all kinds of meat fat, butter, whole milk, cream, and cheeses made from whole milk or cream. Other fats which are unsaturated by nature may become saturated through the process known as hydrogenation. Hydrogenated animal and vegetable products (shortening) are used in many processed foods including commercial crackers, cakes, cookies, chips, and peanut butter. So be sure to *scrutinize those food labels.* A few vegetable fats are also saturated fats. They include coconut oil and palm oil (primarily used in non-dairy creamers, and in some baked goods and frozen desserts) and cocoa butter, the fat found in chocolate. For that reason, these products are not recommended on a regular basis.

Polyunsaturated fats (PUF) are usually of plant origin and are thought to help lower blood cholesterol to a certain extent. But these *should not be overused.* Examples of polyunsaturated oils include canola, safflower, sunflower, corn, soybean, and cottonseed oils. Do not use these with a heavy hand even if they are highly unsaturated. Canola oil, for example, does not make routine frying okay. In fact, recent research indicates that a high intake of polyunsaturated fats can contribute to the occurrence of cancer. This reemphasizes the point that fat intake should be limited in amount and varied in type.

Of the *monounsaturated fats,* olive oil is the most important. At one time (during the PUF craze) this oil was not recommended since it was minimally unsaturated. New studies, however, now indicate that dietary use of this oil can cause a decrease in the total blood cholesterol level but will not cause a concurrent drop in the "good cholesterol" or HDL-cholesterol. Thus, the total cholesterol ratio or profile is improved. We now recommend the use of olive oil when possible, but in limited quantities as with the other sources of dietary fat.

Dietary cholesterol, also considered a fat, is in a group all its own. Cholesterol is generally found in foods of animal origin. Foods restricted on a low cholesterol diet include egg yolk, organ meats (especially liver—one of the highest sources of cholesterol), and meat fat. (For more on cholesterol, see pages 172–175.)

One of the most important factors in determining whether you are consuming the right kind of diet is to *determine your total fat intake in relation to your total daily calorie intake.* That is, you must determine what portion of your total calories are coming from fat sources as opposed to those coming from protein and carbohydrate sources. This sounds complicated, and I am sorry to say that it truly can be. To determine the percentage of calories from fats in your diet, you have two choices:

1. **Computerized Dietary Analysis.** This is being done by many dietitians, or you can do it yourself on a home computer if you have the right software.

2. **Daily Fat Counter.** By using Table 9.4 and Appendix 2, determine the fat content of your own diet. This can be time consuming, but it will be very informative.

Determining Fat Percentage in Packaged Foods

A much simpler way to determine fat content of packaged, prepared foods, or single item foods (assuming you have access to the nutrition information on the label) is to use the following formula:

$$\frac{\text{grams of fat} \times 9 \times 100\%}{\text{total calories}} = \% \text{ fat}$$

This formula can be particularly handy in determining the fat content of mixed food items such as a frozen dinner. *If the percentages of any single combination food exceeds 30 percent, you may want to make another selection.*

Optimal Amounts and Types of Dietary Fat

From the preventive health-care standpoint, the optimal level of fat in the diet is between 20 to 30 percent of the total calories you consume each day. You will decrease your chances of heart disease and other forms of cardiovascular disease, obesity, hypertension, and cancer (especially cancer of the breast, uterus, and colon). Unfortunately, the average American consumes a diet which easily contains 40 percent of the calories as fat; but in our own experience, we more often see patients whose diets contain 45 to 55 percent of the calories as fat.

Holding your total fat intake to 20 to 30 percent of your total calories will be the hardest of all the dietary recommendations for you to accomplish. You will have to use new recipes and consistently purchase lower-fat food products. When food products say "Lite," it usually means a lower fat content, although it can refer to the use of an artificial sweetener. You will have to use these routinely or drastically reduce the full-fat products. This will become easy for you, but you must be willing to do things differently from the way you have done them in the past.

The *amount* of fat in your diet is much more important than the *type* of fat you consume. Though it was a popular belief in the 1960s and '70s that polyunsaturated fatty acids (PUFA) such as those found in corn and safflower oil were healthy in any amount, research has not borne this out. In fact, it is recommended that you equally divide the source of your dietary fat between meat fat or other saturated fats, monounsaturated fats (i.e., olive oil), and polyunsaturated fats (i.e., corn, soybean, sunflower oils). This is usually a surprise for most of our patients who assume that polyunsaturates should be used for everything.

To reiterate the main points:

Total fat intake in your diet should be decreased to no more than 30 percent of your total calorie intake and sources of fats should be varied.

Note: This prescription may vary if you have a medical problem such as elevated blood cholesterol or triglycerides.

Now let's turn our thoughts toward counting the grams of fat actually present in our diets. As stated earlier, many registered dietitians

(R.D.) now use computerized dietary analyses as part of their regular counseling procedure. The cost for a complete dietary analysis may vary from ten to fifty dollars, depending on the number of days analyzed. In this book, however, you will find all the tools you need to calculate your own fat intake. The Daily Fat Counter in Table 9.4 used in conjunction with Appendix 2 (Nutrient Content of Selected Foods) will help you determine your daily sources of fat. This tool is also designed to facilitate selection of low-fat alternatives. A thorough discussion of good grocery store selections will be presented in the next chapter. You may find it helpful to review that chapter before filling out the Daily Fat Counter.

(NOTE: The Daily Fat Counter is optional material. It is provided to answer specific questions about the sources of fat and cholesterol in your own diet. However, if you prefer less involvement, you can simply follow the diet plans provided in chapter 12.)

Instructions for Using the Daily Fat Counter (Table 9.4)

1. Make several photocopies of the Daily Fat Counter Chart.
2. Determine how many grams of fat you need per day in order to consume no more than 30 percent of your calorie intake as fat. To do this, multiply the number of calories you consume per day by 0.3 and then divide that number by 9. We have done the calculations for you at the most common calorie levels.

Calories Consumed Per Day	Grams of Fat Needed for 30% Level
1200	40
1400	47
1600	53
1800	60
2000	67

3. On the Daily Fat Counter Chart, record all foods and drinks consumed in a 24-hour period, including information on quantity.
4. Determine the grams of fat you consumed, taking into account the portion sizes eaten and information supplied in Appendix 2 of this book as well as nutritional labels on food packages.
5. The milligrams (mg) of cholesterol in your diet may also be calculated if this is of interest to you. Daily intake of cholesterol should usually be below 150 to 200 mg for the preventive medicine approach.
6. Find the foods in your diet containing the highest amounts of fats and cholesterol. Choose low-fat alternatives from Appendix 2 or the Grocery Shopping Checklist to substitute for the high-fat items.

Table 9.4. Daily Fat Counter

Food and Quantity Eaten	Calories	Grams of Fat	Mg of Cholesterol	Low-fat Alternative

TOTAL		gm fat		mg cholesterol
Goal		gm fat		mg cholesterol

$$\frac{\% \text{ Fat}}{\text{in diet}} = \frac{\text{total gm fat} \times 9 \times 100\%}{\text{total calories per day}} = \boxed{}$$

Cholesterol Counts

Many people seem to think that fat and cholesterol are the same. This is a misconception we frequently encounter in our work as health-care professionals. Although cholesterol is indeed a type of fat, it is very different from the saturated and polyunsaturated fats we talked about previously. Cholesterol is primarily found in foods of animal origin and is present in notably high concentrations in egg yolk, meat fats, poultry fat and skin, and organ meats such as liver, kidney, brain, and others. *It is not necessarily true that all high cholesterol foods are also high in fat.* Consider this: one egg yolk contains approximately 250 mg of cholesterol; yet it contains only 5 grams of fat. It would take at least three big, thick, juicy cheeseburgers to equal that amount of cholesterol (250 mg), but the fat content of the hamburgers would exceed 100 grams. (The extra saturated fat in the cheeseburgers would also add to serum cholesterol levels.)

High serum cholesterol levels among Americans are a great concern to public health and medical professionals alike. Consequently, so much has been written about this topic that knowing your own blood cholesterol level has become a national pastime. Yet, as a nation, we continue to have higher serum concentrations than many other industrialized countries. Your own goal should be to keep your blood cholesterol level at least below 200 mg/dl. And it is the opinion of many experts that cholesterol levels should be kept below 180 mg/dl.

Serum cholesterol is influenced both by the cholesterol you eat and by the cholesterol produced within your own body. Serum cholesterol is also contingent upon how well specific cells in your liver are able to break down (metabolize) cholesterol in your blood. If you have many of these specialized cells, then your blood cholesterol level will be normal to low. If you don't have as many of these cells then your blood cholesterol may be normal to high. The ability of your liver to metabolize cholesterol appears to be a genetically inherited trait. Therefore, *if other people in your family have had elevated levels of serum cholesterol, then you should have yours checked as a precautionary measure.*

If your blood cholesterol has always been low (below 180 mg/dl), we do not recommend any cholesterol restrictions. If your cholesterol is between 180 and 200, you might just use some care in your food selections. If your cholesterol is over 200, and certainly if it is over 220, then you should try to limit your average daily cholesterol intake to 150 mg. This usually means that you do not consume egg yolks, liver (of any kind), and organ meats. It also means that you are careful to eliminate as much meat fat from the diet as possible. Additionally, you should avoid foods which are high in saturated fats, as these will increase the production of cholesterol within your body.

Table 9.5. Low-Cholesterol and Low-Fat Alternatives for the Healthy Diet

Avoid These	Include These
Whole milk, 2% milk	skim, ½%
Whole milk cheese	skim milk or part skim milk cheese
Butter	soft margarine
Regular ice cream	ice milk, fruit sorbet, frozen yogurt, sherbet
Egg yolks, whole eggs	egg whites,* egg substitutes
Fatty meats, canned meats, processed chopped meats, shrimp, organ meats	lean fish, turkey, chicken (no skin), beef (no visible fat), pork, lobster, crab
Lard, bacon fat, cream	olive oil, vegetable oils
Biscuits, doughnuts, croissants	English muffins, bagels, bread, French bread, muffins, pita bread
Commercial chip and dip, nuts, and other high-fat snack foods	baked chip alternatives, pretzels, homemade dip

*Two egg whites may be substituted for one whole egg in most combination recipes.
Note: For specific information concerning the cholesterol content of selected foods, see Appendix 2.

Table 9.5 gives a comprehensive list of foods which should be included or avoided in a fat and cholesterol restricted diet.

Vitamins for Vim and Vigor

Vitamins are divided into two classifications—water soluble and fat soluble. The *water soluble vitamins* include the B vitamins, folate, and vitamin C. For most of these nutrients, there are only small reserves within the human body, and they must be replenished frequently to avoid depletion. The *fat soluble vitamins* include vitamins A, D, E, and K. Of these, vitamins A and D are stored so efficiently that large overdoses can actually act as a poison because neither can be easily excreted or metabolized once inside the body.

Your total vitamin/mineral requirements (with the exception of iron and sometimes calcium) can be easily obtained from a nutritious diet. We would also like to point out that excessive supplement intake is not synonymous with "Super Nutrition." Your best edge on good nutrition is a varied and well-rounded diet which meets your nutritional needs according to the guidelines established in the Recommended Dietary Allowances (NAS-NRC, 1980). The bottom line is this:

> **You will never make up for a poor diet by taking a vitamin pill.**

Our usual policy is to recommend that *most women over 40 (especially those on calorie-restricted diets) should take a vitamin/mineral supplement which does not exceed 100 percent of the RDA for any nutrient, from two to five times per week.* Some nutritionists would disagree with this statement and would indicate that vitamin supplementation is totally unnecessary for a healthy person consuming a nutritious diet. We feel that it is important for the following reasons:

1. With increasing age, there is a decline in nutrient absorption in the intestine. Thus, a greater percentage of vitamins and minerals pass through the body and are eliminated in the stool instead of being incorporated into the body.

2. As your basal metabolic rate (BMR) drops, your need for calories drops as well. However, your vitamin/mineral requirement remains the same or can even increase, as in the case of calcium. Thus, you must consume the same amount of nutrients in fewer calories, leaving very little if any of your diet allotted to "empty calories." Realistically, though, most Americans commit dietary indiscretions at least weekly, if not daily. A modest vitamin/mineral supplement allows for this reality and helps promote improved nutritional status.

3. Iron supplementation for menstruating women is also an important issue. In the typical Western diet, it is almost impossible for a female to consume 18 mg/day of dietary iron. And, with the added emphasis on less red meat, lower protein diets, and avoidance of liver (usually the best dietary sources of iron), even a healthy diet may be very low or even inadequate in iron and other trace minerals as well (i.e., zinc, chromium).

4. It may be beneficial to have slightly increased tissue saturation levels for a few vitamins, including vitamins A and C. There is some evidence that shows that this may give you a slight edge in disease prevention. These may be obtained from a combination vitamin/mineral supplement which contains *no more than 100 percent of the RDA. Don't allow an untrained, health-food store salesperson to talk you into any extras.* Remember, your best and most readily absorbable sources of vitamins will always be found in the foods you eat. For this reason, we have included a chart describing the best food sources of all the vitamins.

Table 9.6. Food Sources of Vitamins

Vitamin	Best Healthy Food Sources*
Fat Soluble Vitamins	
Vitamin A and retinol	fortified milk and margarine, green and yellow vegetables, yellow fruits
Vitamin D	fortified milk and margarine, fish oils, sunlight on skin
Vitamin E	vegetable oils
Vitamin K	green leafy vegetables, mainly synthesized in the intestine by bacteria
Water Soluble Vitamins	
Thiamin (B_1)	pork, beef, whole or enriched grains, legumes
Riboflavin (B_2)	milk, enriched cereals
Niacin (nicotinic acid, nicotinamide)	meat, peanuts, enriched grains
Vitamin B_6 (pyridoxine)	wheat, corn, meat
Pantothenic acid	egg, milk
Biotin	egg yolk, other foods, mainly synthesized in the intestine by microbes
Folic acid	green leafy vegetables
Cobalamin (B_{12})	meat, milk, egg, cheese
Vitamin C (ascorbate)	citrus fruits, peppers, green vegetables

*We have not included sources we consider to be unhealthy. Also, don't eat the recommended eggs unless your serum cholesterol level is under 200 mg/dl.

Nature's Best—Dietary Calcium

Of all the minerals in the human body, calcium is present in the largest amount. Ninety-nine percent of the body's calcium is contained in the bones, and the other one percent is distributed throughout the rest of the body. The most interesting thing about the large calcium reserves in our bones is that they are constantly being reabsorbed (broken down) and remineralized (built back up). If the calcium taken away from the bones is greater than the new calcium which is being laid down in the bones, then the result is called "negative calcium balance," a situation which results in osteoporosis. *Osteoporosis can be defined as a gradual demineralization and weakening of the bones resulting in bone fractures from even a minimal amount of stress.*

The body's need for calcium and its role in the prevention of osteoporosis will be discussed in greater detail in chapter 17. Generally speaking, the premenopausal woman and the estrogen-treated postmenopausal woman need 1000 mg of calcium per day. *Postmenopausal women not being treated with estrogen require 1500 mg of calcium per day* (Heaney et al., 1978). These requirements, based on relatively new studies by Dr. Robert Heaney and colleagues, contradict the current RDA for calcium which is not thought to preserve bone integrity at the time in life when the process of bone loss or osteoporosis is accelerating.

To achieve this high intake of calcium in your daily diet, dairy products are a must. (We have had many patients in our practice who have eliminated dairy products from their diets when a well-meaning physician recommended that they decrease their intake of fats, sodium, or calories.) However, it is important for you to consume primarily, if not exclusively, low-fat dairy products. For example, one cup of whole milk is twice the calories of one cup of skim milk; yet, the skim milk has more protein, calcium, and phosphorous than the whole milk and is missing only the cream (which is high in cholesterol and saturated fats). *Do not eliminate dairy products from your diet.* The only exception is for persons with some sort of milk allergy. However, you must find out whether it is the milk sugar (called lactose intolerance) which bothers you or a true allergy to the milk protein itself. In both cases, it seems to be a dose-related disorder. That is, small amounts can often be tolerated while large amounts do cause significant problems with bloating, gas, diarrhea, and the like.

In Table 9.7, calcium-rich food sources are listed. Check the items you enjoy and find the total amount of calcium you have consumed at the end of one day. *Remember, you will need 1000 mg of calcium per day if you are premenopausal or if you are on an estrogen supplement. You will need 1500 mg of calcium per day if you are postmenopausal and not on an estrogen supplement.*

Other Minerals

Many other minerals are important to your health. Usually there is not a problem with these nutrients, with the exception of iron. In the past, nutritionists recommended that everyone should eat liver once a week to insure an adequate iron intake. Liver is very high in iron as well as in many other essential nutrients. Unfortunately, however, it contains more cholesterol than almost any other food; therefore, *we do not recommend that you eat liver on a regular basis, or at all.* Four ounces of

Table 9.7. Calcium-Rich Food Sources

Food and Quantity	Calcium Content (mg)	Amount Eaten	Calcium Consumed
Milk, 8 oz. (all kinds)*	300		
Cheese, 1½ oz.	300		
Yogurt, 8 oz.	400		
Pudding, ½ cup	150		
Ice milk, ½ cup	100		
Frozen yogurt, ½ cup	100		
Beans, cooked, 1 cup	100		
Oysters, raw, 7–9	100		
Salmon, canned 3 oz.	150		
Sardines with bones, 3 oz.	350		
Shrimp, 3 oz.	100		
Bokchoy, ½ cup	100		
Turnip greens, ½ cup (and other very green vegetables)	150		
Pizza, 2 slices, medium	250		
Blackstrap molasses, 1 Tbsp.	100		
Cream soup, 1 cup (made with milk)	150		

Your Daily Total _____ mg calcium
Your Daily Requirement _____ mg calcium

*While "all kinds" of dairy products contain calcium, only the low-fat choices are recommended for women over age 35 because the full-fat choices contain too much cholesterol and saturated fat.

pan-fried liver contains over 550 mg of cholesterol. Four ounces of simmered chicken livers contain over 850 mg of cholesterol. That is almost a week's worth of dietary cholesterol in one sitting. We do recommend that you eat other food sources which are high in iron, as shown in Table 9.8. As already stated, we also suggest that a vitamin/mineral supplement containing no more than 100 percent of the RDA be taken

Table 9.8.   Minerals and Their Healthy Food Sources*

Mineral	Food Source
Calcium (Ca)	milk, cheese, green leafy vegetables
Phosphorus (P)	dairy products, meat, whole grains
Magnesium (Mg)	dairy products, meat, seafood, legumes
Potassium (K)	fruits, vegetables, legumes, whole grains
Sulfur (S)	meat, egg, milk, legumes
Iron (Fe)	meat, egg, whole grains, dark green vegetables
Iodine (I)	iodized salt, seafood
Zinc (Zn)	widely distributed, seafood, whole grains
Copper (Cu)	meat, seafood, whole grains
Manganese (Mn)	cereals, whole grains, leafy vegetables
Chromium (Cr)	cereals, whole grains, brewer's yeast
Selenium (Se)	seafood, legumes (in plants, varies with soil)

*Choose low-fat products whenever possible. Do not include eggs unless your serum cholesterol is less than 200 mg/dl.

two to five times per week—or every day if you are on a calorie restricted diet. Make sure this preparation contains 100 percent of the RDA for iron (18 mg).

An Added Note: If you were once told during pregnancy or at some other time that you had iron-deficiency anemia, don't assume that you will always have it and should continue a large iron supplement (i.e. 45–60 mg iron/day). In fact, you can overdose on iron and cause a liver problem called hemosiderosis. Thus, do not take large iron supplements unless you currently have anemia.

FIBER AND FITNESS

Most people talk about dietary fiber as being one particular element of the diet. In reality, there are many different types of fiber, and each serves various functions within the human body. Much of the confusion over fiber is a matter of semantics (Williams, 1988). No single term adequately covers all the meanings involved. *Roughage,* an older word, and *fiber,* the newer facsimile, both create pictures of an abrasive material which might even be woody in nature. The mere thought of something rough and woody sliding down the intestine is intolerable for some persons who suffer from diverticulosis or hemorrhoids. Actually, however, a number of the nondigestible materials in foods are soft and have gel-like qualities.

Fiber, as we now understand it, is a diffuse term applied to a variety of nondigestible carbohydrates. These foods are nondigestible because

Table 9.9.   High-Fiber Foods

Food	Amount	Grams of Fiber
Breads and Crackers		
Graham crackers	2 squares	1.4
Whole-wheat crackers	6 crackers	2.2
Whole-wheat bread	1 slice	1.3
Cereals		
Fiber One	½ cup	12.0
All Bran Extra	½ cup	11.0
All Bran, 100%	⅓ cup	8.0
Bran Chex	½ cup	4.1
Corn Bran	½ cup	4.4
Bran Flakes	⅔ cup	4.0
Shredded Wheat	1 biscuit	2.8
Grapenuts	¼ cup	2.7
Pasta and Rice		
Pasta	½ cup	1.0
Rice, brown (cooked)	⅓ cup	1.6
Rice, white (cooked)	⅓ cup	0.5
Fruits		
Apple	1 medium	2.0
Banana	1 small	1.5
Blackberries	¾ cup	6.7
Cantaloupe	1 cup	1.6
Figs, dried	1 medium	3.7
Peach	1 medium	2.3
Prunes, dried	2	2.4
Strawberries	1 cup	3.1
Vegetables		
Broccoli	½ cup	3.5
Brussels sprouts	½ cup	2.3
Cabbage	½ cup	2.1
Turnip greens	½ cup	3.5
Carrots	½ cup	2.4
Potatoes, baked	½ medium	1.9
Green beans	½ cup	2.1
Winter squash	½ cup	3.5
Beans, dried	½ cup cooked	3.8
Tomatoes	1 small	1.5

humans do not have enzymes to break them down in the intestine and retrieve the basic elements for metabolism. Consider, for example, the fact that cows gain weight and get fat by eating grass and hay. For humans, grass and hay would not be digestible and therefore would be considered dietary fiber. Cows get fat on grass because they have the appropriate enzymes to break down the basic constituents and use the carbon atoms which are present in this particular carbohydrate to produce energy. In fact, grass is to cows as potatoes are to humans.

The two most important forms of dietary fiber for humans are the *celluloses* and the *noncelluloses*. Cellulose is the chief constituent of plant framework. Human beings cannot digest cellulose (but cows can). It remains in the digestive tract and contributes important bulk to the diet. The bulk helps move the digesting food mass along and stimulates intestinal movement. The main sources include stems and leaves of vegetables, seed and grain coverings (such as wheat bran), and vegetable skins and hulls. *Most physicians who specialize in disorders of the intestine and colon recommend that we consume at least 25 grams per day of this kind of fiber.* Some preventive health-care specialists have speculated that this could decrease the incidence of colon cancer by 50 to 90 percent. For a list of foods high in cellulose fibers see Table 9.9.

The other kind of fiber is the noncellulose polysaccharides—hemicellulose, pectins, gums, and mucilages. These fibers absorb water, slow gastric emptying time, bind bile acids, and provide bulk for the stool (Williams, 1988). Binding the bile acids is a very important feature of this group of fibers. Bile acids are made in the body from existing cholesterol. *An inclusion of 5 grams of this type of fiber daily may lower the blood cholesterol by 5 percent (Berkeley Wellness Letter, 1988).* Examples of this type of fiber are found in oat bran and in fruits. Table 9.10 gives more detailed information concerning oat bran products. Increased levels of dietary fiber are considered to be therapeutic for several major diseases. The importance of fiber in the role of preventing these diseases is yet unclear in some cases, but future research should reveal this relationship. The diseases listed in Table 9.11 may be affected by dietary fiber.

OTHER CONCERNS

Sodium

The restriction of dietary sodium to 3000 mg or less per day is a good idea for all adults. This is not hard to accomplish and allows for many salty tasting foods to be included with the diet. In the past, sodium

Table 9.10. Fiber Content of Oat-Bran Products*

Food Product	Grams of Fiber	Nutritional Information
Oat bran, Quaker, 1 oz.	4	Pure oat bran. Can make into hot cereal, muffins, bread.
Oat bran, Erewhon, 1 oz.	3	Also contains wheat germ.
Oat-bran flour, 1 oz.	4	Made from pure oat bran and a little oatmeal ground to a fine texture. Found in specialty food stores.
Quaker Oats, all types, 1 oz.	2.7	No additives. Make cereal, muffins, or bread.
Instant Oatmeal, Quaker, 1 oz.	2	Contains added artificial flavors, sugar, fat, and sodium. Avoid.
Instant Oatmeal, Arrowhead Mills, 1 oz.	4	Oats only. Good choice.
Cheerios, 1 oz.	2	Oat and wheat flour with fortified vitamins and minerals.
Cracklin' Oat Bran, 1 oz.	5	Contains wheat bran, too. High in sugar, coconut and palm oil. Avoid cereals with saturated fats.
Oatmeal bread, 1 slice	1.5	Mostly white flour and wheat flour with a little oatmeal.
Oat-Bran Graham, Health Valley	3	Mainly whole-wheat flour, oat bran, soy oil, and fruit juice. A delightful snack choice.

*Adapted from the *University of California, Berkeley Wellness Letter*, October, 1988, p. 3.

Note: The inclusion of 5 grams of daily soluble fiber (this usually means that which is found in fruits and oat bran) will decrease your cholesterol by 5 percent. The best sources of oat bran are the ones which are plain and natural instead of those which have been "fixed up."

Table 9.11.   The Effect of Fiber on Health Problems*

Problem	Effect of Fiber
Diabetes	Reduces blood sugar levels. Reduces sugar in the urine. Increases insulin sensitivity.
Obesity	Reduces hunger. Reduces fat absorption from food. Reduces caloric value of food. Increases hormonal response to food.
Coronary Heart Disease	Reduces serum triglycerides. Reduces serum cholesterol.
Cancer	Reduces incidence of colon cancer. Reduces incidence of breast cancer.
Diverticulosis, Constipation, Hemorrhoids	Increases diameter of the intestinal lumen, thus allowing the intestinal tract to contract more, propelling contents more rapidly and inhibiting segmentation.

*Taken in part from *Essentials of Nutrition and Diet Therapy* by Sue Rodwell Williams, 1988, pp. 48–49.

restriction was the only means of controlling high blood pressure. Therefore, great emphasis was placed on the low-salt diet. Modern research seems to indicate that *for persons who have never had a problem with their blood pressure, salt restriction is not a major concern.* Nevertheless, it certainly remains a significant part of the treatment program for the hypertensive.

To control your sodium intake, learn to read labels. Try not to consume more than 500 to 800 mg of sodium per meal (1000 mg at most). Also, choose low-sodium alternatives when possible and when palatable—most of them taste good. For a list of foods to avoid or use sparingly when restricting the sodium in your diet to 3000 mg a day see Table 9.12.

Caffeine

More research on caffeine must be completed before any health expert can make exact recommendations. However, in many reports, caffeine has been found to stimulate the nervous system, increase the heart rate and basal metabolic rate, promote secretion of stomach

Table 9.12.   Foods to Avoid on a
Mildly Sodium-Restricted Diet

Salty meats such as bacon, sausage, ham*
Salty or smoked fish, anchovies, caviar, salted cod, sardines
Regular peanut butter
Sauerkraut or other pickled vegetables
Breads and rolls with salt toppings
Regular salted popcorn
Potato chips or other salted chips and snack foods
Salted pretzels
Olives
Salted nuts
Canned soups, stews, or bouillon
Cooking wine
Pickles and relishes
Celery salt, garlic salt, and onion salt
Catsup and chili sauce
Barbeque sauces and meat sauces
Meat tenderizers
Soy sauce
Worchestershire sauce
Some cheeses (check the labels)

---

*Rinsing ham or other allowed luncheon meat and blotting dry on paper towels will reduce sodium content by almost half.

Adapted from *Handbook of Clinical Dietetics* (ADA, 1981).

Note: You will find many items on this list which have been recommended as being good food choices in previous chapters. This table merely serves as a guide to show you which foods are salty enough to limit to occasional use. If you do not currently have blood pressure problems, it will do you no harm to eat some of these on occasion—just don't live on them.

acid, stimulate production of urine, cause insomnia and the "caffeine headache," and with increased quantities, it may cause irregular heartbeats. These are the same effects caused by anxiety, which you can read about in chapter 23.

Caffeine restriction is indicated under the following circumstances:

1. High blood pressure.

2. Pregnancy.

3. Stomach ulcers or irritation.

4. Fibrocystic breast disease (both caffeine and methyl xanthene have been linked in some research to painful fibrocysts in the breast. Methyl xanthene is found in coffee, decaffeinated coffee, tea, chocolate, and caffeinated soft drinks.)

5. Premenstrual tension.

If you do not suffer from any of the above, it is still advisable to hold your caffeine intake down to two servings per day (equivalent to two cups of coffee or four cups of tea). Tea and sodas usually contain half as much caffeine as brewed coffee. Also, many over-the-counter pain relievers contain a combination of ingredients including caffeine.

Sugar versus Artificial Sweeteners

If you are not a diabetic and are within twenty pounds of your ideal bodyweight, we feel that small amounts of sugar are a much better choice than a continual flow of artificial sweeteners in your bloodstream. One teaspoon of sugar in a beverage or on the morning cereal contains only 17 calories. That is hardly going to make or break a diet program. Again, we come back to the same theme—almost any food eaten in moderation is acceptable in a health-oriented menu.

Other natural sweeteners such as honey and fructose may be somewhat helpful for the diabetic or hypoglycemic. However, this too should be used in moderation since both of these are not very different from white table sugar.

The two artificial sweeteners available in the U.S. market are saccharine (i.e., Sweet 'n Low) and aspartame (i.e., Nutrasweet or Equal). Both have been found to be moderately related to the production of cancer in laboratory animals. Our feeling is that you should use them sparingly. To be on the safe side, do not exceed two servings per day.

Fish Oils and Other Supplements

Fish oils are a popular supplement touted as the cure for high serum cholesterol and triglyceride levels. In fact, they do help to lower your blood levels of both cholesterol and triglycerides. However, as these oils lower your total cholesterol, they may also lower your HDL cholesterol (good cholesterol). Therefore, your total risk remains unchanged. To date there are no major studies that indicate fish oil supplements will reduce your risk of heart disease. Our recommendation is that you consume more fish in your diet rather than take unnatural amounts of an oil supplement.

Other popular supplements which are frequently displayed in the vitamin section of "health-food" stores include single amino acid preparations and trace minerals such as selenium and chromium. These minerals can be particularly dangerous and toxic if taken in too large a quantity. Therefore, we do not recommend the consumption of individual supplements of this kind. Please be aware that people selling these vitamins are not usually trained nutritionists. In fact, many times they are sales personnel for a large corporation that has spoon-fed them just enough information on each product so that they sound authoritative. Let the buyer beware!

CHAPTER 10

Supermarket Smarts

Many of the important food choices you make occur before you actually sit down to the table for a meal. The old physician's quip about the best dieting exercise being the "push away" (push away from the table, that is) is only half true and very naive. Granted, we have patients who gain weight by eating healthy foods to excess and forgetting when to stop. But the greater majority have gained weight or contributed to their blood cholesterol and triglyceride problems by making poor food choices and by using heavy, high-fat cooking methods. In this chapter we hope to explore every facet of grocery shopping and food selection that might make your health-oriented diet plan even more palatable, convenient, and affordable.

GROCERY SHOPPING TIPS

1. Do not go to the grocery store when you are hungry, tired, or craving chocolate or some other poor food choice. Break habits of selecting poor food choices by going to a new grocery store where you do not have a subconscious habit to make poor food selections or by avoiding certain aisles or areas of the store which cause you problems. Let us add, there is nothing wrong with an *occasional* chocolate bar, bag of chips, etc.; however, if you find yourself making these selections continually, then it will possibly lead to something less than your own optimal health potential.

2. Read labels. Know what you are getting. If it contains a lot of hydrogenated fats, sugar, salt, and numerous artificial additives, then you don't want it. Also, if you have a choice between a natural product (i.e., no artificial flavorings or preservatives) and a similar product with additives, choose the natural one. Though most of the harmful additives have been removed from our food supply, this still seems like an easy, prudent choice to make as an extra precaution against new findings that these additives may not be as safe as we think.

3. *Shop for light, reduced calorie, or low-fat alternatives.* We highly recommend most light products as long as you do not use twice as much of them because they usually contain half the calories. The term *light* can mean one of two things—a reduced fat content or a reduced sugar content. Everyone needs the lower fat alternatives such as the reduced calorie versions of mayonnaise, margarine, salad dressings, and dairy products. Even if you are at your ideal weight, these products should be considered so that you can reduce the overall fat content of your diet and replace those fat calories with increased portions of complex carbohydrates.

The sugar substitute products are recommended for those who are diabetic or those who are trying to reduce their weight. We would much prefer that you have a teaspoon of sugar (at a mere 17 calories) than a sugar substitute if there is no medical reason for its restriction. One further note, read labels on light products, too. For some products, many of the calories have been replaced with artificial additives. Try to find light but natural products when you are shopping.

4. *Don't overbuy or overstock.* If you have too many perishable groceries in the house, the natural tendency is to eat them more quickly and in greater quantity to avoid wasting food. Also, resist the temptation to buy poor food choices simply because they are at bargain basement prices—that may be all they're worth!

5. *Your family does not need "junk food," either.* But, as parents and hosts, this has been a difficult lesson for us to learn. We are tempted to keep things in the house "for the kids" because the television and other sources say that is what we must do to be good parents. After all, they will only be kids once. In actuality, the only people on earth who *might* qualify as needing the extraordinary calorie-concentrated foods we have at our fingertips today are adolescent boys between the ages of 13 and 18. Many of them are calorie annihilators at this age, but unfortunately no one else in the family can claim this same title.

Here is something else to consider—if you are buying high-cal, nutrient-poor foods for your family and then consuming them yourself, perhaps you need to reexamine your motives. For whom are you really buying or making these foods? Does your family want them or do you want them? Who eats them the most during the middle of the day when everyone is at work or at school? We have fallen into this trap many times. Luckily, this is a trap you can dismantle by simply leaving those items out of the grocery basket.

6. *Take time to shop*. On the first visit to the grocery store after reading this book, assess every food label you can. Spend at least an hour and try to understand what you are really putting into that food cart.

GROCERY SHOPPING CHECKLIST

Now that we have talked about *how* to buy, let's discuss *what* to buy —an equally important question. In this section, we will give specific information on what to look for in your own grocery store. However, to avoid confusion, we will not use brand names unless they are nationally recognized. As you go through the list, check off the items which might be good food choices for you.

Breads

_____ *Whole-Grain Breads.* For these you must buy breads called "100 percent Whole-Wheat Bread" or other types of whole grains. When you buy anything else (i.e., cracked wheat, wheat sandwich, etc.) you are really getting a partial whole grain, caramel food coloring, and a lot of white flour in the product.

_____ *Light Breads.* These are particularly useful for calorie-restricted diets. Calorie content per slice of bread is between 35 to 40 calories compared to an average of 80 to 120 calories per slice for regular bread. Light breads are also low in fat and high in fiber (usually 2 to 3 times higher in fiber than 100 percent whole-wheat bread).

Margarine/Butter/Butter Substitutes

_____ *Diet Margarines.* Though these are primarily tub margarines diluted with water, they still save you calories and decrease fat intake. They are 50 calories per tablespoon which is half the caloric and fat content of regular stick or tub margarine. Examples include Diet Mazola, Diet Parkay, and Kraft Touch of Butter. These are good choices for someone requiring a low-cholesterol, reduced-calorie diet.

_____ *Tub Margarines.* Tub margarines are less hydrogenated than stick margarines and are a better choice. They have the same caloric value per tablespoon as butter. Use sparingly.

_____ *Whipped Butter.* This product generally contains 1/3 fewer calories, fat, and cholesterol than regular butter. Since margarine is basically a vegetable oil which has been artificially hardened by hydrogenation, some physiologists believe butter to be a better choice than margarine. We recommend that whipped butter may be used by those who are at their correct weight and do not have a problem with blood cholesterol. Even then it should be used judiciously.

———— *Butter Substitutes.* These are usually yellow powders which are essentially defatted, dehydrated butter extracts. We find them to be useful flavorings in cooked foods. Some brand names include Butter Buds and Molly McButter.

Cooking Oils

———— *Polyunsaturated Oils.* These include canola, safflower, corn, soybean, cottonseed, sesame, and peanut oils, listed here in order of decreasing polyunsaturation. The main focus is that you should use as little as possible of all varieties. (NOTE: If you prefer peanut oil for wok cookery, for example, there is not much difference in using this rather than safflower oil as long as it is used in small amounts.)

———— *Non-stick Sprays.* Don't be without these. They can save you fat and calories when used to coat your cookware, and they can be used as a light flavoring as well. They are now available in a butter flavor.

———— *Olive oil.* New research has indicated that this monounsaturated oil may actually help improve your overall cholesterol profile to a greater extent than do the polyunsaturates. It contains the same amount of fat and calories as other oils. Use sparingly.

Eggs/Egg Substitutes

———— *Whole Eggs.* Since one egg yolk contains an entire day's supply of cholesterol (250 mg), we usually recommend that whole eggs be eaten no more than one time per week (if at all), and even then only by those who have serum cholesterol levels below 200 mg/dl.

———— *Egg Whites.* This is one of the best protein sources available and contains no fat or cholesterol. Though scrambled egg whites have never seemed palatable, we use egg whites in all recipes calling for whole eggs. Simply *use two egg whites in place of one whole egg in most recipes* (muffins, pancakes, etc.). You will never know the difference.

——— *Egg Substitutes.* These are usually composed of 99 percent egg whites with enough other additives to make them look like a beaten whole egg. These products work well in combination foods and offer scrambled egg and omelette opportunities for those who must avoid most egg products due to elevated serum cholesterol levels (levels above 200 mg/dl).

Milk and Yogurt

——— *Skim and 1/2 Percent Low-fat Milk.* These milks should be used by all adults (even those who are already at their ideal bodyweight) and by many children over the age of 2. Nutritionally speaking, whole milk is half fat (i.e., half the calories in whole milk come from the butterfat), and 2 percent low-fat milk is still one-quarter fat. The calcium content of whole milk versus low-fat milk is virtually the same. Therefore, skim milk and skim milk products are excellent sources of calcium, phosphorous, and protein and remain low in calories and fat. *Milk is not just for kids.* Do not ignore this important food group.

——— *Low-fat Yogurt.* This can be a very versatile group of foods if you are not intimidated by a little cooking experimentation. You can make desserts, dips, sour cream and cream cheese substitutes, and many other items. If you are eating the eight-ounce, fruit-flavored yogurts, try to choose the lower calorie selections. Even though low in fat, many of the fruity yogurts can be very high in sugar and calories.

Cheeses

——— *Mozzarella and Other Low-fat Natural Cheese.* The low-fat natural cheeses include mozzarella (pizza cheese), mysost (a Scandinavian cheese made from whey), part-skim ricotta cheese (lasagne cheese), and low-fat cottage cheese. Always look for the words "made from part-skim milk" on the label. Some companies are now making low-fat varieties of traditionally high-fat cheeses (i.e., Alpine Lace, Kraft Light Naturals). Traditional high-fat cheeses include cheddar, colby, Monterey Jack, Swiss, Gouda, American, and most other natural, brick cheeses. These high-fat cheeses can be as much as 80 percent fat.

——— *Low-fat Processed Cheeses.* These include both slices, bricks, and spreads made from part-skim milk products. An example of this group is the Borden Lite-line cheese slices, which have half the calories and fat of most of the regular processed cheese slices made from whole milk. Some Weight Watchers products also fit into this category. Velveeta is another cheese which is not quite as high in fat as others, but not low enough to be used routinely. If blood pressure is a problem for you, look for low-sodium versions of these cheeses, as they are characteristically high in sodium.

Salad Dressings and Condiments

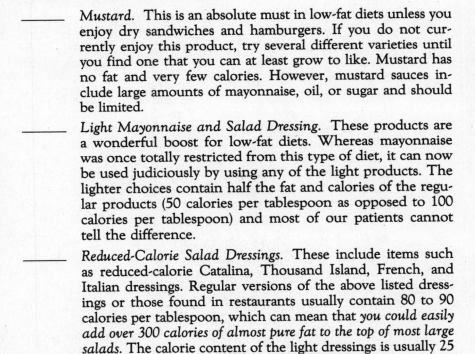

_____ *Mustard.* This is an absolute must in low-fat diets unless you enjoy dry sandwiches and hamburgers. If you do not currently enjoy this product, try several different varieties until you find one that you can at least grow to like. Mustard has no fat and very few calories. However, mustard sauces include large amounts of mayonnaise, oil, or sugar and should be limited.

_____ *Light Mayonnaise and Salad Dressing.* These products are a wonderful boost for low-fat diets. Whereas mayonnaise was once totally restricted from this type of diet, it can now be used judiciously by using any of the light products. The lighter choices contain half the fat and calories of the regular products (50 calories per tablespoon as opposed to 100 calories per tablespoon) and most of our patients cannot tell the difference.

_____ *Reduced-Calorie Salad Dressings.* These include items such as reduced-calorie Catalina, Thousand Island, French, and Italian dressings. Regular versions of the above listed dressings or those found in restaurants usually contain 80 to 90 calories per tablespoon, which can mean that *you could easily add over 300 calories of almost pure fat to the top of most large salads.* The calorie content of the light dressings is usually 25 calories per tablespoon or less. Try several and pinpoint your own favorites.

Meats

_____ *Sandwich Meats.* With the advent of low-fat mayonnaise and reduced calorie cheese and breads, sandwiches are back in style for calorie and fat counters alike. Choose low-fat varieties such as 95 percent fat-free turkey breast, chicken breast, lean ham, and tuna packed in water. Avoid mixed, heavily processed and canned foods such as canned chopped ham, deviled ham, potted meats, and variety meats such as salami and bologna. Also, try to choose meats which do not contain nitrates or nitrites as preservatives since these are cancer-causing agents. Read the label to determine if these are present.

——— *Fish.* Consumption of almost all types of fish is beneficial in reducing your serum cholesterol and triglycerides. If you are not a fish eater, try to develop a taste for this important food group. There is one exception, however. Shrimp is higher in cholesterol than heavy beef and should not be eaten frequently. On the other hand, lobster, clams, oysters, scallops, and crab are all low in fat and cholesterol and can be eaten frequently. Also, remember that frying fish and using tartar sauce defeat the whole purpose. Try the fish recipes in this book—you will love them.

——— *Poultry.* This group is yet another good low-calorie, low-fat, and low-cholesterol alternative. Typically, chicken and turkey are your best bets. Duck and goose are usually higher in fat and cholesterol. Also, remember that poultry skin and fat should be avoided. If using ground chicken or ground turkey as a ground beef substitute, make sure they did not grind the skin into the final product. Ground chicken and turkey are excellent in casseroles, and when used with strong spices (such as chili) they taste almost the same as beef.

——— *Beef and Pork.* These should be used no more than four times per week. However, if you make a very lean choice of beef (i.e., round steak, ground round, eye of the round roast) you don't end up with much more fat than you would with skinless chicken. Likewise, it is necessary to use the very leanest cuts of pork. Cholesterol is equally distributed in both the lean and fatty portion of meats. However, when you trim visible fat, you are cutting away excess amounts of saturated fats which can form cholesterol in the body.

——— *Other Meats.* Generally, game meats such as venison are extremely lean. Lamb is a fattier meat and only the leanest cuts should be used. Be sure to trim all visible fat.

Cereals

——— *Cold Cereals.* There are many good high-fiber choices including very high-fiber sources such as Fiber One (presweetened with Nutrasweet), Bran Buds, and All-Bran. These contain three times more fiber per serving than the medium-fiber-containing cereals such as Raisin Bran, Bran Chex, Bran Flakes, Fruit and Fiber, etc. A mix of the high-fiber and medium-fiber cereals can often improve palatability while increasing the fiber content per serving. At least one serving per day is recommended. See the fiber section of this book for more information.

NOTE: Check the ingredients to make sure that your cereal choice does not contain hydrogenated fat, palm oil, or coconut oil, as these will contribute to cholesterol problems.

NOTE: To consume 25 grams/day of crude fiber, you should try to include 1/2 to 3/4 cup of one of the highest-fiber cereals every day. The remaining dietary fiber can be supplied by fruits, vegetables and whole-grain products. *If you do not consume a very high-fiber cereal on most days, it is doubtful that you will reach the 25 grams/day of crude fiber recommended by most colon specialists.* (See page 202.)

_____ *Hot Cereals.* Of particular importance in this group is the use of oat bran cereals for persons needing to reduce their serum level of cholesterol. Other wheat-bran cereals are merely another way of adding fiber to your diet. Opt for whole-grain products when possible. Oat- or wheat-bran muffins can often be made from these products. But, remember not to use hydrogenated fat or egg yolks—this will defeat the cholesterol-lowering purpose of the oat-bran muffins.

Vegetables and Fruits

_____ *Fruits.* These foods are highly recommended but *not in unlimited quantities.* Fruits have such a good reputation for being nutritious, low in salt, and high in fiber that we find many of our patients overdoing it, especially when it comes to juices. Fresh, whole fruits are much better choices than canned or frozen fruits and certainly better than juices. Juices have lost some of their vitamin/mineral content and provide no dietary fiber.

_____ *Vegetables.* These are your best food choices for obtaining the largest amount of nutrients for the least amount of calories. In our opinion, they are a much more important food group than fruits. Fresh vegetables are usually a better choice than canned or frozen. Use fresh vegetables as soon as possible after purchase and do not eat any portion which has begun to decay. A good quality vegetable brush is a valuable kitchen tool—a must for washing fresh produce. Leave on as many skins as possible since these are particularly high in nutrients, fiber, and flavor. Particularly healthy, nutrient-packed choices include broccoli, spinach (raw or fresh), all types of greens, carrots, and other deep orange vegetables, cabbage, and peppers.

Prudent (but Great Tasting) Desserts

_____ *Frozen Desserts.* There are several frozen desserts which are low in fat, and some are made with Nutrasweet instead of sugar. These include ice milks, puddings made from skim milk and either sugar or Nutrasweet, various frozen bar items made to be low in calories, and frozen yogurt (usually low in fat, does contain sugar).

_____ *Other Desserts.* Additional ideas include angel food cake (contains no fat or cholesterol), baked fruits such as pears and apples, mock cream cheese recipes made with cottage cheese and yogurt, and gelatin desserts (made from unflavored gelatin, fruit juice, and other items). Try one of the many new low-calorie cookbooks now available for specific ideas.

Miscellaneous

_____ *Chips and Dip.* Try the cottage cheese dip listed in the recipe section of the back of this book as an alternative to the high-fat sour cream dips. Baked chips such as Skinny Munchies by Skinny Haven are now available in most areas. Or, to order these call 1-800-826-1911, the number listed on back of all their products. In general, any type snack chip should contain no more than 60 calories and 3 grams of fat per serving.

_____ *Snack Crackers.* There are several lower-fat snack crackers available at most supermarkets. Flavored rice cakes are another good alternative. Crispy crackers such as Craklesnax, Craklebread, or Rye-crisp are usually good low-fat choices. Be aware that just because something is a whole-grain product (such as a whole-wheat cracker) does not insure that it is also a good food choice. In fact, *many of these products contain relatively large amounts of shortening.* Read the labels carefully for fat content.

_____ *Pretzels.* These snack items are usually very similar to tiny loaves of crispy French bread made only from flour, water, and salt. The most important factor is that they do not contain the fat which is prevalent in other "Monday-Night-Football Munchies," such as peanuts and heavy chips. Choose low-sodium pretzels to reduce your salt intake (especially important for persons with heart disease, high blood pressure, PMS, and problems with water retention).

_____ *Popcorn.* This is a great snack choice if cooked properly. The best method is to make it in a microwave popping bowl. You simply pour popcorn in this bowl and place it in the microwave for approximately two minutes. The popcorn will pop beautifully with no oil at all. After the popcorn has popped spray it with a buttery flavored vegetable oil spray and sprinkle with a dry butter flavoring such as Molly McButter. *Most pre-bagged and boxed microwavable popcorn products should be avoided* as they contain large amounts of fat. Don't be deceived; even the ones which indicate "contains no butter" are still loaded with some sort of hydrogenated fat.

_____ *Beverages.* Many great choices are available including *water*, to name the best one of all. Don't ignore this important feature of a healthy diet—*you need at least five glasses of water per day.* Tea, coffee, and many sodas are caffeinated. Caffeine should be avoided by those with stomach ulcers, high blood pressure, fibrocystic breast disease, and premenstrual tension. Otherwise, no more than two servings per day is recommended. Also, instant coffee has about half as much caffeine as either percolated or brewed coffee. And, the less tea is steeped, the less caffeine is present. Sugar-free colas should be limited to about 24 ounces per day (two 12 oz. servings/day) since the long-term safety of Nutrasweet needs more investigation. Use of other sugar-free drinks such as Crystal Lite should also follow these guidelines.

_____ *Alcoholic Beverages.* If you are counting calories, you are better off leaving this group of beverages alone. Alcohol has 7 calories per gram whereas sugar and starch contain only 4 calories per gram. *Alcohol is almost as fattening as fat!* For cocktail hour, we suggest nonalcoholic beverages such as mineral water or club soda with a lime twist. In the way of alcoholic beverages, some health professionals consider one light beer or a single glass of wine to be a moderate choice. We strongly advise no more than two servings per day.

Mixed drinks (which usually include high-calorie mixers) are not recommended.

A FORMULA FOR SUCCESSFUL GROCERY SHOPPING

When shopping for groceries, ask the following questions:

1. How much fat does it contain? Take your calculator to the grocery store, and use this formula

$$\% \text{ fat} = \frac{\text{grams of fat} \times 9 \times 100\%}{\text{total calories}}$$

The items you choose (except for concentrated fats such as margarine and so forth) should be *below 30 percent fat.* This is particularly helpful for mixed foods such as frozen dinners, pasta mixes, and other combination foods. (This formula has also been discussed on page 76.)

2. Is it fresh? Fresh foods that have not decayed are your best sources of nutrients, even better than frozen or canned.

3. Does it contain unnecessary additives? If you can make a choice between something natural or something with colors you don't want anyway, make the natural choice. Read the actual ingredients to make sure the cover is not being deceptive.

CHAPTER 11

Cook It Right

Now that you have the correct ingredients in your kitchen, half the battle is won. The other half is the "how to's" of health-oriented cookery. In this chapter we will discuss the major principles of healthy cooking and, at the back of this book, we even supply you with some of our own favorite recipes. In cooking classes that Sharon gives to nutrition-consultation patients, most are absolutely amazed at the way ordinary recipes can be turned into "good-for-you recipes" with no sacrifices in the eating experience. *Bon appetite!*

COOKING TIPS

1. *Learn to cook well.* I [Sharon] was forced to take a basic food preparation course during my graduate training in nutrition. At first resentful of this time expenditure, I soon came to realize it was one of the most useful things I had ever done. Check out classes at a local junior or community college if you need this type training. Some communities even have professional cooking schools, which can be wonderful, but they are often expensive.

2. *Invest in a good, health-oriented cookbook.* Notice that we did not say "a few" or "several." Buy only one good cookbook and master it well before moving on to another. Before purchasing, scan the book carefully to determine if half or more of the recipes sound appealing and work with your lifestyle.

3. *Cooking methods are important.* To borrow part of a phrase from Nancy Reagan, *"Just Say No" when it comes to fried foods.* When you consider that a single onion contains only 30 calories and that an

order of onion rings contains 350 calories (70 percent of which are from fat), it becomes clear that this type of cooking is not compatible with the health-oriented diet plan. Frying with a heavy batter in some sort of hydrogenated fat (shortening) is the worst cooking method of all. Frying with one coating of cornmeal in vegetable oil is a better choice. Stir-fried and/or sauteed foods cooked in minimal amounts of oil are not very different from steaming food and then adding a little margarine. The best methods of cooking include boiling, broiling, steaming, and poaching. Other good methods include light stir-frying and grilling (good for getting rid of fat, but the blackened portion can be carcinogenic). Also, be careful not to overcook vegetables—this can destroy many of the valuable nutrients they store.

4. *Use the right equipment.* Nonstick pans or ones that will not stick at lower temperatures (stainless and porcelain finishes) are very important. Also, we use the nonstick sprays frequently; this enables us to use less cooking oil. Another helpful and inexpensive piece of kitchen equipment you will enjoy is a stainless steel vegetable steamer which will fit into one of your large sauce pans or a Dutch oven. They are easy to use and clean, and will provide you with cooked vegetables which have not had essential vitamins leached out due to direct contact with boiling water. Bamboo steamers and poachers are also easy to use and readily obtainable at cook shops.

5. *Make use of the microwave.* This cooking method can save you time as well as valuable nutrients. Many new microwave cooking utensils are now available. The microwave popcorn popper has already been mentioned. Other dishes suitable for vegetable cookery allow even the busiest of home chefs to prepare a cooked vegetable from freezer to table in five minutes flat. Microwaving food helps preserve nutrients which can be destroyed by conventional methods of cooking.

6. *Get rid of the fat.* The days of the grease can atop the kitchen stove should be long gone. For every tablespoon of any kind of fat (corn oil, shortening, bacon drippings) that you keep out of your food, you will be saving at least 120 of the wrong kind of calories. Trim all meat fat before cooking so it doesn't melt and become incorporated into the final cooked product. Buy only the leanest meats and especially the leanest ground beef (we recommend ground round). Drain fat from cooked products. Remove chicken skin before cooking if you are making a combination food such as chicken and rice. In recipes, try using half as much fat (margarine, butter, oil, shortening) as is called for. In most instances you will not be able to detect much difference in the taste of your final product.

7. *Start your own recipe collection.* We usually find that with slight alterations, most recipes can be adapted to the basic precepts of health-oriented cookery (with obvious exceptions like walnut fudge). We have

written down most of these old family favorites along with our new recipes and formed our own special recipe collection which meets all our cooking needs from daily family suppers to haute cuisine for dinner parties. (See pages 276–291.)

8. *Use low-fat substitutes.* Be open to new low-fat food products and don't tell your family what is going on in the kitchen until after they have tried your new culinary creation. Let them make a decision on the new recipe without prejudice. Try some of the following substitutes to achieve flavors you thought were only possible when eating the wrong kinds of foods.

For sour cream try substituting low-fat plain yogurt or a combination of low-fat yogurt and the reduced-calorie sour creams which are now available. Another alternative is pureed cottage cheese and lemon juice (16 oz. cottage cheese with 2 tablespoons lemon juice in a food processor until smooth). This is a particularly good substitute for sour cream when making dips.

For cream cheese try draining the whey from plain low-fat yogurt to make a product which is quite similar in texture and somewhat similar in taste to cream cheese. Commercial sieves which make this process easy are now available by catalog or in gourmet cook shops. We have personally made good cheesecakes out of these products and find them to be remarkably delicious. When preparing recipes that call for regular cream cheese, another alternative is to use the lower fat versions of cream cheese which are now commercially available.

For eggs try substituting two egg whites in most combination or baked recipes instead of one whole egg. For example, if you are making oat-bran muffins to decrease your serum cholesterol, but with a whole egg add 250 mg of cholesterol to the mix, you have just defeated your purpose. When whole eggs are required in recipes for quiche or egg casseroles, try one of the commercial, low-cholesterol egg substitutes. Most of these products are made of 99 percent egg white with other substances added to simulate the yolk. If your serum cholesterol is always in control (200 mg/dl or less), there is no need for you to avoid whole eggs in everyday cooking.

9. *Buy a separating cup.* These are wonderful little devices which look similar to measuring cups except that there is a large spout which pours liquids from the bottom of the cup. By using this, you can de-fat any drippings from beef or poultry in order to make a low-fat gravy. For example, after cooking a roast (eye-of-the-round roast is the leanest), pour the drippings into the separating cup. The fat floats to the top while the bouillon sinks to the bottom. You can then pour off the fat-free bouillon, thicken with a cold flour and water paste, cook until thickened, and you will have a wonderful, lump-free, low-calorie beef gravy to put on top of your mashed potatoes (which have been made

with low-fat margarine and skim milk). Your family or guests will never know the difference and will probably praise you for being such a good cook.

10. *Dilute recipes with high-fiber, nutrient-rich, low-calorie foods.* For example, when we make tuna salad, we usually "dilute" the whole recipe with chopped apple and celery. Or when we make chili, taco meat stuffing, or the like, we dilute it with chopped peppers, onions, and carrots. When we make a rice side dish, we often mix in vegetables so that for a 1/2 cup portion, we are getting less fat, fewer calories, and a lot more flavor. This system works. Guests always want our recipes!

11. *Make the most of anti-cancer foods.* The basic foods to include as often as possible in your diet are broccoli; cauliflower; cabbage; Brussels sprouts; spinach; all green leafy vegetables; yellow vegetables, such as sweet potatoes and carrots; citrus fruits; yellow fruits, such as mango and cantaloupe; and wheat bran. We will discuss reasons for including these foods in the chapter on preventing cancer. But for now, seek out recipes which take advantage of these foods without adding a lot of extra fat sources to the recipe. Start this process by using the recipes in the back of this book.

12. Go *natural when possible.* The natural method of preparing food includes many choices. First, when you have an option of choosing a food item which is natural (no artificial flavorings or preservatives), then do so. Also, leave as many skins and peels on your foods as possible. You will need to take greater care in washing everything and may want to purchase a good vegetable cleaning brush. Much of the fiber and vitamin/mineral content of vegetables is contained in the peel. For example, when we make potato salad, we leave the peels on the potatoes. This adds fiber and nutrients to the entire dish. We add chopped celery, green pepper, and light mayonnaise to fulfill the other guidelines of health-oriented cookery.

13. *Be light-handed with the salt.* Salt restriction is not the big issue that it was 15 years ago. The people who really must be careful about salt are primarily those who have been diagnosed as having high blood pressure. For these persons, salt restriction (under 2000 mg per day) is important. However, for persons who have never had a problem with hypertension, and who eat reasonably, there is no indication that salt restriction will be that beneficial. Nonetheless, since the American diet is literally steeped in salt, we recommend that you become an expert with herbs and spices in an effort to ease away from the salt shaker. This procedure is stressed throughout the recipe section of this book. *We do not recommend a salt substitute unless suggested by your physician* since these can sometimes disturb your electrolyte balance. Table 11.1 gives a few suggestions for seasoning various foods with herbs and other flavorings as a replacement for salt.

Table 11.1. Food Flavorings As a Replacement for Salt

Beef	Bay leaf, dry mustard, green pepper, red wine, sage, marjoram, mushrooms, nutmeg, onion, pepper, thyme.
Chicken and poultry	Cranberries, mushrooms, paprika, parsley, poultry seasoning (unsalted), thyme, sage, lemon juice, orange juice, lime juice, white wine.
Lamb	Curry, garlic, mint, pineapple, rosemary.
Pork	Apple, applesauce, garlic, onion, sage, cranberries.
Veal	Apricots, bay leaf, curry, currant jelly, ginger, marjoram, oregano.
Fish	Bay leaf, curry, dry mustard, green pepper, lemon juice, lime juice, marjoram, mushroom, paprika, onion, dillweed, parsley.
Eggs	Curry, dry mustard, green pepper, jelly, mushrooms, onion, paprika, parsley, tomato.
Asparagus	Lemon juice.
Corn	Green pepper, tomato, sugar.
Green beans	Marjoram, lemon juice, nutmeg, dill seed, sugar, unsalted French dressing.
Peas	Onion, mint, mushrooms, parsley, green pepper.
Potatoes	Onion, mace, green pepper, parsley.
Squash	Ginger, mace, onion, basil, nutmeg.
Tomatoes	Basil, marjoram, onion, sugar.

CHAPTER 12

The Eating Plan

For lack of innovative, personalized information, most eating plans and diets fail. Let's face it—people are tired of the old "Four Basic Food Groups" routine because it has rarely been presented with pizazz and flexibility for daily living. There is simply too much information about nutrition and foods to stop at this level anymore. There are many choices to make, and you must be well informed to make the right ones. That is why we have included three other chapters leading up to your prescribed eating plan.

Thus far, we have made the following discoveries about healthy foods:

Chapter 9   *What* we should eat
Chapter 10   *Where* we can buy it
Chapter 11   *How* we can cook it

Now let's look at the quantities and combinations of healthy foods which will be of the most benefit to you.

HEALTHY EATING TIPS

1. *Pre-planning is fundamental.* Although you can make good food choices almost anywhere, a certain amount of premeditated meal planning is usually a must. Consumption of what we call "*desperation foods,*" such as candy bars, soft drinks, chips, and other "machine foods" eaten in haste at three o'clock in the afternoon because you

purposefully skipped or otherwise missed lunch is not pre-planning. Also, ordering a double cheeseburger with fries because everyone else at the table has done this is also a clear-cut case of failure to plan what you want and need before mealtime. Less than two minutes of thought and five minutes of preparation can prepare you for good food choices throughout the next day.

2. *Distribute food throughout the day.* This is all part of the pre-planning. Take time to eat! Eat appropriate portions and eat frequently. See sample menus for examples of how to do this.

3. *Watch your portions.* Have you ever noticed that once you become accustomed to taking seconds at dinner, you somehow feel cheated if you are denied this privilege? Humans are creatures of habit. Unfortunately, we make most of our choices (even food choices) based on these habits. If you are currently eating portions which are too large, it may not be because you are genuinely hungry; it may, instead, be that you are habitually over-eating. As you follow the diet plan listed in this book, we recommend that you initially measure food in measuring cups and on small food scales to ensure accuracy in determining the appropriate food portion sizes for your own diet plan. The fact is, most of us don't need as much food as we think we do, especially women past age 35. Many of us became accustomed to eating larger portions of food during our child-bearing years and haven't cut back yet.

4. *Nutrient intake is key.* On the food lists that follow, circle the foods you like that have a star (*) next to them. These are particularly healthy choices and help keep the nutrient content of your diet high. For example, even though broccoli and lettuce are on the same food list, five pounds of certain types of lettuce will still not match the nutritional content of one-half cup of broccoli.

5. *Good food choices are easy to make.* If you think healthy foods are boring or in some way don't taste good, you are living in the past. You can get great-tasting "light" versions of almost any food, and there are very few natural (unprocessed) foods which should really be avoided except those which are very high in fat. Even then, these may be eaten occasionally in moderation by most people. You are not going to miss a thing.

6. *Throw away your guilt—forever!* There is no room in a positive, health-oriented program for worrying about the past. There is also no reason to be overly concerned about occasional splurges, unless there is a specific medical problem which precludes these splurges. For example, if you fall off the wagon at a Christmas party and eat 3,000 calories in one sitting (*this is a lot of food and drink!*), you will gain less than a pound of fat, technically. However, the far greater

problem is that when you step on the scales in the morning, you may be up three to five pounds from water retention alone. At this point, the guilt which usually sets in may precipitate additional indiscretionary behaviors just because you feel like a failure from the previous day.

The moral of this story is that *it is all right to fall or even willingly jump off that health-food wagon on occasion.* Have fun with this occasional break in the system and never look back. If, on the other hand, you take that fall so hard that you stay on the ground and let the wheels roll over you, then you do have a serious problem—and one which may prevent you from being able to ride on that wagon for some time to come.

DETERMINING YOUR CALORIC NEEDS

Determining how many calories you need is basic to any diet plan. To do this, you must first ask yourself a hard question—"Am I overweight?" If the answer is yes, don't feel alone. Almost two-thirds of all American women want to lose weight—some justifiably and some not.

Being thin is an obsession in America. Let us point out right now that being severely underweight can be just as hazardous to your health as being moderately overweight. Thus we will spend some time now helping you to determine your own best weight.

Finding Your Ideal Bodyweight

The following chart is perhaps one you have seen many times. It is the Metropolitan Life Insurance Company Table of Desirable Weights for women over 25 years of age. *(Note that the weights are based on your wearing a two-inch heel and indoor clothing.)* Have you ever wondered why this large insurance company has spent millions of dollars researching height and weight information? They are definitely not in the nutrition business. And they don't practice medicine. What's in it for them? Actually, they are in the business of *health risk appraisal.* They want to know who has the best chances of living a long, healthy life. They also want to know who is at greatest risk for a catastrophic illness like heart disease or diabetes. If you fall into the suggested weight range for your own height and frame size, then you are considered a better risk than if you are not within the appropriate weight range. Again, being overweight or underweight is not as healthy as being within or close to your correct body weight.

Table 12.1. Desirable Weights for Adult Women

Height (with 2″ heel)		Weight in Pounds (includes 3 lbs. of clothing)		
Feet	Inches	Small Frame	Medium Frame	Large Frame
4	11	95–101	98–110	106–122
5	0	96–104	101–113	109–125
5	1	99–107	104–116	112–128
5	2	102–110	107–119	115–131
5	3	105–113	110–122	118–134
5	4	108–116	113–126	121–138
5	5	111–119	116–130	125–142
5	6	114–123	120–135	129–146
5	7	118–127	124–139	133–150
5	8	122–131	128–143	137–154
5	9	126–135	132–147	141–158
5	10	130–140	136–151	145–163
5	11	134–144	140–155	149–168

My *ideal* weight range is _____.

My *current* weight is _____.

I need to lose (or gain) _____ pounds.

Look at Table 12.1 and draw a line under all weights listed for your height. Remember, this chart is based on your height plus a two-inch heel. If you are 5 feet 4 inches tall, then you should look at the weights under the 5 feet 6 inches category. Now determine what frame size you think you are and circle the correct weight range.

Determining Frame Size

We want to add a note on determining your frame size. Do not assume that your frame size is merely a reflection of your outward appearance. For example, if you are slender, you are not necessarily a small frame size. Likewise, obesity does not necessarily indicate a large frame size. Use the following instructions to find your correct frame size. (Sneed and McIlhaney, 1988; Grant, 1980. Used by permission.) When finished, make sure you have accurately recorded your correct, ideal bodyweight range.

Your height in inches _____.
Your right-hand wrist measurement just beyond (toward fingers) the
    little bone on the outside of your wrist in inches _____.
Height ÷ Wrist circumference = X

Determine frame size as follows:

female	male	frame size
X > 11.0	X > 10.4	small
X = 10.1–11.0	X = 9.6–10.4	medium
X < 10.1	X < 9.6	large

Your X value is _____.   Your frame size is _____.

Knowing Exceptions to the Rule

In women, there are two general forms of moderate obesity—those
who put on weight throughout the entire torso and through the chest
area, and those who predominantly add extra fat through the hips,
thighs and buttocks. It is thought that women of the latter category do
this naturally as a fuel storage for milk production or lactation. Unfortunately, not all this fuel is always used. *Authorities have stated that it is
possible for women to carry as much as twenty extra pounds of fat
through the hips, thighs, and buttocks without increasing their health risk.*
However, if the fat is carried throughout the torso and upper areas of
the body, then it is an increased risk factor for hypertension. By and
large, we do recommend that all patients try to come close to their
calculated ideal bodyweight. We have had patients lose as little as ten
pounds and bring an elevated serum cholesterol level down to normal.

Don't Play the Diet Game

American women have become obsessed with weight control and
thinness; and some of this obsession with thinness is too much to be
healthy. In fact, it's absolutely unnatural. Roller coaster rides from
one diet program to another, with your weight following the same
route is very harmful to your health. Every time you lose a pound of
fat, there are miles of blood capillaries which are also lost. Contrast-
ingly, every time you gain a pound of fat, you add these same blood
networking systems. If your weight is constantly going up and down,
you are putting a tremendous stress on your body in general and your
heart in particular. Our advice is to get on a good eating and exercise
program which concentrates on the right types of foods and adequate
calorie expenditure (exercise). This kind of program works, and it can
stay with you for life.

Additionally, there have been increasing numbers of anorexic/ bulimic women perhaps as a result of the society we live in. The following excerpt describes this more fully.

> Let us say something more about "ideal weight." Far too much emphasis is placed on this single issue, especially by females. Women and girls of all ages are feeling the constant burden of keeping their weight or percentage of body fat at a level that may actually be too low for them. There is an endless barrage of "what we should look like" at every magazine stand, based on fashion-model standards. The result is an epidemic of anorexic/bulimic women who are so obsessed with weight control that they are paranoid about every mouthful and are often endangering their health.*

Choosing a Calorie Level

After determining your ideal bodyweight, you are now aware of whether you need weight loss, weight maintenance, or weight gain. The calorie levels below have been divided into these three categories. After deciding which category you need, you should choose one of the calorie levels provided within that category.

1. To lose weight. 1000 or 1200 calories/day. In most cases 1200 calories is the best calorie level for dieters. This allows for a steady weight loss of one to three pounds per week when coupled with a good exercise program. The 1000 calorie diet is also effective but can be difficult to stick to for long periods of time.

2. To maintain weight. 1500, 1800, or 2000 calories/day. The typical calorie level for most of you who are currently at your correct weight will be 1800 calories per day. If you are active, then you may require more calories per day to match your energy expenditures. If you are very active, you may require even more calories per day.

3. To gain weight. 2200 or 2400 calories/day. If you require weight gain, increase your calorie intake with extra good food choices, especially from the starch and bread group. If you continue to have a problem with being underweight, you should consult a physician.

After determining your appropriate calorie level, you can then refer to the following information on the Exchange Diet to plan your daily menus. *We have included new foods, combination foods, and fast foods to help bring this plan to life for you.* Additionally, there is a 7-day meal plan at the 1200 calorie level and at the 1800 calorie level to assist you in designing your own diets. We chose these two levels because they are the ones most commonly used for weight loss and weight maintenance,

---

*Reprinted by permission. Sneed, S. and McIlhaney, J., PMS: *What It is and What You Can Do About It*, Baker Book House, 1988, p. 90.

respectively. To match the diet plans to other calorie levels, just add or reduce foods according to the daily food allotment.

THE EXCHANGE DIET

Basic Concepts. The exchange diet is a basic program used by dietitians and nutritionists throughout the country as a way of offering more food choices to those on restricted diets. The concept of food exchanges (or food equivalents) has existed for many years and has weathered a barrage of "overnight success" diet schemes. It is equally well respected among the medical profession for its healthful benefits, including simplifying the idea of a "balanced diet" (Sneed and McIlhaney, 1988).

The exchange lists we have put together are our own. They represent a compilation of many other references and take into account the use of low-fat alternatives, low-calorie foods, the best of the fast foods, and the best of other foods. We have not included too many unhealthy choices in the lists. But, as you can see, you won't lack for anything, except that occasional rich dessert like cheesecake or chocolate cake. If you consume items like these infrequently (no more than two times per month) and have reasonable portion sizes, then do so without guilt and enjoy every mouthful. It it what you do on a daily basis that counts—not on special occasions.

Instructions for the Exchange Diet. There are six exchange lists which follow this instruction. They include:

List 1: Starch/Bread
List 2: Meat (includes fish, poultry, eggs, and cheese)
List 3: Milk and Milk Products
List 4: Fruits/Juices
List 5: Low-calorie Vegetables and Free Foods
List 6: Fats (includes dressings and nuts)

In addition, there is a section on combination foods and fast foods and information on vegetarian diets.

Foods are grouped together in an exchange list (see pages 127–136) because they are nutritionally alike. Every food within a list has about the same amount of fat, protein, carbohydrate, and calories in the quantities specified. Therefore, they can be "exchanged" for any other food on the same list. Then, using the exchange lists and following the prescribed meal plans (that is, the number of items from each list you can have per day) you should have the right proportions of nutrients in your diet without spending much planning time. The exchange list we have presented contains a variety of foods; however, some are nutritionally better choices than others because they are higher in vitamin, mineral, and/or fiber content; others are better choices in different ways (i.e., lower in sodium). *In each list, we have placed a star (*) by those foods which are your healthiest food choices.*

The following step-by-step guide will help you set up your own meal plans:

1. From Table 12.2 choose the calorie level which best suits your needs. Note that exchanges are listed per day. If this seems like too much or too little food after a few days, then choose another level more appropriate to your needs. Now, make several photocopies of the Personal Menu Planner in Table 12.3.

2. Notice that Table 12.2 has your prescribed food exchanges distributed throughout the day. This is the healthiest way to eat. It is important that you do not starve yourself at certain times during the day only to overeat at other times. This will cause fluctuations in your blood glucose levels and perhaps contribute to intermittent elevated levels of serum lipids. However, if you prefer to change the food distribution slightly, there is no problem. An example would be adding a snack onto the nearest meal, or saving something from a meal and eating it two hours later.

3. A week's worth of sample menus for the 1200 and 1800 calorie/day plans (pages 120–126) has been provided as a guide for you to use in setting up your own meal plan. Study them carefully.

4. From the food exchange lists on pages 127–136 compile several daily menus for yourself using photocopies of the Personal Menu Planner (Table 12.3), at the calorie level that is appropriate for you.

Table 12.2. Daily Meal Plans

Food List	Calorie Level				
	1000	1200	1500	1800	2000
	(number of exchanges per day)				
Bread/starch	4	5	7	9	10
Meat	4*	4*	4	5	5
Milk	2	2	2	3	3
Fruit	3	3	4	5	6
Vegetables/free foods	free	free	free	free	free
			(at least 4/day)		
Fats	1	3	4	5	6

*Meat choices should be from the low-fat list exclusively in the 1000- and 1200-calorie categories.

Table 12.3. Personal Menu Planner

Number of exchanges	Menu for Day _____	Menu for Day _____
Breakfast		
starch _____		
meat _____		
milk _____		
fruit _____		
veg _____		
fat _____		
Snack		
_____		
_____		
Lunch		
starch _____		
meat _____		
milk _____		
fruit _____		
veg _____		
fat _____		
Snack		
_____		
_____		
Dinner		
starch _____		
meat _____		
milk _____		
fruit _____		
veg _____		
fat _____		
Snack		
_____		
_____		

A WORD ABOUT THE SAMPLE MENUS

1. The 1200-calorie menus are designed for weight loss and will work for most people. The 1800-calorie menus are for weight maintenance.

2. Both diets exhibit the following:

- They are high in fiber (usually over 20 grams/day).

- They meet all nutritional needs for the majority of women (except calories in the 1200-calorie diet plans).

- They include some fast foods and other prepared food items.

- They do not require elaborate preparation.

- They do not always *exactly* match the number of allotted food exchanges for that day, but are at least very close (flexibility makes your diet more pleasant).

Day 1—Sample Menu

1200 Calories (for weight loss)		1800 Calories (for weight maintenance)	
Number of exchanges	Menu for Day ___1___	Number of exchanges	Menu for Day ___1___
Breakfast starch _1_ meat ___ milk _1_ fruit _2_ veg ___ fat ___	¼ cup *Fiber One* cereal ½ cup *Raisin Bran* cereal 8 oz. ½% milk 1 small banana 1 tsp. sugar (optional)	**Breakfast** starch _2_ meat ___ milk _1_ fruit _2_ veg ___ fat _1_	¾ cup *Fiber One* cereal ¾ cup *Raisin Bran* cereal 8 oz. ½% milk 1 small banana 1 tsp. diet margarine 1 tsp. sugar (optional)
Snack 1 starch	3 2½" graham cracker squares	**Snack** 1 starch	3 2½" graham cracker squares
Lunch starch _2_ meat _1½_ milk ___ fruit ___ veg _1_ fat ___	2 pc. lite bread 1 slice turkey breast 1 slice *Lite-line* cheese mustard, lettuce, tomato 2 sm. oatmeal cookies*	**Lunch** starch _3_ meat _2_ milk ___ fruit ___ veg _1_ fat ___	2 pc. rye bread 1 oz. turkey breast 1 oz. low-fat cheese mustard, lettuce, tomato 2 sm. oatmeal cookies*
Snack		**Snack** – 2 *fruit* 1 starch 1 milk	1 cup grapes 6 crackers ⅓ cup cottage cheese dip*
Dinner starch _1_ meat _2_ milk ___ fruit ___ veg _3_ fat _1_	2 cups *Chinese chicken and vegetables* (*Moo Goo Gai Pan*) ½ cup steamed rice sesame oil for stir-fry	**Dinner** starch _2_ meat _3_ milk ___ fruit ___ veg _3_ fat _2_	2 cups *Chinese chicken and vegetables* (*Moo Goo Gai Pan*) 1 cup steamed rice 2 tsp. sesame oil
Snack 1 milk 1 fruit	1 cup plain yogurt ¾ cup fresh strawberries 1 tsp sugar (optional)	**Snack** 1 milk 1 fruit	1 cup plain yogurt ¾ cup fresh strawberries 1 tsp. sugar (optional)

*Indicates recipes included in this book.

Day 2—Sample Menu

1200 Calories (for weight loss)		1800 Calories (for weight maintenance)	
Number of exchanges	Menu for Day ___2___	Number of exchanges	Menu for Day ___2___
Breakfast starch _1_ meat ___ milk _1_ fruit _1_ veg ___ fat ___	8 oz. plain, low-fat yogurt ½ cup fresh blueberries 2 tsp. sugar 1 bran muffin*	**Breakfast** starch _1_ meat ___ milk _1_ fruit _1_ veg ___ fat _1_	8 oz. plain, low-fat yogurt ½ cup fresh blueberries 2 tsp. sugar 1 bran muffin* 1 tsp. butter
Snack 1 vegetable	6 oz. tomato juice	**Snack** 1 vegetable 2 fruit	6 oz. tomato juice 1 large apple
Lunch starch _2_ meat _1_ milk ___ fruit ___ veg _1_ fat _1_	2 slices lite bread ¼ cup tuna 1 Tbsp. lite mayonnaise lettuce, tomato 6 vanilla wafers	**Lunch** starch _3_ meat _2_ milk _1_ fruit ___ veg _1_ fat _1_	2 slices wheat bread 2 oz. tuna 1 Tbsp. lite mayonnaise lettuce, tomato 6 vanilla wafers 8 oz. ½% milk
Snack 1 vegetable	1 cup carrot sticks	**Snack** 2 fruit 1 vegetable	1 med. apple 1 cup carrot sticks
Dinner starch _2_ meat _2_ milk ___ fruit ___ veg _2_ fat ___	½ cup pasta noodles ½ cup tomato & meat sauce salad, no-oil dressing 1 slice angel food cake	**Dinner** starch _4_ meat _3_ milk _1_ fruit ___ veg _2_ fat _2_	1 cup pasta noodles ¾ cup tomato & meat sauce 2 Tbsp. Parmesan cheese salad, low-cal dressing 1 slice bread 1 slice angel food cake
Snack 1 milk 2 fruit	1 oz. mozzarella cheese 1 apple	**Snack** 2 fruit 1 starch	1 banana 1 bran muffin*

*Indicates recipes included in this book.

Day 3—Sample Menu

1200 Calories (for weight loss)		1800 Calories (for weight maintenance)	
Number of exchanges	Menu for Day ___3___	Number of exchanges	Menu for Day ___3___
Breakfast starch __1__ meat __1__ milk ____ fruit __1__ veg ____ fat __1__	½ English muffin 1 egg, cooked, no oil ½ cup orange juice hot tea 2 tsp. diet margarine	**Breakfast** starch __2__ meat __1__ milk __1__ fruit __1__ veg ____ fat __1__	1 English muffin 1 egg, cooked, no oil ½ cup orange juice 8 oz. ½% milk 2 tsp. diet margarine hot tea
Snack _____ _____		**Snack** __2 fruits__ __2 starch__	1 banana 16 animal crackers
Lunch starch __1__ meat __1__ milk __½__ fruit ____ veg __3__ fat __1__	Chef salad w/ vegetables, cheese, ham, low-cal dressing & croutons	**Lunch** starch __1__ meat __1__ milk __½__ fruit __2__ veg __3__ fat __2__	Chef salad w/ vegetables, cheese, ham, low-cal dressing & croutons 1 roll 1 tsp. margarine 1 cup fruit salad
Snack __2 fruit__ _____	1 large apple	**Snack** __1 fruit__ __1 milk__	1 large apple 1 oz. low-fat cheese
Dinner starch __1__ meat __2__ milk ____ fruit ____ veg __2__ fat __1__	1 BBQ chicken breast, no skin ½ cup Skinny French Fries* ½ cup green beans sliced tomatoes	**Dinner** starch __3__ meat __3__ milk ____ fruit ____ veg __2__ fat __2__	1 BBQ chicken breast, no skin 1 cup Skinny French Fries* w/ catsup green beans, sliced tomatoes ½ cup frozen yogurt
Snack __1 starch__ __1 milk__	¾ cup All-Bran cereal 8 oz. ½% milk	**Snack** __1 starch__ __1 milk__	¾ cup All-Bran cereal 8 oz. ½% milk

*Indicates recipes included in this book.

Day 4—Sample Menu

1200 Calories (for weight loss)		1800 Calories (for weight maintenance)	
Number of exchanges	Menu for Day ___4___	Number of exchanges	Menu for Day ___4___
Breakfast starch _2_ meat ___ milk _1_ fruit _1_ veg ___ fat ___	½ cup hot oat-bran cereal 8 oz. ½% milk 2 pc. lite toast 2 tsp. diet margarine 1 tsp. all-fruit jam 4 oz. applesauce	**Breakfast** starch _3_ meat ___ milk _1_ fruit _1_ veg ___ fat _1_	1 cup oat-bran cereal 8 oz. ½% milk 1 pc. whole-wheat toast 2 tsp. diet margarine 1 tsp. all-fruit jam 4 oz. orange juice
Snack _____ _____		**Snack** _1 milk_ _2 fruit_	1 oz. mozzarella 1 apple
Lunch starch _1_ meat _1_ milk _½_ fruit ___ veg _2–3_ fat _1_	Spinach salad with ¼ cup eggs and 2 Tbsp. grated cheese 5 Melba Toasts low-fat dressing	**Lunch** starch _2_ meat _2_ milk ___ fruit ___ veg _2–3_ fat _2_	Spinach salad with ½ cup eggs and 2 Tbsp. grated cheese 5 Melba Toasts 1 roll low-fat dressing
Snack _1 fruit_ _½ milk_	1 small pear ½ oz. mozzarella cheese	**Snack** _____ _____	
Dinner starch _2_ meat _2_ milk ___ fruit ___ veg _2_ fat _½_	2 cups Vegetarian Chili* 2 Tbsp. grated cheese salad, low-fat dressing 6 saltine crackers	**Dinner** starch _4_ meat _3_ milk ___ fruit ___ veg _2_ fat _2_	2 cups Vegetarian Chili* 2 Tbsp. grated cheese 1 pc. cornbread salad, low-cal dressing 2 tsp. diet margarine ½ cup pudding (skim milk)
Snack _2 fruit_	2 cups watermelon	**Snack** _2 fruit_ _1 milk_	2 cups watermelon 1 cup ½% milk

*Indicates recipes included in this book.

Day 5—Sample Menu

1200 Calories (for weight loss)		1800 Calories (for weight maintenance)	
Number of exchanges	Menu for Day ___5___	Number of exchanges	Menu for Day ___5___
Breakfast starch _1_ meat ___ milk _1_ fruit _1_ veg ___ fat ___	1 bran or oat-bran muffin* 8 oz. 1/2% milk 1/4 canteloupe	**Breakfast** starch _2_ meat ___ milk _1_ fruit _2_ veg ___ fat ___	2 bran or oat-bran muffins* 8 oz. 1/2% milk 1/2 canteloupe
Snack ___ ___		**Snack** ___ ___	
Lunch starch _2_ meat _2_ milk ___ fruit ___ veg _1_ fat _1_	Whopper, Jr., no mayo (Burger King)	**Lunch** starch _3_ meat _2_ milk ___ fruit ___ veg _1_ fat _1_	Whopper, Jr., no mayo (Burger King) 1 large oatmeal cookie*
Snack _1 fruit_ ___	4 oz. apple juice	**Snack** _1 starch_ _2 fruit_	6 crackers 1 banana
Dinner starch _1_ meat _3_ milk ___ fruit _1_ veg _2_ fat ___	3 oz. Baked Orange Roughy* 1/2 cup Rice Pilaf* fresh green beans sugar-free gelatin with fruit	**Dinner** starch _2_ meat _3_ milk _1/2_ fruit _1_ veg _2_ fat _1_	3 oz. Baked Orange Roughy* 1 cup Rice Pilaf* fresh green beans gelatin salad with fruit & cottage cheese
Snack _1 milk_	8 oz. 1/2% milk	**Snack** _1 starch_ _1 milk_	1 slice Pumpkin Bread* 8 oz. 1/2% milk

*Indicates recipes included in this book.

Day 6—Sample Menu

1200 Calories (for weight loss)		1800 Calories (for weight maintenance)	
Number of exchanges	Menu for Day ___6___	Number of exchanges	Menu for Day ___6___
Breakfast starch __1__ meat ____ milk __1__ fruit __2__ veg ____ fat ____	³/₄ cup high-fiber cereal 8 oz. ¹/₂% milk 1 whole banana	**Breakfast** starch __2__ meat ____ milk __1__ fruit __2__ veg ____ fat __1__	³/₄ cup high-fiber cereal 8 oz. ¹/₂% milk 1 whole banana 1 pc. whole-wheat toast 2 tsp. diet margarine
Snack		**Snack**	
Lunch starch __1__ meat ____ milk ____ fruit __1__ veg __3__ fat ____	large bowl clear vegetable soup (some potatoes) salad, no-oil dressing ¹/₂ cup fruit salad	**Lunch** starch __2__ meat __1__ milk ____ fruit __2__ veg __3__ fat __1__	large bowl vegetable and chicken soup (some potatoes) salad, low-fat dressing whole-grain roll 1 cup fruit salad
Snack 1 milk	8 oz ¹/₂% milk	**Snack** 1 milk	8 oz. ¹/₂% milk
Dinner starch __2__ meat __4__ milk __1__ fruit ____ veg __2__ fat __2__	4 oz. filet mignon large baked potato 1 Tbsp. light sour cream 2 tsp. diet margarine 2 Tbsp. grated cheese steamed broccoli	**Dinner** starch __3__ meat __4__ milk __1__ fruit ____ veg __2__ fat __3__	4 oz. filet mignon large baked potato 1 Tbsp. light sour cream 4 tsp. diet margarine 2 Tbsp. grated cheese 1 dinner roll steamed broccoli
Snack 1 starch	¹/₂ cup ice milk	**Snack** 2 starch 1 fruit	1 cup ice milk ¹/₂ cup fresh fruit

*Indicates recipes included in this book.

Day 7—Sample Menu

1200 Calories (for weight loss)		1800 Calories (for weight maintenance)	
Number of exchanges	Menu for Day ___7___	Number of exchanges	Menu for Day ___7___
Breakfast starch _1_ meat ___ milk _1_ fruit ___ veg ___ fat _1/2_	1/2 bagel 1 tsp. diet margarine all-fruit jam 8 oz. 1/2% milk	**Breakfast** starch _2_ meat ___ milk _1_ fruit ___ veg ___ fat _1_	1 bagel 2 tsp. diet margarine all-fruit jam 8 oz. 1/2% milk
Snack 2 fruit	1 large orange	**Snack** 2 fruit	1 large orange
Lunch starch _2_ meat ___ milk _1_ fruit ___ veg _1_ fat ___	1 pita bread 1 oz. shredded cheese vegetables no-oil dressing	**Lunch** starch _2_ meat _1_ milk ___ fruit _2_ veg ___ fat _1_	1 pita bread 1 oz. cheese vegetables low-cal dressing 1/2 canteloupe
Snack 1 vegetable	6 oz. vegetable juice cocktail	**Snack** 1 vegetable	1 vegetable juice cocktail
Dinner starch _1_ meat _4_ milk ___ fruit _1_ veg _2_ fat _1_	4 oz. grilled fish 1/2 cup brown rice sauteed vegetables 1 tsp. olive oil 3/4 cup fresh berries	**Dinner** starch _3_ meat _4_ milk ___ fruit _1_ veg ___ fat _2_	4 oz. grilled fish 1 cup brown rice sauteed vegetables 2 tsp. olive oil 1 slice angel food cake 3/4 cup fresh berries
Snack		**Snack** 1 milk 2 starch	8 oz. 1/2% milk 3/4 cup Fiber One cereal 1 small granola bar

*Indicates recipes included in this book.

FOOD EXCHANGE LISTS**

List 1: Starch/Breads

The foods on this list average 70 calories per serving. As you can see, it is a diverse list, including cereals, grains, breads, crackers, and many vegetables. Remember that the starred items (*) are particularly nutritious food choices and should be included frequently, as they are higher in vitamins, minerals, and usually fiber.

Cereals—Grains—Pastas

*bran cereals, concentrated, all types	⅓–½ cup
*bran cereals, flaked	¾ cup
cooked cereals	½ cup
Grapenuts	¼ cup
other ready-to-eat unsweetened cereals	¾ cup
puffed cereals, unsweetened	1½ cup
flour, cornmeal, etc.	2 Tbsp.
rice (cooked)	½ cup
pasta	½ cup
*wheat germ	3 Tbsp.
*(whole-grain varieties of rice and pasta are best choice)	

Crackers—Snacks

animal crackers	8
graham crackers, 2½-in. sq.	3
*matzoth	¾ oz.
Melba toast	5 slices
oyster crackers	24
*popcorn, no fat added (no oil or butter)	3 cups
*pretzels	¾ oz.
saltine-type crackers	6
*whole-wheat crackers, no fat added	¾ oz.

Vegetables—Beans

*beans, peas, cooked (kidney, white, pinto)	½ cup
lentils	½ cup
peas, green	½ cup
corn	½ cup
potato, mashed	½ cup
potato, baked or boiled	1 small
*squash, winter (acorn, butternut)	¾ cup
*yam, sweet potato, plain	⅓ cup

**Taken in part from the *Exchange Lists for Meal Planning*, American Diabetic Association and American Dietetic Association, 1986.

Breads

*bagel	½
bread sticks, crisp	2
*bread, white or whole-grain	1 slice
lite bread, all varieties	2 slices
*English muffin	½
frankfurter or hamburger bun	½
pita, 6-in. diameter	½
roll, small and plain	1
tortilla, 6-in. diameter	1
*(whole-grain varieties are best choice)	

Breads Prepared with Fats
Note: Count these as one bread and one fat

biscuit, 2½-in. diameter	1
chow mein noodles	½ cup
cornbread, 2-in. cube	1
French fried potatoes, 2–3 in. long	10
muffin, very small, plain	1
pancake or waffle, 4-in. diameter	1
stuffing	¼ cup +
taco shell, 6 in.	1

List 2: Meats

Traditional meat exchange lists divide meats into three categories: low-fat, medium-fat, and high-fat choices. On this list, we have only included the two lowest fat groups and have eliminated the high-fat group since we do not feel that these items should be eaten frequently or perhaps ever. In this list, each exchange contains about 7 grams of protein and ranges from 55 to 80 calories. The lower-fat choices will contain the fewest calories. Also, do not be confused by the fact that one meat exchange is one ounce of meat. Remember you will probably have more than one meat exchange per meal in your diet plan.

Low-Fat Meat Exchanges

Meat

*lean beef (esp. round, sirloin, tenderloin) with no visible fat; lean pork or ham; lean veal; venison	1 oz.

Poultry

*chicken, turkey, cornish hen (no skin or fat)	1 oz.

Fish

*any fresh or frozen (not fried)	1 oz. crab,
lobster, scallops, shrimp	2 oz.
*tuna (canned in water only)	1/4 cup oysters6

Cheese

*any cottage cheese	1/4 cup Parmesan
cheese, grated	2 Tbsp.
*special low-fat cheeses (less than 55 cal/oz.)	1 oz.

Miscellaneous

*egg whites	4
*Egg Beaters	1/2 cup
*95% fat-free lunch meats, look for "no nitrates"	1 oz.

Medium-Fat Meat Exchanges

Meat

ground beef, roast, porterhouse and T-bone steak, meatloaf; lamb	1 oz.

Pork

most pork products, pork chops, pork loin, and pork roast, but not sausage and bacon	1 oz.

Poultry

chicken *with skin*, duck, goose, ground turkey	1 oz.

Fish

tuna (canned in oil, drained)	1/4 cup
salmon (canned)	1/4 cup

Cheese

Skim or part-skim-milk cheese, such as ricotta, mozzarella, and "diet" cheeses	1 oz.

Miscellaneous

Whole eggs (no more than 3 per wk.)	1
Tofu	4 oz.
Organ meats (high cholesterol!)	1 oz.
Peanut butter (high fat!)	1 Tbsp.

List 3: Milk and Milk Products

No adult should be drinking anything above a 1% low-fat milk. And, skim milk is even better. If you haven't made that switch to these improved choices, resolve to do so now. Within two months you will be accustomed to the new taste and may actually prefer it. Likewise, if you have avoided dairy products for years because of weight control or medical problems (i.e., high serum cholesterol) then it is time to put this important food group back into your diet. The key here is to choose only low-fat products.

We include cheese on this list even though most exchange lists include cheese within the meat list. We have done this to accommodate women who cannot tolerate milk for one reason or another. If you can drink milk, it is the preferable choice. Most of the low-fat or non-fat choices average 90 calories per serving.

Milk

*skim, 1/2% or 1%	1 cup
*low-fat buttermilk	1 cup
*evaporated skim milk	1/2 cup
*dry nonfat milk	1/3 cup

Yogurt

*plain, nonfat	1 cup

Cheese

low-fat cottage cheese	1/2 cup
part-skim cheeses	1 oz.

List 4: Fruits

Most of the items on this list contain 55 calories per serving in the quantity specified. These servings are small. In many cases, a normal sized piece of fruit would represent 2 fruit servings. For example, when was the last time you had a 2 1/2-inch orange? Most large navel oranges would count as 2 fruit exchanges. If you are wondering about a fruit which is not listed on this page, consider 1/2 cup a standard serving size for most fruits. When choosing canned or frozen fruits, check the label and avoid added sugar or syrups.

Fruit

Fresh (or Canned)

*apple, medium	½ apple
applesauce, unsweetened	½ cup
*apricots, raw, medium	4 apricots
canned	½ cup
banana, 9-in.	½ banana
*berries	¾ cup
*cantaloupe, 5 in. across	⅓ melon
cherries, raw, large	12 cherries
fruit cocktail	½ cup
*grapefruit, medium	½ fruit
grapes	15 grapes
kiwi	1 kiwi
*orange, 2½-in.	1 orange
peach, 3-in.	1 peach
pear, large, raw	½ pear
pineapple, raw	¾ cup
canned	⅓ cup
plum, raw, 2-in.	2 plums
strawberries, fresh	1¼ cups
*tangerines, 2-in.	2 tangerines
watermelon, cubed	1¼ cup

Dried

apples	4 rings
dates	2½ dates
prunes	3 medium
raisins	2 Tbsp.

Juices

apple, grapefruit, orange, pineapple	½ cup
cranberry, grape, prune (higher in sugar)	⅓ cup

List 5: Vegetables and Free Foods

This list of free foods includes all non-starchy or low-starch vegetables as well as seasonings. These foods may be eaten whenever desired as long as the quantities are reasonable (a few exceptions have been noted). Of all food groups, vegetables seem to pack in the most nutrients for the fewest calories and least fat. *We have yet to see a patient who is truly serious about a good diet and has not learned to like vegetables.* If vegetables with every meal has not been a routine in your own life, make some changes, check some new recipes, and try some new foods. You'll love it!

Vegetables

asparagus	mushrooms
beans (green, wax, Italian)	okra
bean sprouts	onion
beets	pea pods (snow peas)
*broccoli	*peppers (all varieties)
*Brussels sprouts	radishes
*cabbage	salad greens (all kinds)
*carrots	*spinach
*cauliflower	*summer squash (yellow
celery	crookneck and zucchini)
cucumbers	tomato
eggplant	tomato juice
green onion	vegetable juice
*greens (all varieties)	turnip
hot peppers	water chestnuts

NOTE: The vegetables listed above are only considered *free foods* when they are *not* swimming in butter or another high-fat sauce. Caloriewise, it does not matter whether they are raw or cooked. Thus, these foods may be used as part of a soup, casserole, or salad; or they may be eaten as a single food.

Other Free Foods and Condiments

Seasonings

Seasonings can be used as desired. If you are following a low-sodium diet, be sure to read the labels and choose seasonings that do not contain sodium or salt.

flavoring extracts (vanilla, almond, butter, etc.)	onion powder
	paprika
	pepper
*garlic or garlic powder	pimento
herbs, fresh or dried	spices
*lemon or lemon juice	soy sauce
*lime or lime juice	worcestershire sauce

Drinks

bouillon or broth, no fat
cocoa powder, unsweetened baking type
    (1 Tbsp.)
coffee or tea
soft drinks, calorie-free, including carbonated
    drinks

Fruits
cranberries or rhubarb, no sugar (½ cup)

Sweet Substitutes
gelatin, sugar-free
jam or jelly, sugar-free (2 tsp.)
whipped topping, sugar-free (2 Tbsp.)

Condiments

catsup (1 Tbsp.)	*mustard
dill pickles, unsweetened	*taco sauce
horseradish	vinegar
hot sauce	

List 6: Fats

Most of the items on this list consist almost entirely of fat, either saturated or unsaturated. Per serving, each item contains about 5 grams of fat and from 35 to 45 calories. Notice that items such as nuts, avocados, and bacon are on this list as opposed to another seemingly more appropriate list. They are, in fact, almost exclusively fat.

If you want to avoid the trouble of counting fat exchanges, use a minimum of these foods and try to use light alternatives at that.

Fats

Concentrated Fats

oil, butter, margarine, mayonnaise, salad dressings	1 tsp.

Low-Fat Alternatives

*reduced-calorie margarine	2 tsp.
*reduced-calorie mayonnaise	2 tsp.
*reduced calorie salad dressings	1–2 Tbsp. (up to 20 cal./Tbsp.)

Nuts

all nuts	1 Tbsp.

Others

avocado	⅛ medium
olives	10 small
bacon	1 strip
coconut, shredded	2 Tbsp.
non-dairy creamer	1 Tbsp.
cream, light	2 Tbsp.
cream, sour	2 Tbsp.
cream, heavy	1 Tbsp.
cream cheese	1 Tbsp.
cream cheese, light	2 Tbsp.

The "Goodie" List

The following items may be eaten as often as once daily in the specified quantities. They make great tasting, light desserts for any occasion. Just delete one of your bread/starch exchanges in place of one serving of the following. (If you are maintaining your weight, you may even have two servings per day.)

Food	Amount
angel food cake	1 in.-slice
cake, no icing	1½ in.-square
cookies	2 small (1½ in. across)
frozen yogurt	⅓ cup
frozen fruit bars	1 bar
gingersnaps	3
granola bars	1 small (100 calories or less)
ice milk	½ cup
ice cream bars, low-cal	1 bar (under 100 calories)
pudding, made with skim milk	½ cup
sherbet and sorbet	½ cup
**snack chips, baked	½ oz.
vanilla wafers	6 small

**As recommended in the grocery shopping list.

Combination Foods

In general, you must learn to use your own judgment about combination foods such as pizza, soups and stews, fast food, and the like. It is important that you become good at this. The best rule of thumb when cooking at home is to use only nutritious ingredients which are light on salt and fat. For example, if a recipe calls for cream cheese, use a substitute or just don't make that recipe. There are certain ingredients which should not be used at all or only sparingly and infrequently (i.e., animal fats, shortening, cream cheese, and other high-fat cheese, etc.). We mention this only because many poor food choices can be hidden inside casseroles or pre-prepared foods. Canned soups (even the creamed variety) are usually a good choice for casseroles, although they are high in salt.

Popular Combination Foods

Food	Amount	Exchanges
Pizza	1 slice (12 in.)	1 starch, 2 meat, 1 fat
Casserole	1 cup	2 starch, 2 meat, 1 fat
Chili, with beans	1 cup	2 starch, 2 meat, 1 fat
Chow mein, no rice	2 cups	1 starch, 2 meat, 1 vegetable
Macaroni and cheese	1 cup	2 starch, 1 meat, 2 fat
Chunky soups, all varieties	10¾-oz. can	1 starch, 1 meat, 1 vegetable
Cream soup, made w/ skim milk	1 cup	1 starch, 1 fat, ½ milk
Cheeseburger	average size	2 starch, 2½ meat, 1 fat

What to Know about Vegetarian Diets

A vegetarian diet is one which includes plant foods but eliminates one or more of the following: meat, poultry, fish, milk, and eggs. *Lactovegetarians* include plant protein and milk products and exclude meat, poultry, fish, and eggs. *Laco-ovo-vegetarians* include plant foods, milk products, and eggs. They do not eat meat, poultry, or fish. *Pesco-vegetarians* include plant foods and fish but do not use milk, eggs, meat, or poultry. Pure vegetarians (or *vegans*) include only plant foods in their diets. Thus, they do not include milk, eggs, meat, fish, or poultry.

Nutritional adequacy for all of the diets listed above is not a problem, assuming you know what you are doing. If you are serious about becoming (or already are) a vegetarian of some type, you should take time to study proper combinations of foods for optimal nutrition. Of particular interest is the fact that a variety of legumes, nuts, and cereal grains will furnish the essential amino acids. When eaten together most cereals and legumes provide the body with a complete protein. These are called complimentary proteins. Examples of plant food combinations which supply a well-rounded protein source equal to that of beef, chicken, or any other meat include:

rice and legumes (dried beans, peas, lentils)
rice and wheat
beans and corn
peanuts and sunflower seeds
soybeans, wheat, and rice
soybeans, wheat, and sesame seeds
soybeans, peanuts, and sesame seeds

The only vitamin (or mineral) which cannot be obtained in a purely vegetarian diet is vitamin B–12, which is found only in foods of animal origin. For *vegans*, a vitamin B–12 supplement should be taken regularly.

While this book was never intended to be a reference for persons planning a vegetarian diet, we will now mention a few exchanges for those already involved in a vegetarian diet.

Vegetarian Diet Exchanges

Food	Amount	Exchange
Dried beans, peas	1 cup (cooked)	2 starch, 1 meat
Tofu	3½ oz.	½ starch, 1 meat, 1 fat

Note that cheese and eggs are on the Meat List.

One further point—a good diet is a good diet whether it is vegetarian or omnivorous. Make the right choices no matter which path you follow. We have seen far too many overweight vegetarians in our office who have gained weight on excessive amounts of bread, butter, beans, rice, and potato chips. If you are eating corn chips in lieu of lean beef, chicken, or fish, you are *not* making a wise health choice. The balanced approach to any kind of eating method is your best bet. Also, remember that all the other rules of the high-fiber and low-fat diet apply to the vegetarian diets as well.

DINING OUT WITHOUT FEAR

Eating outside the home has become a major part of the American lifestyle. Whether you are vacationing, going out with friends, attending a social function, having a business luncheon, or grabbing a quick take-out, more calories are eaten outside the average home every year. Consequently, most of us can no longer approach this part of our lives casually. If we were going out once a month, that occasional splurge would not be very important. However, with our own patients, we see people splurging several times a week because they are not making good choices when they dine out. Eating out is a reality—let's learn to deal with it.

Tips for Eating Out

1. *Plan ahead!* Try to find out where you are going and decide what you will order before you get there. You may lighten up your other meals and snacks if you anticipate a little overeating, but *don't skip*

meals before going to a restaurant. Research studies indicate that this usually backfires and causes you to eat more total daily calories.

2. *Learn portion control.* Many restaurants pride themselves in serving about twice as much food as you really need. To counter this, familiarize yourself with appropriate portion sizes by practicing at home. Small food scales and simple measuring cups can be quite helpful in accomplishing these goals. Measuring out that three-ounce piece of roast beef can be a real eye opener. If you are being served more food than you need, try one of these solutions:

- Split a dinner with a friend.

- Request a take-out carton before you have even taken a bite and save the other half for another meal.

- Don't go to that restaurant again.

3. *Make special requests.* Don't hesitate to ask the cook to do it your way. Examples: ask for low-cal dressing; ask for food without butter or sauce or for these items to be brought in a container on the side so you are in control of amounts used; ask for skin to be removed from poultry dishes; etc.

4. *Order first.* When with a group of people, try to make your selection first. If everyone at the table decides on the fried fish special with loads of tartar sauce and French fries, then you may be tempted to do this, too, instead of the great grilled fish and rice you *were* going to get.

5. *No room for extras.* Many people will make good menu choices at a restaurant and then "blow it" with all the extras such as beverages, cocktails, breads, and desserts. We suggest Artesia water or club soda with a lime twist for cocktail hour. (Some health professionals allow a glass of wine or a single beer.) Hors d'oeuvres, chips, buttery spreads, and dips should be eaten with caution and in most cases in very small quantities as most are high-cal/high-fat foods.

6. *When vacationing, bring your own.* When vacationing, try to avoid eating three full meals per day in restaurants. It is very difficult to maintain a proper diet while continually eating out unless you are extremely disciplined. For example, you might try keeping bagels or muffins and small cartons of juice in your room for breakfast. Or pack a picnic for lunch with all your low-fat sandwich and chip/dip makings. It will be more fun, cost you less money, and keep your healthy lifestyle on track.

NOTE: Have you ever wondered why you can actually get tired, lethargic, and constipated while on vacation? Most likely it is the result of temporarily abandoning your health program, including your improved

What to Order at Restaurants

Order these	Avoid these

Breakfast

Order these	Avoid these
Juices, fresh fruits	Sugary drinks
Hot tea or coffee, 1 tsp. sugar ok if not diabetic	Cream or coffee creamers
One egg, toast, grits (only if your serum cholesterol is less than 200 mg/dl)	More than one egg, biscuits or other high-fat bread, hash browns
Oatmeal, high-fiber cereals, low-fat milks	Sugary, low-fiber cereals, and whole milk
Bagels, muffins, slight margarine or butter and jams	Doughnuts, waffles, rolls, syrups, pastries, large amounts of butter and jams
Lean ham or Canadian bacon, 1 oz.	Sausage, bacon, or grease from these products

Lunch or Supper

Order these	Avoid these
Sandwiches with mustard, lean meats, low-fat cheese, veggies, whole-grain breads, French bread	Sandwiches made with mayo or other so-called sandwich spreads or "special sauces," bologna, salami, potted meat, meat salads, high-fat cheese (cheddar, American, provolone), croissants, grilled sandwiches
Hamburgers, regular-sized, *no mayo, no cheese, no butter*—all other condiments and veggies are good choices on hamburgers	Oversized burgers with mayo, cheese, double meat, French fries, and potato chips
All clear soups, salads with low-cal dressings	Creamed soups or cheese/vegetable soups, salads with regular dressing unless using 1 Tbsp. or less
Chef, salads, including limited amounts of lean ham or other meat, egg, cheese, low-cal dressing	Chef salads with unlimited toppings, potato and pasta salads (usually too high in fat when eaten out, high-cal dressings)
Ask for sliced tomatoes instead of extra side dishes	Chips, potato salad, cole slaw, fries served with sandwiches

exercise and eating habits. This can cause your body to be devoid of energy. Don't let your good habits and health-oriented medical practices disappear while on holiday—frankly, your holidays just won't be as wonderful without them. Just remember: *When you go on vacation, your healthy lifestyle should go with you.*

Ethnic Foods

Italian food. Quantity is the key issue when it comes to dining out on Italian food. *Resist the urge to eat too much just because it is on your plate and tastes great.* The same recipe will still be there the next time you come back. Good choices include spaghetti with tomato sauce, including mushrooms or other vegetables and lean meats. Be careful of mixed dishes such as lasagne and eggplant Parmesan. These selections may be wonderful choices when prepared in your own kitchen; but in restaurants these dishes are usually prepared with too much oil, cheese, and other high-fat ingredients; therefore, they can be unhealthy choices.

Dishes made with cream sauces such as Fettucine Alfredo or pasta primavera should also be avoided unless the menu specifies that they have been made with light ingredients. (You can make great low-fat versions of all of these at home.) Two slices of a medium pizza plus salad with a light Italian dressing is also a good choice. The best pizza choices include vegetarian-style and Canadian bacon. Choose whole-wheat pasta and pizza crusts whenever possible. They are delicious. Be careful of the extras like garlic bread and garlic butter. Moderation is the key.

Mexican/Spanish foods. These foods are notoriously high in calories because they tend to be high in fat, contain too many carbohydrate foods, and are served in prolific amounts. The best orders usually include tacos, tostadas, chalupas, and salads a la carte. Avoid large, complete dinners which include all of the above plus extra side dishes such as rice and refried beans. Fajitas or any kind of grilled meat is also a good choice. Salsa, pico de gallo, and other tomato/pepper blends are almost calorie-free and are very high in nutritional value. However, other condiments such as sour cream, guacamole (high in cholesterol) and grated cheese should be used sparingly. Mixed foods such as enchiladas, burritos, chilis rellenos are not good orders. They usually are packed with high-fat cheeses and are often fried. Be careful and learn to assess what you are really eating.

Chinese food. Except for the sodium content, Chinese food can be among the healthiest choices when dining out. You should order entrees which consist primarily of vegetables and lean meats, preferably chicken. Our personal favorite is Moo Goo Gai Pan or some other facsimile. Chicken and Snow Peas, Beef and Broccoli, and Chop Suey are also good choices. Poor choices include Sweet and Sour Pork or

Chicken, Kung Pao Chicken (has too many peanuts and not enough vegetables), and Lemon Chicken (this entree is fried). Request steamed rice instead of fried rice to accompany your meal. Do not use additional soy sauce (contains more concentrated salt than almost any other condiment), and eat no more than one egg role, or avoid it altogether since it is a fried food.

American foods. The main problem with American foods is that they usually contain too much meat and fat. If you only need three ounces of meat for that meal and nothing on the menu contains less than six, then you should plan on sharing a dinner, leaving half on your plate, or taking the leftovers home. Grilled meats cooked over an open-fire on a metal grill, especially fish and chicken, are great choices. If you select beef, it should be sirloin, tenderloin, or round steak—the leanest choices. Baked potatoes, rice, salads, and vegetables are all good side dishes as long as you are prudent with the butter, sour cream, and other dressings.

FAST FOODS

Fast-food chains have developed a bad reputation among health enthusiasts, and probably deservedly so. Many of these restaurants fry in beef fat, serve milk shakes that don't contain milk, and add many preservatives to extend food life. But let's face it, if you have exactly 10 minutes to grab something, with the only alternative being that you will go for hours without "body fuel," or resort to a candy bar, then you are certainly glad that the corner drive-in is there. Fast foods serve a real purpose in our fast-paced American lifestyle. The trick is to learn to make the best choices at fast-food restaurants. Then you can have the best of both worlds—good nutrition and great convenience! Here are some suggestions for helping you to accomplish this goal.

(NOTE: The best choices are indicated with a star *.)

Jack in the Box

Hamburgers. Order just a hamburger—no cheese, no mayo, no special sauce, no bacon, no double meat. (Exchanges: 2 bread, 3 meat, 1 vegetable, 1 fat)

Pita Pocket Supreme. (Exchanges: 2 bread, 1 1/2 meat, 1 vegetable)

Chef Salad. Use diet dressing only. (Exchanges: 2 vegetables, 1 fat, 1 1/2 meat)

Grilled Chicken Sandwich. Do not add mayo. (Exchanges: 2 bread, 3 meat)

Fajita Pita. Choose chicken as opposed to beef; use salsa instead of guacamole. (Exchanges: 2 bread, 3 meat, 1 vegetable)

Taco Salad. Eat the salad and leave the chips. (Exchanges: 2 meat, 2 vegetable, 1 fat)

McDonald's, Burger King, etc.

Hamburgers. Choose the medium size with no double beef, no cheese, no mayo, and no special sauce. Vegetables, mustard, and catsup are ok. Examples include Quarter Pounder (no cheese), small hamburgers, and the Whopper, Jr. (no mayo). (Exchanges: 2 bread, 3 meat, 1 vegetable, 1 fat)

*Salads. Any of these are good choices as long as a low-fat dressing is used.

Arby's or Other Roast Beef Restaurants

Basic roast beef or turkey sandwich. Choose medium-size sandwiches with no mayo-based sauces such as horseradish, which is really mayo with a little flavoring. (Exchanges: 2 bread, 2 meat, 1 fat)

Wendy's

*Salad bar. This is a good choice if you avoid the potato and pasta salads (laden with oil and mayo); light dressings are usually available. (Estimated Exchanges: 3 vegetable, 2 fat, 1–2 meat)

Hamburgers. Choose medium size, vegetables, mustard, and catsup. (Exchanges: 2 bread, 3 meat, 1 vegetable, 1 fat)

*Chili. A very good choice since Wendy's chili is so low in fat and calories. (Exchanges: 1 bread, 2 meat per serving)

Baked potato. Omit the butter and opt for the chili topping; easy on the cheese, no sour cream. (Exchanges: 2 1/2 bread, 1 1/2 meat)

Taco Salad. similar to the Jack in the Box Taco Salad (Exchanges: 1 bread, 3 vegetable, 1 meat)

Taco Bell

Tacos. Fried in a hydrogenated fat, but not bad for fast food. (Exchanges: 1 bread, 2 meat, 1 vegetable)

Tostados. A small amount of fat is added to the refried beans. (Exchanges: 1 bread, 2 meat, 1 vegetable)

Taco Salad. Eat only a small portion of the shell or none at all. (Exchanges if 1/4 shell is eaten: 2 meat, 2 bread, 2 fat, 1 vegetable)

Pizza Hut

Pizza. Choose thin crust, single cheese, vegetarian and/or one meat such as ham or Canadian Bacon. (Exchanges for 1/4 of a medium pizza: 2 bread, 3 meat, 2 fat)

NOTE: Avoid places that only serve fried foods.

CHAPTER 13

Exercise and Fitness

American women reach the menopausal years with one-third to even one-half of their lives ahead of them. Happiness and vitality during these years will be partially dependent on one's own level of fitness. Other things in life are surely important and can affect your outlook, but if you constantly feel fatigued, frustrated, depressed, or sick (much of which can improve with a realistic and well-planned fitness program), then you are settling for less of the good things in life.

One of the most important parts of a health-oriented lifestyle is consistent exercise. Certainly a good diet and other preventive-medicine health measures impact one's level of fitness; but *without some exercise, you just cannot be fit.* We have already discussed the type of diet that promotes fitness. In this chapter, we will discuss an effective exercise program which will increase your level of fitness and won't waste your time.

BENEFITS OF CONSISTENT EXERCISE

1. Greater strength. To strengthen muscles, you must contract them against a resistive force. Usually this means some kind of pushing or lifting motion, often with the use of weights. Many of our adult female patients have not considered incorporating exercise of this nature because weightlifting for women is relatively new. It is only recently that women's exercise programs have begun to consistently include the use of free weights or other type weight machines. We highly recommend a reasonable amount of this form of exercise to strengthen and tone your muscles. Benefits will include less muscle strain from daily activities and fewer accidents related to falls.

143

How muscles actually work can be a bit confusing. Basically, however, each muscle is made of bundles of tiny, threadlike fibers. When you contract any muscle against resistance (i.e., lifting or pushing), you only use a portion of these fibers. Then, as you continue to resist, an increasing percentage of muscle fibers become involved until the muscle becomes acidic from the accumulation of lactic acid. When this happens, the number of contracting fibers decreases, as does the training benefit. It takes approximately 30 to 50 seconds of strenuous lifting for muscles to accumulate large amounts of lactic acid, and in that period of time you can normally lift a weight eight to twelve times. Therefore, *to increase your strength, you should choose the heaviest weight you can comfortably lift for at least eight consecutive times.* This should be done every other day and you will soon be able to increase to twelve repetitions. When that becomes easy, you can increase your weight by five pounds and decrease your repetitions once again (Shangold and Mirkin, 1985).

At the end of this chapter, we will give specific instructions on how you can strengthen your own muscles with as little investment of time as 45 minutes per week. This can be accomplished either at home or in a health club. One further point, don't be afraid of developing bulky muscles like those of male weightlifters. Women do not have high enough levels of the masculinizing hormone, testosterone, for this to occur. In fact, toning and strengthening your muscles will given them a firmer and more youthful appearance.

2. Decreased bodyfat. When you have a consistent exercise program, stored fat and carbohydrate (glycogen) is burned or metabolized to a greater extent than protein (or muscle mass). This is very important. *The higher your lean body mass and the lower your bodyfat, the easier it will be to control your weight.* Muscle burns more calories than fat.

Also, when on a weight-loss diet, it is important to remember these things. Very low calorie diets, such as those below 1000 calories per day, make the body's metabolism decrease by as much as 45 percent. The body slows down so that it can function on such a low calorie level. There is also a tendency for the body to hold onto fat more efficiently in preparation for what it perceives as a potentially long period of starvation. This conservation of stored energy (fat) causes larger percentages of muscle to be burned, and over time, less weight is lost on the diet. To counteract this process, exercise is definitely needed. In fact, many health professionals go so far as to say, "Don't diet unless you also exercise."

One further piece of interesting information. After about 40 minutes of sustained aerobic exercise, you will begin to burn almost "pure fat" as your fuel source. That thought really helps keep us going to walk that fourth mile (three miles in 45 minutes and four miles in 60 minutes). You must be in very good condition to do this, and it may take 6 months to work up to this level.

3. *Increased flexibility.* Your own flexibility determines how far you can stretch, bend and reach without tearing your muscles (Shangold and Mirkin, 1985). Did you get that—". . . without tearing your muscles"? Have you noticed that the shopping bag you reach for in the back seat of the car is getting farther away and harder to reach? You must work at it to remain flexible as you age, but good flexibility can prevent injury from even simple daily tasks.

Slow, deliberate stretching is the best type of exercise to increase flexibility. The bouncy, jerky type stretching, called *ballistic stretching,* can actually be dangerous in itself. On the other hand, *static stretching* involves a slow, gentle stretch to a feeling of tightness in the muscle and then is held for 30 seconds. It is not meant to be painful. Instead, it should actually feel quite good—unless you are in the process of recovering from an injury (Shangold and Mirkin, 1985).

4. *Improved cardiovascular fitness.* Cardiovascular heart disease is the major cause of death in American women over the age of 50. These deaths are most often caused by coronary artery disease, in which the small arteries delivering blood to the heart are blocked with atherosclerotic plaques and fatty deposits. When the blood supply to the heart muscle becomes completely blocked, oxygen is cut off and the muscle, as well as the patient, will die unless immediate intervention is begun.

Coronary artery blockage increases with age in both sexes, but more commonly in men than in women. This is due largely to the beneficial effects of the feminine hormones in causing increased serum levels of the "good" kind of cholesterol, high-density lipoproteins (HDL). This molecule is composed of cholesterol and a large amount of protein. Higher circulating levels of this hormone decrease a person's risk for heart attack. Conversely, the heart-attack-promoting type of cholesterol, the low-density lipoproteins (LDL), is commonly found at higher serum levels in men.

The important things to remember are these: *Regular aerobic exercise lowers serum concentrations of total cholesterol while raising HDL levels. It will also lower total serum triglycerides and serum glucose levels, which are considered additional risk factors for heart disease.*

5. *Greater physical energy and clearer thinking.* For a period of four to six hours after you finish exercising, your metabolic rate may be operating at a higher level, a process which seems to make concentration easier. This can be explained by the fact that several of the body's natural chemicals and hormones are increased by exercise. They include the catecholamines (i.e., epinephrine and norepinephrine). These are your "fight or flight" hormones, and their purpose is to prepare

you for action. Many patients have asked us about the most productive time of day to exercise. For the reasons stated above, we often recommend the morning hours for a workout. It can serve as a tangible energy boost for the rest of the day and can provide you with clearer thinking, at least through lunch. One thing is certain, if you are not exercising because you are tired, then you are the type of person who needs exercise the most. *A consistent exercise program will eventually provide you with more energy, less fatigue, and greater productivity* (Shangold and Mirkin, 1985).

6. *Decreased stress and increased happiness.* Quite simply, exercise makes you feel good. Not only will you experience a peace of mind about doing something to promote good health, but exercise also causes secretions of several body chemicals that can promote feelings of pleasure, well-being, and even euphoria. Psychiatrists often prescribe exercise as an appropriate treatment for depression, anxiety, and tension.

We have already stated that the body is stimulated to secrete catecholamines as a response to exercise, and this can promote alertness. Other mood-altering hormones secreted within the body following heavy exercise include the *endorphins,* naturally occurring opiates (chemically similar to morphine) which are present in our bodies to prevent and relieve pain. These chemicals, plus another called seretonin, promote a sense of satisfaction and pleasure.

7. *Increased bone strength.* Osteoporosis, or the demineralization of bone, is one of the most serious medical problems facing older women. Twenty-five percent of all Caucasian women over age 60 will break a bone due to this disease, and some will die as a result of the fracture and surgery complications. For men, the process of bone thinning begins at age 50, but in women this process begins at around age 35, the time when most women will attain their peak bone mass (Shangold and Mirkin, 1985). You may feel healthy and wonderful, but your bones could already have begun this thinning process. Osteoporosis is a silent but potentially lethal condition—don't get caught in its far-reaching web.

The many factors that can prevent osteoporosis will be extensively discussed in chapter 17. Exercise is one of those factors. It is also a treatment which can increase the density of your bones by causing more calcium to be absorbed and laid down in the bone matrix. Most of the other processes only slow or halt the process of osteoporosis. Bones that bear a load and those that constantly work against resistance are the ones which benefit most with exercise. For example, there are documented studies showing that professional tennis players have thicker arm bones on their playing side. Your bones will be most benefited by load-bearing exercises such as walking, biking, and working with weights or against resistance.

MOTIVATION

We have spent a great deal of time telling you why exercise can improve your current health status and can even prevent disease. We have done this in an attempt to help motivate you in what you may perceive as an insurmountable task. In fact, studies have shown that it is easier to change someone's diet (and that's no picnic!) than it is to change that same person's exercise habits.

When David and I were in our twenties, we generally hated exercise. It cut into our schedules (although we were not good time managers). It made us hot, sweaty, and tired (probably because we anticipated that it would). In short, we didn't take exercise seriously. Our biggest problem was probably that we didn't have the foggiest notion of what a suitable exercise program might contain. Our usual routine was to watch the Olympics (or something similar), feel the need to "push" our bodies just as the athletes on TV had done, go out and absolutely overdo it (with running, calisthenics, and an aerobic exercise class), and then vow the next day never to do that again. It took us awhile, but we finally discovered that a solid exercise program can be one which is time efficient and very enjoyable. The best and only meaningful fitness progress is that which is attained in small increments.

In reality, no one can substantially motivate you but you. *You* are the one who will set a daily schedule for yourself. *You* are the one who will determine if exercise is a high enough priority that it can take precedence over other important things in your day. *You* are the one who will buy proper exercise shoes and read the rest of this chapter. *You* are the one who will keep up that walking program even when the temperature drops by twenty degrees. *You* are also the one who will reap the bountiful benefits!

GETTING STARTED

Beginning any self-help program can be a little difficult at first because it requires change. Therefore, we recommend that you take things at an easy pace. The tortoise really does win this race—slow, consistent progress pays off every time. A change that requires 10 minutes as opposed to 45 minutes is somehow infinitely easier to accomplish. By the time you have become accustomed and perhaps even bored with your new 10-minute habit, challenge yourself with an upgraded goal, one that seems a very small hurdle in comparison to your original abilities and attitudes.

There are three important preliminaries to accomplish before you begin a new exercise program.

1. *See your doctor.* If you are over age 40 and not currently active in an exercise program, you should see your doctor before beginning. Important risk factors which may affect your exercise prescription include high blood pressure and any past or present chest pain. An assessment of your current cardiac risk factors should be done. Depending on your individual circumstances, your doctor may want you to have an exercise stress test before advising you to begin your new exercise program. This is an excellent idea for *anyone* at increased risk of heart disease. It is much better to push yourself to the maximum in a controlled, monitored situation rather than to have a problem develop while alone on a grassy path.

2. *Like and dislikes.* Determine the sport, activity, or exercise you like best. You will need at least one form of aerobic exercise which works well for you. We most often recommend fast walking. Other forms of aerobic exercise include swimming, biking, stationary biking, jogging, aerobic dancing, and cross-country skiing. The nice thing about walking is that all you need is a good pair of walking shoes and a willing spirit. Also, you should be prepared with alternatives and contingency plans so that minor inconveniences (like bad weather) don't ruin your exercise routine. For example, we have an aerobic exercise video tape in our home for days which do not afford "walking weather." Many people go to the mall for aerobic walking during inclemant weather. Whatever you do, don't go through every winter out of shape because the weather and your schedule get the best of you.

3. *Determine your exercise heart rate range.* To do this simply find your age on Table 13.1 and note the heart rate numbers listed on that line. This is the number of pulses your heart should make in *10 seconds.* When you exercise, you will eventually need to wear a watch with a second hand and learn to take your pulse (at your neck or wrist). After you are five minutes into your exercising, your heart rate should never fall below the low number nor rise above the higher number for the duration of the exercise period.

DANGER—TURN BACK!

As you become an exercise enthusiast, you must be aware of the warning signals of overexertion. Though the possibility of these occurring is fairly remote, don't underestimate them if they should happen to you.

1. *Chest pain.* If you ever have chest pain while exercising, stop immediately and get help if necessary. *Consult your physician about this at once.*

2. *Severe breathlessness.* If you are so out of breath that you literally

Table 13.1.   **Exercise Heart Rate
Ranges in Beats per 10 Seconds**

Age	Pulse Rate Range for Aerobic Exercising (per ten seconds)
15	24–31
20	23–30
25	23–29
30	22–28
35	21–28
40	21–26
45	20–26
50	19–25
55	19–24
60	18–23

Reprinted by Permission. *PMS: What It Is and What You Can Do About It* by Sneed and McIlhaney, Baker Book House, 1988, page 82.

can't say even one sentence, then you are working out too hard for your current state of fitness. In fact, you have gone beyond aerobic exercise into anaerobic exercise. And because of a lack of oxygen, your muscles are building up lactic acid which will cause soreness and discomfort later. To correct this, slow down your pace and check your heart rate to see that it is not over the recommended upper limit. Also, you might try working out for longer periods of time but with less intensity until your stamina has improved.

3. *Lightheadedness.* Stop exercising if this should occur and go into your cool-down procedure of slow walking. Do *not* sit or lie down until your heart rate has fallen below the aerobic exercising pace.

4. *Muscle pain.* The slogan "no pain, no gain" should be outlawed in gyms. There is no need for pain. Small increments of gained strength and increased endurance are the best. You are not supposed to hurt. You may get tired and winded, and you may be a little sore the next day; but, *if you are experiencing significant muscle pain while exercising, it is not beneficial.* (NOTE: Don't confuse pain with exertion.)

5. *Dizziness and nausea.* These are other signs of overexertion. They are especially prevalent if you have not drunk enough fluids, if you are exercising on a very hot and/or humid day, or if you are simply doing too much.

6. *Loss of muscle control.* This is a sure sign that your muscles are running out of immediate energy. As you become more consistent in

your workouts, this will occur less frequently. When this does happen, slow your pace and begin a cool-down sequence.

THREE STEPS FOR SUCCESSFUL EXERCISING

STEP 1: *Warming Up*

Warm-ups can ease your body into exercising, reduce muscle stiffness, protect you from injuries, and increase your heart rate gradually. Since most warm-ups revolve around progressive stretching, you can

Table 13.2.   Sample Warm-ups and Cool-downs

Start and end your workout first with light exercise (i.e., moderate walking or slow jogging) for about 5 minutes, and then some stretches. When stretching, concentrate on relaxing, particularly the muscles being stretched. Stretch until you feel a slight pulling sensation (not pain) and hold it for 10–20 seconds.

Stretches

Calf and achilles tendon. Lean against a wall or tree with one foot back and flat on the ground. Keep knee locked first (upper calf), then unlocked (lower calf and achilles tendon). Do other leg. Repeat.

Quadriceps. Support yourself and grasp one foot. Pull up to stretch the front of your leg. Do other leg. Repeat.

Lower back, hamstrings, calves and groin. Sit on the ground with feet together and legs flat. Reach for your toes, pointing your feet to meet your fingers. Do also with feet wide apart. Repeat 2 times each way.

Ankles. Rotate ankles 10 times in each direction.

Reprinted by permission. Princeton Pharmaceutical Products, E. R. Squibb & Sons, Inc., Princeton, 1988.

also take this opportunity to improve your flexibility. Warm-ups should take from 2 to 5 minutes. Even on that morning walk, don't leave home without stretching calves, achilles tendons, quadriceps, lower back, hamstrings, and ankles. (See Table 13.2 for sample warm-ups and stretches.)

STEP 2: Working Out

The best examples of aerobic exercise include walking, jogging, swimming, biking, and aerobic dancing. The exercise program you choose for yourself should fit in with your lifestyle and your budget. If you can't afford more time than 30 minutes, four times a week, you will probably have to choose something you can do at home. However, if you have time and enjoy exercise with a support group, you might enjoy going to a gym or aerobic exercise class. Just remember these words of wisdom: *Start slow, push a little every workout, and be consistent.*

STEP 3: Cooling Down

Cooling down reduces your heart rate safely and gradually. After you have completed your workout, you should begin the cool-down with light walking (don't just stop). Follow this with 3 to 5 minutes of stretching as shown in Table 13.2. As you stretch, deliberately try to relax the muscles being stretched. Stretch only far enough to feel a slight pull (not pain), and hold it for 10 to 20 seconds. Remember this stretch should be a steady pull, not a bouncing or ballistic one.

YOUR EXERCISE PRESCRIPTION

Any exercise prescription must be a progressive one which begins with the basics and eventually builds to a workout routine which should last a lifetime. At level one you will begin with a pleasant 10-minute daily walk and eventually progress to level seven which involves a complete workout three times per week. Note the following instructions pertaining to the Progressive Exercise Program (Table 13.3).

1. The duration of the workout does not include time for your warm-ups or cool-downs. You will need at least 7 additional minutes for these activities once you have reached levels four, five, six, and seven. That is, you should allow a minimum of 2 more minutes for pre-exercise stretching and at least 5 more minutes of slower walking for your cool-down.

2. Calisthenics, weight training, and the correct procedure for walking are discussed later in this chapter.

Table 13.3.   Progressive Exercise Program

Level	Duration	Frequency	Suggested Exercise
1	10 min.	7 times a week	Walking
2	10 min.	6 times a week	Fast walking or other aerobics
3	15 min.	5 times a week	Fast walking or other aerobics
4	20 min.	5 times a week	Fast walking or other aerobics
5	25 min.	4 times a week	Aerobics*: 20 min. Calisthenics: 5 min.
6	30 min.	4 times a week	Aerobics*: 25 min. Calisthenics: 5 min.
7	45–60 min.	3 times a week	Aerobics*: 30–40 min. Calisthenics and weight training: 15–20 min.

*Aerobic exercises include fast walking, jogging, swimming, biking, or any other activity which elevates your pulse rate for at least 20 minutes without intermittently dropping.

Adapted in part from PMS: *What It Is and What You Can Do About It* by Sneed and McIlhaney (Baker Book House, 1988), page 81.

3. Aerobic exercise may be taken every day if you prefer. However, weight training and any other exercise which requires strength should be limited to an every-other-day routine. Many people find that alternating their aerobic routine with strengthening exercises every other day also works well.

NOTE: If you think you don't have time for this routine, consider the time you spend watching television. In the same amount of time it takes to watch a 2-hour television program, you could achieve level five, including the warm-up and cool-down section.

CALISTHENICS, WEIGHT TRAINING, AND WALKING

1. *The Oldies are the Goodies.* Go back to basics when you are considering which calisthenics you want to include in your exercise program. Here are a few recommendations for each muscle group:

- *50 modified sit-ups.* With knees bent, hands folded across chest, raise only your head and shoulders off the ground—do not come to a full sitting position. Do 25 looking at your knees and the other 25 looking at the ceiling.

- *20 leg lifts.* While lying on the back do 20 leg lifts with each leg. Then do 20 while lying on the side and 20 more while lying on the stomach. You may bend your non-working leg. Ankle weights (small one-pound weights strapped to your ankles) may be used for added resistance.

- *10 push-ups.* From the modified (knees on the floor) position, keep back straight, weight on arms, and push up from floor and lower again.

In fact, just these in the quantities specified would be the basis of a wonderful program. Then just add a few exercises with weights and you are set.

2. *Using weights is fun and easy.* You can begin with small one pound weights and progress to five- and ten-pound dumbbells. We would recommend that you choose a few of the basic exercises in the instruction book which accompanies the weights, such as curls and butterflies. Do these at the end of your workout after the calisthenics. Ankle weights may also be used to help tone and strengthen leg muscles. These are available in one- to three-pound increments and may be worn as ankle bracelets when doing your leg lift routine. This helps with toning the muscle which is underneath the fat layer. As you lose fat tissue and bodyweight, this will improve the appearance of your skin and figure in these areas and help to reduce *cellulite* (which is nothing more than fat popping out from the sheath that covers it underneath the skin).

NOTE: *There is no such thing as spot reducing.* That is, exercising your thigh will not cause your thigh to lose fat tissue. However, in the course of your exercise routine, you will burn more calories, and when enough calories are burned, eventually weight loss will occur. The exercising will tone the muscle and skin underneath the fat to help you have a sleeker look when the fat on top is lost from dieting.

If you have high blood pressure, you should not be lifting any heavy weight. Talk with your physician about what kind of exercise program you need until your blood pressure normalizes.

3. *Walking, not strolling.* We often see people in our neighborhood that are not taking their walking seriously. Walking works as an aerobic exercise only if you push yourself. Here are some tips:

- Exaggerate your arm movements. Swing them with gusto and feel the pull on the back of the arm when they swing back.

- Stretch your legs and feel a pull in your thighs and buttocks. Tense these muscles for more isometric tension.

- Try to walk under a 15-minute mile. Measure off the distance of your course in your car and then try to walk one mile in 15 minutes or two miles in 30 minutes. Stay on your pace. Once this is easy, walk the same distance in a shorter period of time.

WHAT TO WEAR

1. *Loose-fitting clothing* is a must. Articles of clothing which constrict your circulation will limit your physical activity. They can also make you hotter and less able to perspire normally. Vinyl workout suits designed to hold body heat and make you sweat more are a big mistake. There are really no shortcuts to physical fitness, and this kind of clothing is particularly dangerous, especially in the heat.

2. *Gloves* can be helpful, especially in the winter when your hands will tend to chill while on a brisk walk.

3. *A good, support bra* is a must to prevent supportive breast tissue from breaking down during aerobic exercise. If you have a large cup size, you may even consider wearing two at once for added support.

4. *High absorbency socks and underwear*, preferably cotton, are also a priority in athletic attire. You must let your body sweat during exercise, so wear something that is absorbent.

5. *Sunscreen, sunglasses, and a hat* are advised for persons walking in sunny climates to protect their skin from harmful ultraviolet radiation.

6. *Good shoes* are a must whether they are made for walking or aerobics. Try on several pairs. You will probably spend *at least* $40 for a good pair of exercise shoes, but you will be able to use them for years.

Disease Prevention

CHAPTER 14

The Health-Oriented
Medical Examination

Promoting wellness and a healthy lifestyle are the basis for disease prevention. If your relationship with your physician is limited to just correcting what is wrong on that particular visit, you are missing the boat for optimal health and disease prevention. Think about the possibilities of totally preventing certain diseases or using screening examinations for the early detection of others. It sounds great because it is great. In this section of the book, we will show you how to work with your physician to achieve these goals.

But first, you must know the right questions. As your doctor is giving you a checkup, you should be checking up on his knowledge and commitment to preventive medicine. *Don't allow yourself to be short-changed with just gynecologic concerns—there is much more to a woman's health than an annual Pap smear and breast exam.* To achieve your maximum health potential, you need a health-oriented medical plan for your entire life and a considerate, caring physician to help you implement these ideas.

CHOOSING YOUR PERSONAL PHYSICIAN

Selection of a personal physician is of great importance. First, look for someone you can feel comfortable with, someone easy to talk with. *We would recommend that you find a board-certified family physician or a gynecologist.* Board certification means the doctor has extra training beyond medical school in his particular field. The family physician can take care of most of your health needs as well as those of the rest of your family. Or you may prefer to have a gynecologist. *Whomever you* choose, make sure he/she understands your desire for preventive health care and that you expect your health professional to help you establish a long-range, personal plan to accomplish these goals.

COMPONENTS OF THE
HEALTH-ORIENTED MEDICAL EXAM

There is no "cookbook answer" to the question of what comprises a complete and thorough preventive, health-care examination. There are, however, some essential elements of all health-oriented examinations.

Your Medical History

Each individual must be carefully assessed for risk factors she may have which predispose her to develop certain diseases. The first element of a good physical is *the patient's medical history*. The doctor will ask you various questions and you should answer as completely and truthfully as possible. Sometimes there may be incidents from the past or even the present you would rather not discuss. It would be a mistake to withhold any information from your doctor. Many times we have had to ask patients personal but very pertinent questions and have not been able to get the complete story until much later. This unfairly handicaps your doctor and may adversely affect your medical care and health.

So tell the whole truth—even the part about not having had a Pap smear for the past 5 years or occasionally eating a half gallon of ice cream at one time. There must be a detailed account of significant events in your past medical history, with special emphasis on any obstetric or gynecological problems. *Your family health history, especially with regard to significant diseases such as cancer, high blood pressure, heart disease, and diabetes in close relatives, is essential.*

Breast cancer is a good example of the importance of your family history. Having a relative with breast cancer puts you at two to three times greater risk of this illness than the general population. About 45 percent of women whose close relatives had cancer in both breasts will develop this type of cancer themselves. Therefore, your doctor would be much more vigilant in screening for breast cancer with this kind of family history.

Your Social History

Your doctor needs to know who you are, what you do, and what your immediate family is like. Do you smoke or drink alcohol? Don't cheat on your answers—you will only be hurting yourself. In case you haven't noticed, your doctor needs to be pretty nosey and ask you some very personal questions. The next thing you know he'll be asking about your sex life—and he should. The more your physician initially knows about you, the easier it will be for him to formulate a complete, individualized health plan.

Additional Information

There are many other questions concerning what *allergies* you have, what *medications* you are taking, and the status of your *immunizations*. Your physician needs to know if you *exercise* regularly and *which preventive medical tests* you have had performed in the past (there's no need repeating tests unnecessarily). Finally, you should have an opportunity to discuss any particular health concerns you may have. We encourage our patients to write down these questions so they won't forget anything. Your concerns are very important and may prompt a more thorough evaluation in certain areas.

Obviously, it takes a fair amount of time to complete a comprehensive physical exam. Allow your doctor enough time to do the job right, and tell his receptionist to schedule your appointment accordingly. Also, leave your children at home or with a sitter so you won't be distracted.

THE HEALTH-ORIENTED PHYSICAL EXAM

Let's talk now about the actual examination and what the doctor is looking for. There is usually quite a difference in the complexity of an exam given to someone the doctor is seeing for the first time versus an exam given to a patient who has been receiving regular, preventive health-care exams. To begin with, the history-taking will not need to be as extensive on subsequent exams, and the physician can focus on areas of particular concern. For example, your physician may not look in your ears every time you come in for a Pap smear unless you ask him/her to; but if your mother and older sister each had a heart attack in their 40s, on each visit, your doctor would want to check you for similar tendencies. There's not a particular standard to be applied to the physical exam except that it should be tailored to the individual and her particular circumstances. With these things in mind, we will outline the components of a complete physical and highlight those areas particularly important in the preventive medicine approach.

A comprehensive, preventive medical exam can be performed in an efficient and cost-effective manner. The exam should be head to toe;

and as some of you will no doubt agree, must unfortunately be done with the patient completely disrobed. Unlike the ancient Chinese who used small dolls to indicate the parts of the body which were hurting, your doctor needs to see, feel, and listen carefully to your body. Anything less is simply a disservice to you. Health professionals want to protect the individual's privacy and modesty as well as provide a comfortable environment for the examination. If your doctor is not paying attention to these needs, tell him or her. It will be welcomed information.

Above the Shoulders

Generally, the physician will start with the head and work down. The *head, ears, eyes, mouth, throat, and neck* are first. The *eyes* can be checked for cataracts and evidence of disease on the retina (the covering of the inside rear of the eye). This is one of the only places on the body where you can actually observe the blood vessels. Here, certain changes associated with high blood pressure and diabetes can sometimes be detected. The pressure in the eye itself or intraoccular pressure needs to be checked regularly in anyone over 40. *Glaucoma*, an abnormal increase in this pressure, can cause damage without your even realizing it. There are two ways of checking for this disease, one with an instrument which is placed on your eye, and the other with a special device which reads the pressure from a puff of air directed onto the surface of your eye.

The *mouth* should also be carefully examined as oral cancer is a real threat, especially in those who smoke. Your dental health is of concern because healthy teeth contribute greatly to your overall well-being. The *neck* needs to be carefully examined for any abnormal enlargement of the lymph nodes and any abnormality of the thyroid gland. Your doctor should listen to the large carotid artery in the neck area for a bruit. This is an abnormal swishing sound in the artery caused by a partial obstruction or narrowing of this blood vessel. Should this be present, it could indicate hardening of the arteries and increased potential for a stroke.

Cardiopulmonary Checkup

Next comes a careful evaluation of the *heart and lungs*. During your physical, the doctor will probably ask questions about the part of your body that is being examined. Do you ever get short of breath? Do you ever have chest discomfort?—questions of that sort. But when the doctor is listening to your chest and has the stethoscope in his ears, he can't really hear or respond to your questions. So just save the questions for a moment. With the stethoscope the physician will listen to your lungs and then to your heart. He is checking to make sure your lungs are clear and that the beat of your heart is regular with no abnormalities.

Breast Examination

Examination of the *breasts* should be done carefully and systematically. This includes an exam of the nipples and the breast tissue extending from the breast into the axilla or armpit area. We always inquire as to whether or not a patient is performing breast self-exams on a regular basis. Many times women will say they really don't know what they are feeling for. There are numerous pamphlets available which explain the correct way to perform this very important part of preventive medicine. Certainly your physician or his nurse can easily explain this procedure to you. We have included information on breast self-examination in chapter 16. Be sure and tell the doctor if you have noticed any lumps or other changes in your breasts or nipples.

The Abdomen

The *abdomen* must be checked for any unusual tenderness or masses that should not be there. The abdominal organs can be felt for and any enlargement noted. These organs include the *liver and gallbladder, the stomach, intestines, pancreas, and spleen.* Sometimes the doctor will listen to your abdomen with a stethoscope. This is important, especially if you have high blood pressure, as a narrowing of the blood vessels going to the kidneys can sometimes be the cause of hypertension.

Pelvic Exam

As far as the *pelvic exam* goes, most women are well aware of the circumstances involved. However, many are unsure of what is actually taking place during that pelvic exam. First the doctor checks the opening to the *vagina* with careful inspection of the *vulva and labia*. This remains an important area to be checked throughout your life, even in the woman who has had a hysterectomy. It's difficult to examine this area on your own and it can be a site where cancer could develop. Next, the doctor will use an instrument called a speculum to open up the vagina and check the cervix. The *cervix* is the lower part of the uterus or womb and is where the Pap smear sample is taken.

We think *the annual Pap smear has done more to establish the need for regular, preventive medical care than almost any other procedure.* There is some controversy concerning the proper frequency for this procedure and which patients should be checked (we'll discuss this issue in greater detail later). For now, understand that the Pap smear is used to screen for cervical cancer by obtaining a few cells directly from the cervix itself. This test should usually not be performed if you are on your menstrual period, as the bleeding can interfere with the interpretation of the smear. Next, the internal pelvic organs—the uterus and ovaries—are felt through the vagina to determine any unusual enlargement. If you are having any urinary problems such as difficulty holding your urine, be sure to tell your physician so he can assess the support tissues in the vagina, bladder, and rectal area.

The Rectal Exam

As unpleasant as it may seem, a yearly *rectal exam for all persons over the age of 40 is a necessity.* By checking with his finger, the doctor can feel for any rectal masses, hemorrhoids, and also obtain stool to determine the presence of any blood in the stool. Colon cancer is the third leading cause of cancer death and in many cases can be cured if discovered in an early stage.

The Skin

Throughout the exam your physician has probably been noting any skin lesions which appear abnormal. The skin is actually our largest organ and a survey of the entire surface is in order annually. The incidence of some skin cancers seems to be increasing. The area of the skin which you cannot easily see yourself should receive careful attention. The back is a good example of an area not easily seen by one's own self. We'll talk more in depth about skin cancers and the changes which can accompany them in chapter 16, but for now be sure and tell your doctor of any place on your skin which seems to be unusual.

This concludes our outline of the basic components of a complete health-oriented exam, detailing what the doctor is doing and why. A more comprehensive physical examination would no doubt go on to a complete neurological examination, and your doctor may feel it necessary on the basis of your medical history or particular complaints to do a more thorough evaluation. Now let's talk about the ancillary tests which may be required.

SCREENING LABORATORY AND PHYSICAL TESTS

There are a number of other tests which help screen for certain diseases. If used properly, these tests will allow early detection of illness or cancer at a stage where it can be cured. Other tests may indicate certain risk factors for the development of an illness. Early recognition of these factors can be helpful in modifying, reducing, or eliminating the threat of that illness altogether. There is really no point in doing tests which will have no impact on modifying the outcome of an illness. Nor is it prudent to recommend testing which is unlikely, except in very rare circumstances, to detect an illness. Preventive medicine procedures should be based on evidence that indicates the test on a particular patient is likely to be worthwhile.

Electrocardiograms

The EKG or electrocardiogram is a test that your physician may order at various times in your health-oriented medical program. The electrocardiogram is a tracing of the electrical activity of your heart. By analyzing this electrical conduction from twelve different directions, the doctor can determine a number of things, including the rate of your heartbeat, the regularity or rhythm of the heart, and possibly any previous damage to the heart muscle. Sometimes, the EKG indicates a possible abnormal enlargement of the heart which can be further investigated. *A baseline EKG should be obtained on every person 40 years old or older—this includes women.* A second EKG would not be done routinely until age 50 unless you develop a problem which warrants it. After age 50, a prudent approach calls for a new EKG every 5 years or as needed clinically.

The reasons for these early EKG's are twofold. Some heart attacks can occur without any symptoms and would be recognized only on a screening EKG. These "silent MIs" (myocardial infarction) were obviously not fatal, but indicate a significant problem and present a warning of things to come if action is not taken. Also, there is a need to have a baseline EKG at a time when you are well. Then should you ever develop chest pain, the EKG taken during the episode of pain can be compared with your baseline EKG. We have found this to be helpful on several occasions when trying to decide whether or not a person's pain was cardiac in origin or unrelated to the heart. There are many reasons for chest pain that are not caused by a diseased heart. However, *all chest pain must be taken seriously and every effort made to determine its cause.*

Exercise Stress Test

The *exercise stress test* is a very important tool in screening for and diagnosing heart disease. This exam is usually performed while the patient walks on a treadmill. The patient is connected to a 12-lead electrocardiogram (EKG), and the heart is monitored continuously throughout the exercise. At first the treadmill starts moving slowly and with no incline at all. In stages, the treadmill speed increases and the incline of the treadmill elevates. Thus, it forces you to walk uphill quickly after a short warm-up. Your doctor will have calculated your predicted maximum heartrate based on your current age. Hopefully, you can achieve 80 to 100 percent of this predicted maximum as this will give the most meaningful information.

We try to have patients who are in relatively good health push themselves in this test to their maximum effort. This provides two important pieces of health information. First, if there are no abnormalities, you can be assured with about 85 percent certainty that there is no significant heart disease present. Second, you can have the confidence that maximal exertion during other forms of exercise probably will not harm you.

Most likely you have read from time to time about some individual, in apparent good health, who collapsed and died while exercising. This sort of thing is very disturbing when you consider that premature death is the very thing you are trying to prevent with a good exercise program. That is why a careful evaluation by your doctor is so important before you begin a vigorous exercise program.

Anyone over the age of 40 who is just beginning a fitness program which includes aerobic conditioning should have a thorough physical exam, an assessment of her cardiac risk factors, and consider having a maximal exercise stress test before starting the exercise program. Anyone over the age of 35 with significant cardiac risk factors should likewise have a pre-workout stress test.

The exercise test can be performed in your physician's office if he has the proper equipment or on an outpatient basis at your hospital. Or your doctor may prefer to send you to a cardiologist for this testing. During the test, the doctor watches your heart tracings and looks for any subtle changes which could indicate a blockage of the coronary arteries. Several complete EKG's will be taken and your blood pressure monitored frequently. When you have done as much as you can, you will be asked to lie down (you'll probably be grateful for the rest), and you'll continue to be monitored until your vital signs are back to normal. The risks of doing this test are very low, and the benefits of discovering unrecognized heart disease are potentially very great. It is far safer to have this test under carefully monitored conditions than to perform the same stress test on yourself while running alone in the park.

Sigmoidoscopy

We have already discussed the importance of an annual rectal exam for anyone over 40. *Screening for colon cancer is an extremely important part of any complete, preventive health-care program.* This test becomes increasingly important for those individuals with a family history of colon/rectal cancer or colon polyps. The digital rectal exam can obviously examine only the rectal area and not the upper colon. The evaluation of your stool for blood is an important test and should be done yearly, but it may not detect a non-bleeding polyp or tumor. For these reasons a more thorough examination of the colon is required. Within the past few years increasingly widespread use of the flexible sigmoidoscope has greatly enhanced our ability to diagnose colon cancers and pre-malignant polyps at a very early stage.

The flexible sigmoidoscope, available in lengths of 30 or 60 centimeters, is now the clear choice in instruments for colon screening. You may have heard about an exam with the older rigid sigmoidoscope in which the patient had to be turned on her head. In this older procedure, insertion of the scope was difficult to say the least. Now the patient lies on her side, and in most cases, the scope is passed easily, and with *much less discomfort*, two to four times farther than with the older method. The procedure usually takes about 20 minutes and is usually done without anesthesia in your doctor's office. If any abnormal polyps are seen, a biopsy can be taken without additional discomfort.

If rectal bleeding has been present or if it was found on examination of the stool and the source of that bleeding is not found with the flexible sigmoidoscope, than a *barium x-ray* should be done to check the area of the colon above the limit of the scope. Should any polyps be found or any source of bleeding still be undiscovered, then an exam called *colonoscopy* should be done. This is similar to sigmoidoscopy except the scope is much longer and some anesthesia is usually required.

The American Cancer Society recommends an annual rectal exam in all people over 40, including a check of the stool for blood. After age 50, they recommend a screening sigmoidoscopy with a repeat of the test a year later, and again every 5 years after that unless the patient develops symptoms which require investigation. Although a rectal exam is probably not high on your list of birthday presents, the early detection of pre-malignant polyps can prevent complicated surgical procedures and save lives.

X-ray Examinations

The annual *chest x-ray* is a good example of a test that is no longer recommended on a routine basis. Previously, high-risk individuals were advised to have a chest x-ray every year. Now, according to the American Cancer Society, even those people at high risk—such as smokers —needn't have an annual chest x-ray. This is not to imply that chest x-rays are worthless or that having them is harmful. It's just important that any testing you have done be meaningful and that your health-care dollars be spent as wisely as possible. We do not order chest x-rays routinely now, but we are careful to listen to the health complaints which our patients voice and especially those who are at greater risk for the development of lung disease.

Sometimes other x-ray studies are ordered as part of a routine physical exam. These might include an *upper gastrointestinal series* (upper GI) and a *lower gastrointestinal series* (lower GI), also known as a barium enema. These are excellent tests with which to evaluate the intestinal tract but should be ordered only when specific disease conditions are suspected. These tests are expensive and involve multiple x-rays, which increase your total radiation exposure. However, if your doctor suspects that you may have a stomach ulcer, then an upper GI series would be very helpful. Or, if blood is found in your stool during a routine exam, then a barium enema should be done, along with a flexible sigmoidoscopy to determine the cause. These tests should be used in specific circumstances but not for general screening purposes in a preventive health-care exam.

Spirometry

Spirometry is the evaluation of your lung capacities and the functional ability of your pulmonary system. Testing of this sort can help detect damage to your lungs or disease states such as emphysema and asthma. This is especially important in people who smoke or who breathe potentially harmful fumes on the job. There are really no specific guidelines, but a baseline testing for high-risk patients, followed by testing every year or two is helpful in detecting damage at the earliest possible stage.

Audiogram

The *audiogram* is used to test hearing. If you think you have a hearing problem, then your doctor will probably recommend this procedure. *Don't settle for hearing less than others are hearing.* Modern hearing devices are small and fit right inside your ear. As a preventive or screening device the audiogram is primarily helpful for individuals who work in loud-noise environments so that ongoing records of hearing levels may be kept and that protective measures can be taken to prevent permanent hearing loss.

Glaucoma Testing

Glaucoma is the second leading cause of blindness in people over the age of 40, and in almost all cases the harmful effects of this disease can be prevented. It is a condition in which the fluid inside one or both eyes builds up to a dangerously high level. Unfortunately, glaucoma symp-toms are often not detected until some damage has already occurred. These harmful pressure changes in your eyes can be found easily by using simple testing procedures. *Tonometry* is a test designed to check the pressure in your eyes either directly by placing a meter on your eye or indirectly by using a puff of air directed against the eyeball. *All persons over the age of 45 should be screened every 3 years for glaucoma.*

LABORATORY BLOOD TESTING

Blood testing is probably one of the most frequently used compo-nents of a complete health evaluation. Used properly, several disease conditions can be found at an early stage or perhaps even before any symptoms have appeared. On an initial screen the following tests should be done:

Biochemical/metabolic screen (SMAC, lipid profile)
Complete blood count
Urinalysis
Thyroid function

The *metabolic screen*, sometimes called a SMAC, includes a battery of tests to check for diabetes, kidney function, bone metabolism, liver function, blood electrolytes (sodium, potassium, chloride, and bicar-bonate), and blood lipids (cholesterol, HDL and LDL cholesterol, and triglycerides).

The *complete blood count* or CBC checks for anemia and in some cases may indicate a nutritional problem such as iron or vitamin defi-ciency.

The *urinalysis* screens for kidney problems, infection, renal and bladder cancers, and diabetes.

In Table 14.1, we have listed the specific laboratory tests, what they determine, and what abnormalities they can suggest. Please note that this table only scratches the surface with regards to diagnosing differ-ent disease states from laboratory tests.

Testing for *thyroid function* can sometimes detect thyroid dysfunc-tion, which by its slow and gradual onset may otherwise go unnoticed. Thyroid dysfunction is particularly difficult to notice in older individu-als, and screening tests can help avoid the possibility of an oversight in this area.

After an initial database of laboratory tests has been gathered, it is probably not necessary to retest completely every year. Tests should be individualized according to each patient's needs. However, it is often

Table 14.1.   Laboratory Tests and What They Can Mean

Test	Purpose	Possible Disease Conditions
glucose	blood sugar	diabetes, hypoglycemia
BUN	blood urea nitrogen	kidney function
creatinine		kidney function
uric acid		gout
sodium	electrolyte	water balance
potassium	electrolyte	lost with diuretics
chloride	electrolyte	lost with vomiting
bicarbonate	pH of blood	acid or alkaline conditions
protein		nutritional and kidney
albumin	major protein	nutritional
LDH	liver enzyme	hepatitis
SGOT	liver enzyme	hepatitis
SGPT	liver enzyme	hepatitis
alkaline phosphate	liver and bone	hepatitis, gallbladder, bone
calcium	bone	parathyroid disease
phosphorous	bone	parathyroid disease
iron	red blood cells	anemia
cholesterol	lipid level	heart risk
HDL cholesterol	lipid level	heart risk
LDL cholesterol	lipid level	heart risk
triglyceride	lipid level	heart risk

no more expensive to order the entire metabolic screen than to order just two or three individual tests.

WRAPPING IT UP

Once you complete your health-oriented medical examination and the follow-up consultation with your physician, you should have a much better idea of just where you stand concerning your present and future health risks. By taking action to correct circumstances which pose increased risk to your health and careful monitoring of your physical condition, you should live longer and certainly healthier.

CHAPTER 15

Preventing Cardiovascular Disease

Cardiovascular disease is the number one cause of death in the United States, and it has been the principal cause of death to Americans for over 40 years (Amler and Dull, 1987). Coronary heart disease and stroke comprise the vast majority of deadly cardiovascular events. In young women, death from coronary heart disease is much less likely than it is in young men. However, with advancing age, both men and women are at greater risk of heart disease, but the risk to women increases at a much faster rate than that of older men (see Table 15.1). Why these differences exist and how to reduce the rate of cardiovascular disease in women, as they get older, is the primary focus of this chapter.

Years of careful research and clinical study have resulted in better treatment and prevention of cardiovascular disease. For example, early

Table 15.1. Death Rates for Cardiovascular Disease for Men and Women in the United States in 1979 (Annual rate per 100,000)

Age	Coronary Heart Disease		Stroke	
	Men	Women	Men	Women
30–34	9.4	2.2	3.4	3.4
35–39	29.4	6.5	6.9	6.2
40–44	74.4	16.3	12.5	12.6
45–49	160.6	34.8	21.1	19.8
50–54	288.0	70.0	35.5	29.1
55–59	468.1	131.9	57.8	44.3

Adapted in part from Mishell, 1987.

intervention in persons with high cardiac risk has resulted in a significant decrease in deaths due to cardiovascular disease compared with other diseases. Death due to stroke has declined by 5 percent a year since 1972, and death due to coronary heart disease has dropped by more than 30 percent in the same period of time (Amler and Dull, 1987). However, more than half of all deaths in the United States are still due to cardiovascular disease, and further efforts are needed to prevent premature death and disability.

IDENTIFICATION AND TREATMENT OF CARDIOVASCULAR DISEASE RISK FACTORS

To begin with let's look at the cardiovascular risk factors for women:

Advancing age
Cigarette smoking
Elevated blood pressure
Elevated cholesterol
Glucose intolerance and diabetes
Menopause
Family history of cardiovascular disease
Alcohol excess
Use of oral contraceptives *if you are over 35 and smoke*
Obesity
Physical inactivity

Advancing Age

Advancing age is a risk factor for cardiovascular disease in both men and women. Growing older with good health and vigor is the goal of preventive medicine, and although you cannot turn back the hands of time, increased awareness of potential cardiac symptoms such as unexplained chest pain, shortness of breath, and easy fatigue may facilitate treatment before the permanent damage of a heart attack occurs. Nevertheless, age is not an avoidable risk factor. We tell our patients who complain about another birthday that "being another year older looks pretty good when you consider the alternative."

Prevention strategy. Learn the warning signs of heart disease.

Smoking

Smoking is responsible for over 350,000 premature deaths annually (Amler and Dull, 1987). We usually think about smoking causing cancer, especially lung cancer. The fact is that *smoking causes more deaths from cardiovascular disease than from all the annual cancer deaths combined.* Although the number of smokers is declining, up to one-third of adult Americans still smoke cigarettes (Amler and Dull, 1987). Proportionately speaking, more women than men are smoking now than ever before, especially in the 20-to-24-year-old age group.

Of all people who die from cardiovascular disease, 17 percent of the deaths can be attributed to smoking (Amler and Dull, 1987). *Women who smoke have a two to six times greater risk of heart attack as compared to women who do not smoke* (U.S. Dept. Health and Human Services, 1985). And of all the years lost due to premature death from heart disease before the age of 65, smoking accounts for 30 percent of the total (Amler and Dull, 1987). The increased risk of cardiovascular disease in smokers on birth control pills is so great that most physicians will not prescribe oral contraceptives for their patients who are 35 and older if they smoke.

Prevention strategy. If you smoke—stop, quit, cease, and desist. Many fine programs and medications are now available to help you accomplish this goal. If you can't (or won't) stop, at least cut down!

Hypertension

Elevated blood pressure is a "silent killer." Gradual increases in blood pressure can be unnoticed physically until the damage presents itself as a stroke or heart attack. Women with elevation of the systolic (upper) or diastolic (lower) blood pressure run about a two times greater risk of coronary heart disease than women with normal blood pressure (*Women's Health*, 1985).

It is generally advised that your blood pressure be kept below 140 systolic (top number) and 85 to 90 diastolic (bottom number) to avoid increased risk. Proper diet, exercise, and maintenance of ideal bodyweight should be first-line efforts to control hypertension. Your doctor can monitor your blood pressure and prescribe medication if needed.

Additional ways of controlling blood pressure without medication include reducing stress, limiting caffeine and alcohol (less than 2 oz. daily), and not smoking. There has been recent interest in the role of calcium in controlling blood pressure. Calcium supplementation has been found to produce mild reductions in blood pressure (McCarron and Morris, 1985). This adds further potential benefit to calcium supplementation in women.

Proper diet is very important for control of high blood pressure both in low-sodium intake (less than two grams daily) and weight control. *Weight loss of as little as 8 to 10 pounds is as effective as the use of medication in controlling mild hypertension* (Imai, 1986). Also, regular exercise alone can control blood pressure in up to 70 percent of young adults with hypertension (Cade and Marrs, 1984). Those of you who persist in smoking despite having hypertension run a much greater risk of having a stroke. The combined effect of smoking and high blood pressure gives you a twentyfold increased risk of having a stroke (Bonita and Scagg, 1986).

Control of hypertension is having a dramatic effect on the decreased rate of strokes in the United States. No doubt much of the success is due to the use of anti-hypertensive medication. However, even though many of the newer medications have significantly less adverse side effects, it is still much better to control your blood pressure by nonmedical means, if possible. The following list gives examples of *nonmedical ways of controlling blood pressure:*

Regular aerobic exercise
Proper diet
—Limit salt to less than 2 grams daily
—Adequate calcium intake: 1–2 grams daily
Maintain ideal bodyweight
Don't smoke
Limit caffeine
Control stress

Prevention strategy. Check your blood pressure annually and keep it below 140/85; or better yet, below 120/80. Initiate a self-help program to keep this in check.

Cholesterol and Blood Lipids

Suppose I offered to *double* your money after just one year for a 100 percent investment return? I suspect you would either consider the investment too risky or figure we were doing something illegal. There is a way you can double your money, so to speak, in terms of reducing your risk of heart disease. Interested? Read on.

Cholesterol and blood lipids (fats) in your body are major risk factors for heart disease. *For every percent you lower your blood cholesterol, you reduce your risk of heart disease by 2 percent* (Levy, 1986). That's a 100 percent return on your health care investment and, in most cases, it can be easily accomplished by dietary change alone.

When we consider the risk of heart disease from elevated blood lipids we are talking about total serum cholesterol, low density lipoprotein (LDL) cholesterol, high density lipoprotein (HDL) cholesterol, and triglycerides. All of these blood lipids play a role in your risk of cardiovascular disease. *Every woman should at least know her cholesterol level.* This can easily and inexpensively be checked without prior preparation in your doctor's office. *If your cholesterol is elevated, then a complete lipid profile should be obtained.*

New guidelines for acceptable levels of cholesterol and blood lipids have been set by the National Heart, Lung, and Blood Institute's National Cholesterol Education Program. It is estimated that 60 percent of Americans have cholesterol levels which are too high. The current guidelines which are recommended for all adults regardless of age or sex include:

Cholesterol Level	Risk of Heart Disease
less than 200 mg/dl	safe level for all adults
200 to 239 mg/dl	borderline
above 240 mg/dl	high risk

For those persons with an elevated cholesterol (greater than 200 mg/dl), further testing should include LDL, HDL, and triglycerides. Low-density lipoprotein cholesterol (LDL) level is another way of assessing your risk of heart disease. The recommended levels for LDL cholesterol are as follows:

LDL Cholesterol	Risk of Heart Disease
less than 130 mg/dl	safe for all adults
130 to 159 mg/dl	borderline
above 160 mg/dl	high risk

HDL cholesterol is the so-called *good cholesterol.* The higher the level, the better off you are. In fact, many experts consider the total cholesterol to HDL cholesterol ratio (called the "HDL Ratio") to be a more significant indicator of coronary heart disease than total cholesterol alone. Your cholesterol to HDL ratio should be a maximum of 4.5 or less; the ideal ratio is 4.0 or lower. Your HDL ratio may be determined by the following equation:

$$\text{HDL Ratio} = \frac{\text{Total Cholesterol}}{\text{HDL Cholesterol}}$$

Triglycerides are merely circulating fats (such as corn oil or beef fat) in your bloodstream. Many experts believe that severely elevated levels of triglycerides increase your risk for cardiovascular disease. Generally, triglyceride levels can be variable and should always be checked after you have fasted for 12 hours or more. Current recommendations for triglycerides stand at less than 200 mg/dl and ideally less than 150 mg/dl (Leaf, 1988).

Correction of elevated blood lipids is first and foremost treated with diet therapy and weight control. If careful diet modification, including professional nutrition counseling, are unsuccessful in lowering blood lipids, then your doctor may consider adding a lipid-lowering medication. However, careful attention to your diet is still needed even though you are on these medications.

Dieting for some may be difficult, and it seems attractive to just take a pill, sit back, and watch your cholesterol level decline. Unfortunately, it's just not that easy or simple. We have several good and safe medications now which can effectively lower the blood lipids, but they tend to be expensive, are not totally free from side effects, require frequent follow-up lab testing, and simply cannot replace the healthful effects of a proper diet. For treatment recommendations see Table 15.2

Seek Nutritional Help. For nutrition information, look for a Registered Dietitian (R.D.) who is innovative and well-respected in the medical community. Many (like Sharon) now have their own private practices. An advanced degree in nutrition such as an M.S. or a Ph.D. will also be a benefit, as this usually indicates a higher level of understanding on the subject. However, *you must beware of "pseudo-nutritionists."* Ask for credentials and call medical references before seeing anyone.

As you grow older, an interesting thing happens to cholesterol levels. After about age 45, women in general tend to have higher cholesterol levels than men on the average (Mishell, 1987). It seems that after menopause, whether natural or surgical, the cholesterol level rises. Numerous research studies have documented the lowering of coronary

Table 15.2. Treatment Recommendations for Elevated Serum Cholesterol Levels

Cholesterol Level	Recommendation
Less than 200 mg/dl	Recheck level every 5 years
200–239 and *no* risk factors	Diet therapy and recheck yearly
200–239 with heart disease, or with HDL less than 35, or with 2 risk factors (+ family history, smoker, obese, diabetes, hypertension)	Check all lipids (LDL, HDL, triglyceride), begin diet 1, if that fails then diet 2, if that fails add medication
Over 240 mg/dl	As above with 3-month trial of careful diet before medication

heart disease among women who use estrogen replacement therapy. The beneficial effects of estrogen appear to act on the improvement of the cholesterol to HDL ratio (Mishell, 1987).

Cholesterol elevation is the cause of about 36 percent of all cardiovascular disease (Amler and Dull, 1987). If these guidelines are accepted and achieved by the 60 percent of you who have high cholesterol, as many as 300,000 lives could be saved annually.

Prevention strategy. Know your blood cholesterol level, and try to keep it below 200 mg/dl. Keep your HDL Ratio under 4.5 and your triglycerides under 200 mg/dl.

Borderline Diabetes and Diabetes

Diabetes is a disease in which the blood sugar or glucose level is abnormally elevated. Glucose intolerance or borderline diabetes is a problem for susceptible people who, when under stress of illness or pregnancy, develop abnormal blood sugars. Many women may have glucose intolerance during a pregnancy and then have their blood glucose return to normal after delivery of their baby. Diabetes primarily affects organs with a large supply of blood vessels such as the eyes, kidneys, and heart. *Untreated diabetes doubles the risk of death from heart disease in women* (*Women's Health*, 1985) *and is responsible for 36 percent of cardiovascular deaths* (Amler and Dull, 1987).

Effective treatment is readily available for diabetics, but the problem is making people aware of this disease. It is estimated that only half of the 6.5 percent of the population with diabetes are aware of their health problem. Easy fatigue, excessive thirst and urination can be early signs of diabetes. But many women may have no symptoms at all. Annual screening for diabetes with urine tests and periodic blood tests may uncover women with asymptomatic diabetes.

Most women who develop diabetes after age 40 have what is known as type II diabetes, adult-onset diabetes, or non-insulin-dependent diabetes. This type of diabetes usually does not require insulin shots but is controlled in most cases with proper diet and, if needed, a glucose-lowering medication. A proper diet is the one which we have outlined for you in chapter 9 with special attention to achieving and maintaining your ideal bodyweight. Women with a family history of adult-onset diabetes, obesity, or a history of glucose intolerance during pregnancy are at special risk and need regular screening for diabetes. Tight control of the blood glucose is proven to significantly lower the risk of heart disease and other complications of diabetes.

Prevention strategy. Keep your weight as close as possible to your ideal bodyweight, and check your blood or urine for glucose annually.

Menopause

Menopause is now considered a major coronary risk factor.

As we have already discussed, women are initially less vulnerable to cardiovascular disease than men, but with advancing age this relative immunity subsides, especially after menopause. The only definite effect on heart disease by menopause is on blood lipids which appear to increase after menopause and can sometimes be lowered with estrogen therapy. Menopause has no apparent effect on blood pressure or bodyweight (Mishell, 1987).

Prevention strategy. Estrogen replacement therapy is now considered to be a significant factor in reducing the risk of coronary artery disease in postmenopausal women. In light of this benefit and numerous others, we recommend hormone therapy for virtually all women.

Family History

Those women with close blood relatives who have had serious heart problems such as a heart attack, bypass surgery, and angina are at increased risk themselves for cardiovascular disease. This is especially true if the relative was younger than 55 when the event first occurred. If you have a positive family history, then increased surveillance of other potential risk factors and correction of those risk factors which do exist is advised.

Prevention strategy. Be aware of your family health history and increase your risk factor surveillance if needed. Correct other cardiovascular risk factors whenever possible.

Alcohol

You may have heard of medical studies completed in the last 10 years which suggested that drinking moderate amounts of alcohol (defined as three beers a day) might reduce the risk of coronary heart disease. This effect seems to be mediated by elevating the HDL cholesterol and in one study was as effective at raising HDL as was jogging (Hartung and Forey, 1983).

However, we need to examine this data and subsequent studies in their entirety. The study by Hartung and others showed no improved effect on HDL with moderate drinking of wine, and furthermore, in premenopausal women, the effect of exercise was greater than the effect of alcohol on HDL levels. Keep in mind that while alcohol may possibly have a good effect on HDL, it has a definite detrimental effect on blood pressure, bodyweight, and glucose intolerance (Eichner,

1988). Exercise has a significant beneficial effect on all these parameters as well as HDL levels.

In view of the facts that *alcohol* (even social to moderate drinking, as has been suggested) *increases a woman's risk for breast cancer, high blood pressure, and risk of alcoholism*—a truly devastating disease— we do not recommend that you drink in hope of increasing your HDL ratio.

Preventive strategy. For those who choose to drink, moderation is certainly advised, and is clearly no substitute for regular aerobic exercise in improving your lipid profile.

Oral Contraceptives

Birth-control pills clearly increase your risk of developing blood clots and subsequent heart attacks or strokes *if you are over age 35 and smoke.* With the use of low-dose pills, the overall risk to healthy women under 40 who do not smoke is minimal. For most women over 40, a barrier method of contraception or permanent sterilization is the preferred method of birth control.

Preventive strategy. Take the lowest effective dose pill possible and don't smoke.

Obesity

Being overweight is a risk factor for high blood pressure, elevated cholesterol, elevated triglycerides, stroke, heart disease, and the development of diabetes. Obese individuals are often less physically active compared with normal weight individuals. This inactivity presents yet another cardiac risk factor. Additionally, women who carry their excess weight in the torso and upper part of the body are at a greater risk of hypertension than those women who carry their extra weight primarily in the hip, thigh, and buttocks areas. All of these factors play a major role in the development of heart disease.

Prevention strategy. Maintain as close to ideal bodyweight as possible. Also be relaxed instead of frantic about weight loss. A steady one pound loss per week on the way to your goal is great!

Physical Inactivity

Recent surveys have concluded that *60 percent of Americans do not get enough exercise. This low level of activity is considered to be as great a risk factor for heart disease as smoking, elevated cholesterol, or hypertension* (Eichner, 1988). Some experts even feel that exercise is our most powerful weapon in the fight against heart disease.

Many of you will have a multitude of excuses for not exercising regularly. Overcoming the inertia problem of a sedentary lifestyle may be difficult at first, but the potential benefits are certainly worth every effort. *Regular exercise is proven to reduce your risk of coronary heart disease.* In fact, even low-intensity exercise such as gardening, if done regularly, can be beneficial (Rippe et al., 1988).

Throughout this book we have emphasized the various *favorable effects of aerobic exercise.* The following is a summary of these benefits:

- Reduced anxiety and stress
- Weight control
- Reduced cholesterol
- Blood pressure control
- Improved cardiopulmonary capacity
- Prevention of osteoporosis

Walking is by far the easiest and safest aerobic exercise. It is really never too late to begin a walking program for anyone in good health. The key point is don't delay, *start now!*

Prevention strategy. Inactivity is hazardous to your health; activity is beneficial. See Table 15.3 for an exercise prescription for healthy adults. Also see chapter 13 for complete exercise details.

SUMMARY AND PERSONAL OPINIONS

According to the American Heart Association, *prevention is the greatest need in the fight against heart disease* (Grundy and Greenblad, 1987). Let's face it, more than one out of every two Americans will die from some form of cardiovascular disease. Statistics show that it is not the rare cancers, auto accidents, or even AIDS that is killing most of us.

Table 15.3. Exercise Prescription for Healthy Adults

Frequency	3 to 7 days per week
Duration	20 to 60 min. continuous activity (or for shorter periods of time when first getting started)
Intensity	70 percent or greater of your maximal heart rate
Activity	brisk walking, jogging, cycling, aerobic dance, or swimming

Instead, it is a deadly disease so common that we have become too complacent about it.

Periodic health examinations with an emphasis on identification of cardiovascular risk factors, coupled with a preventive diet and exercise program, is your best way of avoiding this number one killer of women. The benefits of a cardiovascular disease prevention program will also spill over into other areas and further improve your general well-being and physical condition.

The following list summarizes *cardiovascular risk factors and our recommendations:*

Risk Factor	Recommendation
Smoking	Don't
Hypertension	Keep below 140/85
High cholesterol	Keep below 200 mg/dl
	Keep HDL Ratio below 4.5
Diabetes	Control weight and blood sugar
Menopause	Consider estrogen therapy
Family history	Know about it, if possible
Oral contraceptives	Take low dose; don't smoke
Obesity	Maintain ideal bodyweight
Physical inactivity	Do aerobic exercise at least 20 min. 3 times a week

CHAPTER 16

Prevention and Early Detection of Cancer

Cancer is the second most common cause of death in women and the leading cause of death in women age 35 to 64 (*Women's Health*, 1985). *In the past 50 years, death from cancer has increased 250 percent and currently one of every three Americans will develop cancer during his or her lifetime* (Lippman, 1988). Although there are over 1300 different subtypes of cancer, the National Cancer Institute reports that lung, breast, colon, and prostate cancer account for more than 50 percent of the cancer cases in the United States. Fortunately for women, you don't have to worry about prostate cancer, but the risk of lung, breast, and colon cancer is significant. Melanoma, a skin cancer, is also being discovered at alarming rates in today's woman. Of course, cancer of the reproductive organs, the uterus, cervix, and ovaries continues to be of major concern to women. Prevention of disease and early detection so that treatment can be more successful will significantly improve your overall quality of life.

While advances in the treatment of cancer with chemotherapy and radiation therapy have occurred and substantially improved survival in certain types of cancer, *prevention and appropriate screening tests clearly appear to be the most effective ways of reducing cancer deaths.* The National Cancer Institute has a goal of reducing cancer deaths by 50 percent by the year 2000. Believe it or not, this could really happen, but only if *you* take personal responsibility to make the changes in your lifestyle which reduce your risk of cancer and if physicians will encourage the proper use of cancer-screening procedures.

PREVENTING BREAST CANCER

One in eleven women will develop breast cancer at sometime in her life. This is a sobering thought when you think of ten or eleven close friends and realize that one of them will probably develop breast cancer, possibly even yourself. Breast cancer has for years been the most common malignancy in women, only recently surpassed by lung cancer. It is the most common cause of cancer death in women.

Unfortunately, the incidence of breast cancer seems to be slowly increasing while the mortality or death rate from breast cancer has remained essentially unchanged at 27 women per 100,000 annually for the past 50 years. This grim statistic points out the critical importance of early detection and preventive measures. Personal involvement by you and your physician will make the difference in reducing deaths from breast cancer.

Risk Factors for Breast Cancer

While there is no one known cause of breast cancer, several significant risk factors have been identified.

1. *Advancing age.* The older you are the greater your risk for breast cancer. Eighty-five percent of all breast cancers occur in women older than 40, and 65 percent occur in women over age 50. Less than 1.5 percent of all breast cancers are found in women under age 30 (Lippman, 1988).

2. *Family history of breast cancer.* Next in importance among the major risk factors is a family history of breast cancer. Several medical studies have shown that there is a definite increased risk (fivefold increase) for women whose mother or sister had a breast cancer. The earlier they developed the cancer (especially if both breasts were involved) the more significant the relationship.

3. *Benign breast disease.* Women with *benign breast disease* appear to be at increased risk by two- to threefold.

4. *Age at first pregnancy.* There is a clear relationship between age of first pregnancy and breast cancer. It is more common in women who never have children and in those who deliver their first baby after age 35. The relative risk could be as high as a one- to twofold increase. Incomplete pregnancies, either miscarriage or abortion, do not carry any protective benefit against breast cancer (Mishell, 1987).

5. *High-fat diet.* Diet has now been identified as one of the major environmental factors in the development of breast cancer (Amler and Dull, 1987). It appears that the total fat content of your diet is what increases the risk, not the calorie content. *The National Academy of*

Sciences has recommended reducing the fat content of your daily diet to no more than 30 percent of the total calories consumed.

6. *Alcohol.* There is a definite correlation between drinking alcohol and breast cancer. *A study of more than 7000 women showed a significant increased risk of breast cancer for women who drink any alcohol* (Schatzkin et al., 1987). This increased risk was particularly significant in those women who consume more than three drinks per week. The message is that *alcohol increases your risk of breast cancer* and should be considered along with other risk factors, in assessing your potential risk of breast cancer.

Hormone Therapy and Breast Cancer — Increased Risk or Not?

The issue of hormone therapy and the possibility of its increasing the risk of breast cancer has been a concern for many women. In fact, some will not even consider taking estrogen because of this perceived risk. However, because many women will need estrogen replacement after menopause, we want to examine this problem a bit more closely.

First of all, what about birth-control pills? A review of five recent studies on this subject shows that *there is a slight increased risk of breast cancer when taking birth-control pills,* **but only in women over the age of 46** (Mishell, 1987). We never recommend taking birth-control pills after age 45 and usually recommend stopping oral contraceptives before age 40. The risk factor of breast cancer simply provides another reason for not taking birth-control pills permanently.

Now let's consider postmenopausal hormone therapy. With over 30 million postmenopausal women in the United States and strong recommendations for most of them to be on estrogen replacement therapy to prevent hot flushes, osteoporosis, tissue atrophy, and even heart disease, the issue of estrogen and breast cancer cannot be ignored. Many medical research studies have been done on this issue, and some conflicting results have been obtained.

A recent study by the Centers for Disease Control showed no increased risk of breast cancer with estrogen replacement therapy in postmenopausal women. Other studies, however, have shown a slight increase in the risk of breast cancer with long-term use of high-dose estrogen in women with spontaneous menopause (Mishell, 1987). Smaller doses of estrogen for long periods of time do not seem to carry an increased risk. The use of progesterone along with estrogen does not protect the breast against cancer as it does with the endometrial lining of the uterus. *Our recommendation is to consider the relatively small risk, if any, of developing breast cancer as a direct result of estrogen therapy against the much greater potential benefits of estrogen replacement therapy for most women.* You should take only the amount needed for prevention of estrogen deficiency symptoms (.625

mg of Premarin if possible), and do not take progesterone (Provera) unless you have a uterus.

EARLY DETECTION OF BREAST CANCER

Now for the good news! Early detection of breast cancer is highly successful in minimizing the surgery and additional therapies required to effect a cure. Early detection can literally save your life. *Breast self-examination, clinical examination, and screening mammograms are the basis for a successful breast cancer detection program.*

Breast Self-Examination

Every woman over the age of 21 should be practicing breast self-examination at least once a month. A large number of abnormal breast masses are found by women themselves. Breast self-examination is easy to learn and takes very little time to perform (see diagram). Although usually painless, any breast lump or mass which appears and does not quickly go away should be considered suspicious. This finding should prompt a visit to your doctor, who can further evaluate the mass.

When performing breast self-examination, you should check the breast tissue leading up under your armpit and also your nipples. Any unusual skin or nipple change, skin dimpling, nipple discharge or bleeding, pain, ulceration, or reddening of the skin should be viewed with great suspicion and prompt a visit to your doctor. *A complete breast examination by a physician each year should be part of every adult woman's preventive health care.*

Mammograms

The good word regarding the importance and effectiveness of screening mammograms is finally reaching most women in the United States. However, the National Cancer Institute recently reported that *45 percent of women over the age of 40 who have heard about mammograms have still never had one performed on themselves.* Are you one of them?

Mammograms can detect small lesions in the breast usually before they can even be felt by you or your doctor. Detection of cancer this early can save your breast and your life as well. The real questions are how often do you need a mammogram and when should you have your first one. The answers, of course, depend on the individual woman and an assessment of her risk factors.

There is little dispute with the current American Cancer Society recommendations which suggest that *every woman over the age of 50*

How to examine your breasts

This simple 3-step procedure could save your life by
finding breast cancer early when it is most curable.

1

Before a mirror:
Inspect your breasts with arms at your sides. Next, raise your arms high overhead. Look for any changes in shape or contour of each breast, a swelling, dimpling of skin or changes in the skin or nipple.

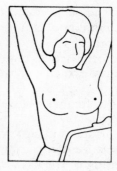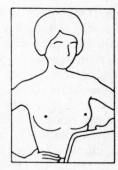

Then, rest palms on hips and press down firmly to flex your chest muscles. Left and right breast will not exactly match —few women's breasts do.

Regular inspection shows what is normal for you and will give you confidence in your examination.

2

Lying down:
Lie down. Flatten your right breast by placing a pillow under your right shoulder. Fingers flat, use the sensitive pads of the middle three fingers on your left hand. Feel for lumps or changes using a rubbing motion. Press firmly enough to feel the different breast tissues. Completely feel all of the breast and chest area from your collarbone to the base of a properly fitted bra; and from your breast bone to the underarm. Allow enough time for a complete exam.

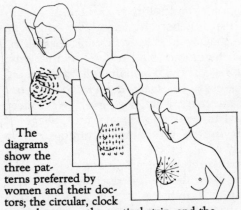

The diagrams show the three patterns preferred by women and their doctors; the circular, clock or oval pattern, the vertical strip, and the wedge. Choose the method easiest for you and use the same pattern to feel every part of the breast tissue.

After you have completely examined your right breast, then examine your left breast using the same method. Compare what you have felt in one breast with the other.

Finally, squeeze the nipple of each breast gently between the thumb and index finger. Any discharge, clear or bloody, should be reported to your doctor.

3

In the shower:

Examine your breasts during bath or shower; hands glide easier over wet skin. Fingers flat, move gently over every part of each breast. Check for any lump, hard knot or thickening.

WHAT YOU SHOULD DO IF YOU FIND A CHANGE

If you find a lump or dimple or discharge during BSE, it is important to see your doctor as soon as possible. Don't be frightened. Most breast lumps or changes are not cancer, but only your doctor can make the diagnosis.

Reprinted by permission of the American Cancer Society, Texas Division, Inc. *How to Examine Your Breasts*, May, 1988.

should have an annual mammogram in addition to the monthly self-examination and annual breast checks by her physician. The American Cancer Society, The American Academy of Family Physicians, and the American Medical Association all recommend a *baseline mammogram at some time between age 35 and 39.* They also recommend *repeat mammograms for women age 40 to 49 every one to two years.* However, other groups, including the National Cancer Institute, the American College of Obstetricians and Gynecologists, and the American College of Physicians do not recommend routine screening mammograms in women under the age of 50 (Eddy et al., 1988).

This matter of when to start routine screening mammograms has become an important issue to the 14 million women age 40 to 49 here in the United States. An estimated 16 percent of new breast cancers (about 18,300 per year) will occur in this age group. And screening mammograms can greatly improve the early detection of cancer and prolong their life expectancy. However, mammograms do involve a certain amount of expense and some small risks.

The more mammograms that are performed, the more early cancers that will be discovered. On the other hand, the number of false positive tests will also be greater. False positive mammograms are exams which indicate a suspicious breast mass; but when the mass is removed, it is benign and not cancerous at all. However, the mammograms today are so good that the false positive rate is only about 1 percent (Eddy et al., 1988). A false positive test is what every women with an abnormal mammogram hopes she has.

Some women may be concerned about the risk of radiation exposure from mammograms, especially when you start getting them every year. Today, the radiation from a mammogram is actually very low—so low in fact, that the risk of its actually causing a breast cancer is negligible. Estimates are that out of one million women who have a mammogram done every year for 10 years, there might be an increase of 40 new breast cancers. This amounts to a risk of 1 in 25,000 (Eddy et al., 1988). Remember that your overall risk of developing breast cancer is 1 in 10 or 11. Doesn't it make more sense to go with the odds and give yourself the greatest chance of early disease detection?

The costs for mammograms vary widely. In our community they range from a low of 60 dollars to more than 150 dollars. Some insurance plans cover screening mammograms while others do not cover the cost of preventive-medicine tests. This situation is changing, but clearly there is a need for economical and accurate mammogram availability.

A final argument or complaint that we sometimes hear from patients when we suggest a mammogram is that the procedure is painful. With most radiology centers now having specialized rooms and experienced technicians for mammograms, this should be a rare problem. In fact, an article in the *Archives of Internal Medicine* from March, 1988, stated that actual pain was uncommon and that 88 percent of women experienced no pain at all or only mild discomfort during mammography.

Our recommendations regarding screening mammograms and breast examinations tend to follow the guidelines of the American Cancer Society and the American Academy of Family Physicians. *Mammograms are safe and effective at detecting early malignant breast changes.* We believe that the higher your individual risk for breast cancer, the more aggressive your health program should be in screening mammograms.

Prevention strategy. Eat a low-fat diet (30 percent or less total fat). Avoid entirely or drink limited amounts of alcohol (fewer than three drinks per week). Avoid birth-control pills after 45. If menopausal, take only the dose of estrogen needed to control hot flushes; then reduce to .625 mg conjugated estrogen (Premarin or its equivalent) if possible.

Screening strategy. Monthly breast self-exam for life. Annual breast exam by your physician. Mammogram and breast biopsy if needed to evaluate any suspicious breast mass. Routine mammograms every 2 to 4 years age 40 to 49 (discuss with your physician). Annual mammogram after age 50.

PREVENTING LUNG CANCER

The prediction several years ago that lung cancer would become the most common cancer among women has sadly enough, come to pass. In 1988 there were over 152,000 new cases of lung cancer and 139,000 deaths due to this disease (Lippman, 1988). In 1980 there were only about 88,000 deaths due to lung cancer, at a cost of 1.6 billion dollars (Amler and Dull, 1987). Today the costs in terms of personal suffering, deaths, and treatment are much greater; and for the most part, preventable.

We may have "come a long way, baby," but it is all in the wrong direction in terms of smoking liberation. Sure, you've got the right to smoke, but why would you want to? Lung cancer rates for women increased 276 percent between 1952 and 1979, compared with a 167 percent increase for men (Amler and Dull, 1987) simply because more women now smoke.

In addition to being a major risk factor for heart and lung disease, it is estimated that smoking accounts for 76 percent of lung cancer and significantly increases the risk of several other cancers (Lippman, 1988). See Table 16.1. Take a look at these figures—*did you realize that 24 percent of all cervical cancer can be attributed to smoking?*

Several factors influence the effect of smoking on cancer development. Smoking less than nine cigarettes a day increases your cancer risk by four to five times. Those smoking more than two packs a day

Table 16.1. Percentage of Cancer
Attributed to Smoking

Location	Percentage
Lung	76
Cervix	24
Pancreas	26
Bladder	29
Larynx	74
Esophagus	74

have a 20 times greater risk of cancer. Smoking filter cigarettes carries a 25 percent lower risk of lung cancer than smoking non-filter cigarettes. The younger the smoker, the greater the risk of developing cancer. However, the major risk factor is the *duration* of one's smoking habit. *The number of years (length of time) one smokes is a greater risk than the total number of cigarettes smoked.*

Don't kid yourself by saying "it's too late to stop." Moderate smokers (less than two packs a day) who quit for 5 years reduce their increased-risk factor to almost zero. Heavy smokers (more than two packs a day) must have stopped for 10 years before their increased-risk factor falls to almost zero.

There are a number of occupational hazards which increase the risk of lung cancer. Asbestos, primarily, but also arsenic, radon, chromates, and coke oven emissions are associated with increased cancer rates. All of these relatively rare environmental exposures are compounded by any concurrent exposure to smoking.

There are no generally accepted screening procedures for lung cancer. The American Cancer Society no longer recommends annual chest x-rays. Certainly those people who are at greater risk for lung cancer need to give careful attention to any suspicious symptoms, particularly any change in their pulmonary habits.

Prevention strategy. Do not smoke (don't even think about it). If you already do smoke, quit. And support legislative efforts to curtail smoking and control air pollution.

Screening strategy. None have proven effective.

If you are unable to stop smoking, the following list are things you can do to improve your risk factors:

- Eat increased amounts of food high in beta-carotene (all dark green and deep yellow to orange fruits and vegetables).

- Take a vitamin/mineral supplement containing at least 100 percent RDA of Vitamin A and C.

- Don't take birth-control pills.
- Don't use artificial sweeteners.
- Use filtered, low-tar cigarettes.
- Try to eliminate other risk factors.
- Look for a good "Quit Smoking" program.

PREVENTING COLON AND RECTAL CANCER

Cancer of the colon and rectum is a common disease and a significant cause of death. About 140,000 new cases are diagnosed in the United States every year, and about 60,000 people die from this cancer annually. Men and women are affected equally and *colon-rectal cancer strikes one out of every 20 women.*

As unfortunate as any cancer is, colon cancer is almost 100 percent curable if found early. And there is increasing evidence that this type of cancer is also highly preventable. This is great news, but why are so many people dying from a disease which is both preventable and potentially curable? The cold, hard facts are that many people are not getting proper health-oriented checkups and refuse to change their eating habits. If you can change this trend in your own life, then you can probably avoid this devastating disease.

Diet. The role of diet in the development of colon cancer has been under careful study for several years. A diet high in fat seems likely to promote cancer formation in the lower intestine, while a reduction in saturated fats reduces your risk of colon cancer. Increasing dietary fiber also reduces your risk of colon cancer, possibly by speeding up transit time of food in the intestine so that potential cancer-causing agents in our diet have less contact time with the colon. Most colon specialists recommend an intake of 25 grams of crude fiber per day to make a difference. Practically speaking, this means that you will need to consume a very high-fiber cereal (i.e., Bran Buds, All-Bran, Fiber One) on a regular basis. Fortunately, these high-fiber cereals are very low in calories and can almost be thought of as a dietary supplement rather than as a food. For example, 1/2 cup of Fiber One cereal plus 1/2 cup of skim milk is only 100 calories and provides 12 grams of fiber, not to mention the calcium and protein content of this healthful snack.

Cruciferous vegetables such as cauliflower and broccoli act directly to reduce colon cancer risk. Those people whose diets do not include these types of vegetables have a threefold increase in the risk of colon cancer (Amler and Dull, 1987). However, newer studies have not been able to completely reproduce these findings. Other cruciferous vegetables include cabbage and Brussels sprouts. Heavy beer drinkers (more than 15 liters per month) and persons with diets deficient in Vitamin A also increase their risk of colon cancer. The presence of nitrates and nitrites in foods are also cancer-causing agents. These are widely used food preservatives and should be avoided whenever possible. Be sure to read the labels on the foods you buy! Currently about 20 percent of colon cancers are attributed to dietary factors, and research seems to indicate increases in that figure every year.

Early detection. Although many people discover they have colon cancer after noting some change in bowel movements or bloody stools, the cancer itself probably developed over a long period of time. In many cases, colon cancer develops from the malignant change of colon polyps. Since this is the case, early detection and elimination of colon polyps should significantly reduce the incidence of colon cancer. See Table 16.2 for screening guidelines.

Identification of individuals at high risk for colon cancer is important, as screening measures may need to begin at an early age in some cases. A family history of polyps or cancer is significant. If you have had ulcerative colitis, there is also an increased risk. If you personally have had a colon polyp or previous colon cancer, there is also a greater risk. Now it is evident that women with a history of these high-risk factors may need to begin screening procedures at an earlier age.

The American Cancer Society recommends that everyone over 40 should have his/her stool checked annually for blood. This is important because microscopic bleeding from a small polyp or tumor may not be noticed by the individual. Your doctor may choose to perform this test during your annual gynecologic exam or you may be given some stool cards to take home and bring back to the office for testing. The

Table 16.2. **American Cancer Society Screening Guidelines for Colon Cancer**

Age	Recommendation
40 and up	Check for blood in the stool annually.
50 and up	Sigmoidoscopy every 3 to 5 years after two normal tests 1 year apart.
High risk 20 and up	Annual stool check and sigmoidoscopy when there is family history of polyps or bowel cancer, personal history of polyps or cancer, and other medical conditions.

whole point of this procedure is to find potentially cancerous polyps in the colon at an early stage.

If the stool test is positive or if you are over 50 years old, you will need periodic screening sigmoidoscopy. This is usually the point where doctors start losing their patients' interest. Most people consider checking their stool unpleasant enough, but being subjected to a sigmoidoscopy and paying to have it done—you've got to be kidding!

Well, we're *not* kidding. In fact, this is really a very important issue in preventive medicine. Although no one looks forward to this exam, the discomfort is minimal. Most physicians now use a flexible sigmoidoscope which is essentially a lighted tube smaller than your finger which is passed into the rectum. Your doctor can check for polyps or other sources of bleeding and take a biopsy if needed. This is usually done in the doctor's office or outpatient surgery and requires, in most cases, no anesthetic or pain medication. If your doctor does not perform this test, ask for a referral to someone who does do flexible sigmoidoscopy.

The results of careful screening are clear. *Early detection of precancerous polyps and small malignant tumors saves lives* and prevents surgical complications such as a colostomy. Is it worth it to you to undergo such tests once a year to prevent such a devastating disease? We hope so.

Prevention strategy. Decrease dietary fat. Increase dietary fiber. Eat more cruciferous vegetables (broccoli, cauliflower). Eat more vegetables high in Vitamin A (carrots, squash). Limit beer consumption. Avoid nitrates and nitrites.

Screening strategy. Women over 40 should have an annual rectal exam and annual stool guiac test. Those over 50 should have a sigmoidoscopy every 3 to 5 years after two negative exams 1 year apart.

PREVENTING SKIN CANCER

Skin cancer is by far the most common malignant disease. *Up to one-half of all people who live to be 65 will have at least one skin cancer in their lifetime.* Fortunately not many people die from skin cancers, but the majority of these deaths are preventable.

Most skin cancers (95 percent) are *basal cell carcinomas.* About 500,000 of these cancers occur annually and most of them are due to ultraviolet radiation from sun exposure (Lazar and Lazar, 1988). If a basal cell cancer is found and treated early, almost 100 percent are totally cured. *Squamous cell carcinomas,* which are less common, are almost equally as curable if found early.

Melanoma, on the other hand, is a very dangerous skin cancer with a death rate of 30 to 40 percent of those affected (P. Rubin, 1983). Dr.

Charles Balch of the M.D. Anderson Cancer Center in Houston, Texas, has stated that the rate of melanoma occurrence is rising faster than any other cancer except lung cancer in women. It is projected that 27,000 new melanomas will be found in 1988, and about 7000 people will die from the disease (Lazar and Lazar, 1988). If this rate continues, one of every 100 people born in the year 2000 will develop a melanoma at some time during his/her life.

Sun-worshipers beware. Skin cancer prevention can essentially be summed up by the simple advice of avoiding excessive sun exposure. For years skin cancer was primarily a problem of people who made their living outdoors, such as farmers, sailors, or construction workers. Now, with so many enjoyable outdoor activities and our cultural emphasis on seeking a deep tan, the incidence of skin cancer is increasing in all groups of people.

Sun prevention methods. Here are a few tips on how to protect yourself from the sun:

- *Proper clothing*—Wear hats, long sleeves, long pants.

- *Sun avoidance*—Limit exposure. Avoid outdoor activity from 11 A.M. to 3 P.M. Extra precautions on the beach or snow.

- *Use sunscreens*—Don't use "tanning oils;" they can actually cook your skin. Use at least SPF 15. Apply 30 minutes before exposure and every hour thereafter.

Although skin cancer and melanoma can occur in anyone, they are less common in blacks and much more likely to occur in people with fair skin or red hair. A small number of people have an inherited tendency to develop melanomas. There is also evidence now to suggest that serious sunburns at an early age may be more likely to promote skin cancer.

Prevention of the consequences of skin cancer also depend on early detection and treatment. You should have your doctor examine and biopsy any suspicious lesion. Any changes in a skin lesion's shape, size, borders, or color must be checked. Lesions which begin to itch or bleed should also be checked. Skin ulcers which don't heal or changes within an old scar are also concerns.

Avoidance of excessive sun exposure and periodic surveillance of the skin by your doctor will certainly help win the battle against skin cancer. Prompt attention to changes in your skin or individual moles is very important. Early detection and treatment could almost totally eliminate deaths from skin cancer and melanoma.

Warning signs of skin cancer. Be alert to any of the following signals of skin cancer:

- Change in size, color, or thickness of a mole.
- Irregularity of the margin of a mole.
- Itching of a mole.
- Bleeding of a mole.
- Non-healing skin ulcers.
- Change in an old scar or burn.

Prevention strategy. Avoid excessive sun exposure. There is no such thing as a "healthy tan."
Screening strategy. Annual skin surveillance in high-risk individuals.

PREVENTING CERVICAL CANCER

Every year 16,000 new cases of invasive cancer of the cervix are diagnosed in the United States. Of these women, 7000 will eventually die from the disease (P. Rubin, 1983). This is a tragic statistic in light of the fact that *most of these cancers could have been diagnosed at an early and very curable stage with a simple office procedure called a Pap smear.* In part, because of the effectiveness of screening Pap smears, the incidence of invasive cervical cancer has dropped over the past 40 years by about half. At the same time, deaths from cervical cancer have dropped by more than 50 percent to only 6 deaths per 100,000 women annually (P. Rubin, 1983).

Risk Factors

The causes of cervical cancer and just what is considered a risk factor for the disease are becoming clear. Increasing evidence suggests that one potential risk is that of sexually transmitted disease. *Women at higher risk for cervical cancer are those with multiple sexual partners, early onset of sexual intercourse, or a partner who himself has multiple sexual contacts.* Several studies indicate that a sexually transmitted virus called *human papillomavirus* (HPV) may be responsible for some cancers (Amler and Dull, 1987). The use of barrier contraceptives such as the diaphragm or condom has proven effective at decreasing the risk of HPV transmission. Sexually-transmitted HPV is a growing concern, as 95 percent of all cervical cancers contain HPV and this infection is becoming increasingly common. For a more detailed discussion of sexually-transmitted disease, see chapter 6.

Smoking and other drugs. Smoking doubles the risk of developing cervical cancer, and this risk increases to 400 percent if you begin smoking before age 15 (Amler and Dull, 1987). Exposure to diethylstilbestrol (DES) is an additional risk factor for cervical cancer. Some women were exposed to DES as a fetus when their mothers took the drug during their pregnancy. There is a clear association of increased cancer risk and DES exposure, but 91 percent of these cancers are found early, between the ages of 15 and 27. Yet, some cases have been found as late as the mid 30s. The actual risk is still low, however, at only 1 case per 1000 exposed women.

High-risk factors for cervical cancer. If any of the following factors are present in your life, you are at an increased risk for developing cervical cancer:

- Multiple sexual partners
- Onset of sexual intercourse at an early age
- High-risk male sexual partner
- Human papillomavirus (HPV) infection
- Smoking
- Exposure to DES

Pap Smears

In 1941 the Papanicolaou smear, better known now as the Pap smear, was developed. Since then, it has become one of the most important medical discoveries of the twentieth century. With the Pap smear, most cervical cancers can be found in their earliest, even precancerous stages. This is particularly important since there are absolutely no symptoms in the earliest stages of most cervical cancers.

Although most of you are well aware of what Pap smears are, you may not realize the full importance of this test. Unfortunately, only 10 to 15 percent of women in the United States have a Pap smear done annually (P. Rubin, 1983). Perhaps some of the difficulty in getting women to have the test is that there is some controversy over who should have Pap smears and how often they should be done.

Recent criticism of the accuracy of Pap smears has some women concerned about this test. However, the facts remain that *deaths from cervical cancer have dropped by 70 percent since the beginning of Pap smear screening (Piver, 1988) and most of these deaths could have been prevented by early detection and treatment.*

An additional tool called the *colposcope* is now being widely used to evaluate the cervix when an abnormal Pap smear is reported. The colposcope is an instrument which magnifies the cervix and when combined with special staining techniques can identify suspicious areas on the cervix for direct biopsy.

In 1957 the American Cancer Society began recommending annual Pap smears. Since then, modifications in this initial proposal have been made several times as new information became available. In 1988 the American Cancer Society, American College of Obstetricians and Gynecologists, the National Cancer Institute, and American Medical Association all stated that *initial Pap smear tests should begin at age 18 or at the onset of sexual activity if earlier. After three consecutive normal smears, Pap smear tests may be done less often at the discretion of the physician.* The reliability of Pap smears is also in question. Some experts fear that as many as 20 to 40 percent of results may be falsely negative. That is, the Pap smear, while an excellent test, is far from being 100 percent accurate on every exam.

In light of the variable speed of progression in cancerous cervical changes and the lack of 100 percent accuracy, we cannot recommend anything less than annual Pap smears for any high-risk woman regardless of age. You also need to consider that the addition of a Pap smear to your annual exam is a relatively low-cost item which yields important, potentially life-saving, screening information.

What about older women? Are Pap smears and pelvic exams still important? Consider that 25 percent of all the new cervical cancers in 1987 and 40 percent of the 7000 deaths annually are in women older than 65 (Piver, 1988). Although the American Cancer Society has now apparently left the issue of Pap smears in women older than 65 up to their physicians, it is important to realize that a significant percentage of older women will have positive results on their Pap smears. *We recommend that screening every 1 to 3 years continue even after age 65.*

If you have had a hysterectomy and obviously no longer have a cervix for a Pap smear to be done, do you still need this type of exam? The answer is yes. Pap smears of the vagina after hysterectomy are important to screen for vaginal cancer. *It is recommended that a Pap smear be done every year for the first 2 years after hysterectomy and every 3 years thereafter when the results are consistently normal* (Bell, 1984).

Prevention strategy. Maintain a monogamous (one-partner) sexual relationship. Avoid sexual intercourse at an early age. Don't smoke. Treat HPV infection if detected on the Pap smear.

Screening strategy. The following table shows our recommendations for screenings of cervical cancer:

Initial Pap smear	Age 18 or onset of sexual activity.
High-risk women or age 35 to 65	Annual Pap smear.
Low-risk women younger than 35	After three consecutive normal Pap smears, then every 3 years.
DES exposure	Every 6 to 12 months after age 14, onset of menses, or initiation of sex.
Older than 65	Every 3 years if previous Pap normal.
After hysterectomy for benign disease	Every 3 years.
Following treatment of cancer	Every 3 months for 2 years and then every 6 months for 3 years and annually thereafter.

PREVENTING CANCER OF THE OVARY

Cancer of the ovary is the fourth leading cause of death from cancer in women after breast, lung, and colon cancer. About 18,000 new cases are found each year, and approximately 1 in 80 women will develop this cancer (P. Rubin, 1983). Fortunately, new cases of this cancer seem to be declining over the past 10 years.

Very little is known about what causes ovarian cancer, but women who are near menopause appear to be at greatest risk. Two factors seem to provide some protection—childbearing and birth-control pills.

Early diagnosis seems to be the best way to effect a cure. Annual pelvic exams and ultrasound studies of the pelvis as needed may help detect early ovarian problems.

Prevention strategy. There are no practical prevention measures.

Screening strategy. Annual pelvic exams.

PREVENTING CANCER OF THE UTERUS

We discussed cancer of the endometrium or the lining of the uterus when we considered hormone therapy in chapter 3. There are numerous risk factors associated with this cancer, and about 38,000 new cases are discovered in the United States each year.

Obesity, diabetes, hypertension, infertility, late menopause, and irregular periods are all predisposing factors. *Currently, about 1 woman in*

1000 can expect to develop endometrial cancer. However, the use of progesterone with estrogen replacement therapy significantly reduces your risk of this cancer.

The other good news is that if you do develop endometrial cancer while taking estrogen therapy, the cancer is typically less malignant and invasive. It is believed that the risk of this cancer can approach zero with regular exams and cyclic estrogen/progesterone therapy.

Prevention strategy. Use cyclic progesterone (Provera) with estrogen at least 10 days a month. Have pretreatment endometrial biopsy at menopause. Control bodyweight.

Screening strategy. Have annual pelvic exams. Have careful endometrial biopsy for any abnormal bleeding followed by a D and C if symptoms persist despite therapy.

PREVENTING CANCER OF THE VULVA AND VAGINA

These cancers are a problem for older women. The peak age for this disease is from 50 to 70 years, and unfortunately the lesion may go undetected for a long time. Although this area of your body is difficult for you to personally see, there are certain warning signs.

Early warning symptoms may be itching, pain, bleeding, an ulceration that will not heal, or an unusual discharge. Any suspicious lesion should be biopsied, and annual pelvic exams with a thorough vaginal inspection and Pap smear should be done as well.

Prevention strategy. There are no proven preventive measures.

Screening strategy. Have annual pelvic exams and Pap smears regardless of age or prior surgery. A biopsy should be made of any suspicious lesion.

FOODS, ADDITIVES, AND CANCER

In 1982 the relationship between diet and cancer was the current rage of the medical community. Preliminary epidemiological studies indicated that this might be the preventive cure for America's most dreaded disease. Initial studies were based on population groups and general information about what foods they ate. For example, many of the original colon cancer studies showed that as the fiber intake of the entire population increased (that is, the average intake of the average citizen), as compared to the intake of other populations, the incidence of colon cancer decreased. It seemed simple—fiber intake goes up and cancer occurrence goes down.

It is important to realize that not all the evidence is in. While we personally believe that diet plays a major role in cancer prevention, some of our colleagues believe otherwise. Many feel that it is too early to make sweeping statements as to the importance of these relationships because there are very few long-term human studies to back up these suppositions. Our response to this argument is that if we had waited for the "official word" that a low-fat, low-cholesterol diet was good for us, there would no doubt be fewer of us to hear the good news. *Research scientists base their recommendations on unequivocal facts.* They do not want to be told later that their assessments were premature. Thus, they outwardly maintain a very conservative approach.

Our feeling is this: *There are many reasons to make healthy food selections, one of which is to prevent cancer. As long as the recommendations are reasonable and would otherwise be healthy food choices in preventing other types of diseases, we feel that a cancer-prevention diet is warranted based on existing evidence.*

A *Government Report.* In 1984 Margaret Heckler, the Health and Human Services Secretary, launched a new cancer-prevention campaign. She was quoted as saying, "Changes in people's lifestyle and behavior could save 95,000 lives per year by the year 2000. We know that fully 80 percent of cancer cases are linked to lifestyle and environmental factors, and we know that the most important causes of cancer are the ones we can control or influence. *We are not always at the mercy of our environment.*" The following chart from the National Cancer Institute clearly indicates that at the time proper diet was considered to be as important as tobacco cessation in terms of cancer prevention (National Cancer Institute, 1984).

Cancer-Causing Agents in Foods and Food Additives

As you can see from Table 16.3, dietary imbalances seem more important in explaining the relationship between food and cancer than specific cancer-causing additives. The 35 percent bar on top by the word "diet" indicates that these particular researchers think that a proper diet is the single-most important factor in preventing cancer. By diet, they are referring to the fact that most typical Americans consume a low-fiber, high-fat diet and should be doing exactly the opposite. By comparison, food additives are only estimated to cause 1 percent of all cancers. Think of it this way—*it's not the red food dye that's getting us, but the cheeseburgers with mayo and a side order of fries.* Of course that makes it a more difficult problem because it puts more responsibility on the individual for proper food selections.

Indeed, chemicals are formed in foods, as in the processes involved with smoking, pickling, or salt-curing. However, foods which have been poorly preserved can contain carcinogens (cancer-causing

Table 16.3.   Estimated Percentages of Cancer Cases Related to Lifestyle and Environmental Factors*

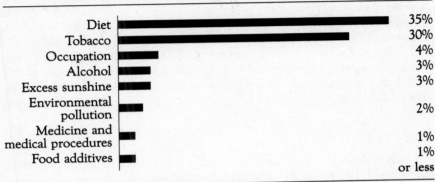

Diet	35%
Tobacco	30%
Occupation	4%
Alcohol	3%
Excess sunshine	3%
Environmental pollution	2%
Medicine and medical procedures	1%
Food additives	1% or less

*Public domain information from the National Cancer Institute, 1984. Also printed in *American Journal of Family Practice*, May 1984, p. 385.

agents), themselves. Refrigeration, canning, and improvements in transportation and the food marketing process are probably responsible for the dramatic decline in gastric cancer noted in developed countries over the last 50 years.

Over the last 10 years, an enormous amount of public concern has been generated about the potential dangers of food additives and preservatives. These include commonly known chemicals such as saccharin, aspartame, BHA, and BHT. Because many food additives are used for their antioxidant properties, it may be possible that the net effect on cancer risk is beneficial even though some of the additives are known carcinogens.

Hundreds of carcinogenic and mutagenic (causes changes in the body's cells) chemicals occur naturally in our foods—even in the fruits, vegetables, and grain products we promote as being anti-cancer foods. But most of this information is based on rat and mice studies, and we are certainly different from these tiny creatures. Fortunately, our bodies have a built-in detoxifying system to protect us (most of the time) against these harmful substances. These protective mechanisms work on both naturally occurring and food-additive carcinogens.

To summarize, here are five major points:

1. Try to choose natural foods (no additives) whenever possible. However, when you cannot, it is not a significant health risk.

2. Be more concerned about general dietary imbalances which are prevalent in the average American diet, such as eating too much protein; too many calories; excessive amounts of fat; overly processed foods, and too little fiber, fruits, and vegetables.

3. Eat only fresh foods. Do not eat any foods (including vegetables) which have begun to deteriorate as these may contain mutagens or carcinogens.

4. Avoid foods with pesticides whenever possible. Wash fresh fruits and vegetables before eating them. A good vegetable brush will help.

5. Be careful of the food packaging. Glass containers are the very best in terms of no chemical contamination. Do not store opened foods in the original cans. Do not microwave plastics which were never intended for this purpose.

Calories and Cancer

Caloric restriction was shown to be a powerful cancer-preventing factor over 50 years ago in animal experiments. However, it has only been of late that there is evidence to suggest the opposite—and, again this evidence is based only upon rodent studies. *We once thought that fat intake was the major factor in dietary promotion of cancer; we now believe that an excess of calories may really be the culprit.* For example, rodents consuming a very high-fat diet do not develop breast cancer as readily if calorically restricted and/or if calorie expenditure is increased with exercise.

In humans, increased physical activity in the workplace has been shown to decrease colon cancer risk. The real question for us is whether or not we should reduce calories or fat from our diets. The answer to that question is quite simple. Fat constitutes the most concentrated calories that humans consume. If we reduce our fat intake from 40 percent to the recommended 25 to 30 percent of our total caloric intake, then we will reduce both at once.

Fats and Cancer

The strongest evidence that excessive fat intake increases human cancer risk comes from epidemiological studies of the dietary habits of population groups. These correlations are particularly strong for breast, colon, and prostate cancers. Some reports have even suggested that you might decrease your chances of acquiring breast cancer by as much as 50 percent when changing to a low-fat diet. The age at which you make this change would surely be significant. That is, the earlier in life you make these changes, the greater your decrease in risk.

More research is necessary before we can be assured of this relationship. In the meantime, it seems that fat restriction is necessary for a multitude of reasons, including weight control, caloric restrictions for cancer prevention, and control of heart disease. In short, everyone wants us to control fat intake! Why wait until there is positive proof in this area if fat restriction is good for so many other reasons?

Fiber and Cancer

Fiber in the American diet is a hot topic. There is widespread public support that colon cancer can be prevented by including a good source of dietary fiber. Supporting this relationship is an impressive group of epidemiological data; but again, there has been no definitive evidence with American people over several years of study.

Dietary fiber is also healthy for reasons other than preventing colon cancer. First, insoluble fibers add bulk to the stool and thus aid in normal bowel function and elimination. Creating larger, softer, and more frequent stools will reduce the incidence of such common conditions as irritable bowel syndrome, diverticular disease, and hemorrhoids. It will also help prevent intestinal polyps, which can become cancerous. Fiber also seems to help regulate blood sugar levels somewhat and are highly recommended in the diabetic diet. Finally, by pushing intestinal materials through at a faster rate, less fat from dietary foods is absorbed when consuming a high-fiber diet.

As we previously stated, the recommended amount of dietary fiber is 25 grams per day. The question is, how do you know what this means in terms of real food?

In chapter 9, we have given a more thorough discussion of fiber with charts to help you determine your actual fiber intake. Now look at the healthy menu on page 202 and note the amount of fiber that each dietary component provides. We think you will be amazed to find that it is indeed difficult to get 25 grams of fiber even in a healthful diet with good food choices. And if you are on a calorie-restricted diet, the fiber content will be even lower simply because you are consuming fewer foods.

Vitamin Supplements, Antioxidants, and Cancer

Vitamin A is an important chemical in many bodily functions, including the maintenance of normal epithelial cell reproduction. Epithelial cells form outer coverings both inside and outside the body. Although vitamin A has been shown to have a weak anti-cancer effect in animal experiments, it is also very toxic to humans when consumed in larger than recommended quantities for prolonged periods of time (more than 2 months). Therefore, we do not recommend a supplement of vitamin A other than those which may be taken in a regular vitamin/ mineral pill containing 100 percent RDA levels.

Beta carotene is the precursor of vitamin A and is the orange pigment found in so many of the fruits and vegetables characteristically thought to be high in vitamin A. They are actually high in beta carotene. To name a few, these foods include cantaloupe, sweet potatoes,

Healthy Menu

	Food Product	Fiber Content
Breakfast:	corn flakes and milk	2.0
	orange juice	0
	1 piece whole-wheat toast	1.3
Lunch:	turkey sandwich on whole wheat	2.6
	lettuce, tomato, mustard	.5
	1 large apple	2.0
Snack:	2 oatmeal cookies	2.5
Dinner:	1 cup whole-wheat pasta	3.0
	1 cup sauce	.3
	large salad	1.0
	garlic bread	.8
	light ice cream	0
	TOTAL grams of fiber from diet alone	16.0 ⟵ LESS than recommendation
	ADD ½ cup Fiber One (or equivalent)	12.0
	TOTAL grams of fiber with a high-fiber cereal	28.0 ⟵ MEETS the recommendation

carrots, and winter squashes. Beta carotene is split in the intestine to form two vitamin A molecules, called retinol.

Beta carotene has antioxidant properties that may be important in cancer prevention apart from being the vitamin A precursor. One of the most consistently observed relationships between diet and cancer is an apparent association between the intake of carotene-containing foods and protection against cancers in the lining of the lungs (Byers, 1988). A large clinical trial involving more than 25,000 American physicians is currently under way to determine if a modest supplement of beta carotene can reduce the occurrence of lung cancer (Hennekens, 1984).

In the previous paragraph, we mentioned the word, *antioxidant*. This is a substance which prevents deterioration by hindering oxidation. Antioxidants can be useful because they help maintain the body's cells, especially the outside cellular membranes, and keep them from breaking down. In addition to the carotenes, there are other naturally occurring antioxidants in our food system. They include vitamin C, selenium, and vitamin E. In animal studies, each of these substances has exhibited some anti-cancer qualities. However, at high doses, both selenium and vitamin E can be very toxic. We do not recommend supplementation with these products beyond a preparation which includes 100 percent of the RDA.

Cruciferous Vegetables

Early studies relating the cruciferous vegetables (broccoli, cauliflower, cabbage, Brussels sprouts, and kohlrabi) to cancer revealed that they had a protective effect against colon cancer due to a particular chemical they contained. More recent studies, however, seem to indicate that these particular vegetables may be no better than any of the other vegetables in terms of cancer prevention (Byers, 1988). However, we feel that these vegetables are extremely high in many nutrients and should be consumed for these reasons as well as any anti-cancer effects they may be found to have in the future.

Alcohol and Cancer

Heavy alcohol consumption has long been recognized as a causative factor in cancer of the oral cavity, larynx, and esophagus. We realize that cancer prevention may be the least concern for the heavy drinker. But, what about the social drinker? A growing body of evidence suggests that a few ounces of alcohol per day may be enough to increase a woman's chances of contracting breast cancer. It is not yet clear what type of alcohol may be the major offender. However, *if you are at high risk for breast cancer, you might want to consider abstinence from alcoholic beverages.*

DIET AND CANCER—A SUMMARY

Foods to Cut Back On or Eliminate Entirely (Creasey, 1985)

1. Most Americans consume a diet which contains 40 percent fat or more. Ideally we should consume a diet in which 20 to 30 percent of the calories are contributed by fat.

2. Salt-pickling, smoke-curing, nitrate-curing, and frying or broiling at very high temperatures produce substances in foods which are

potentially carcinogenic. Foods preserved or cooked in these ways should be eaten infrequently or not at all. Read your labels and check for these ingredients.

3. Alcohol intake greater than amounts equivalent to one or two glasses of wine per day should be avoided, especially for smokers. Concurrent smoking and alcohol consumption multiply the risk of esophageal and pharyngeal cancers.

4. Artificial sweeteners such as saccharin are carcinogenic under certain conditions in animals, but evidence is sketchy in humans. Studies showing the safety of aspartame (Equal or Nutrasweet) are incomplete. If you do not need an artificial sweetener for diabetic or weight-loss purposes, we recommend judicious uses of natural sweeteners—even white table sugar. Pregnant women and children should particularly minimize their intake of artificial sweeteners until more evidence concerning their safety is found. (Most sugar-free drinks for example, would not be a good choice because they use artificial sweeteners.)

5. Most hazardous additives, flavors, and food dyes have been eliminated from our food supply. However, be cautious and choose foods without additives or attractive colors whenever possible.

6. Meat and calorie intake in the United States is too high. We have simply become accustomed to overeating and eating too many rich foods. The limitation of excesses in terms of total protein and calorie intake has been linked to cancer prevention.

Foods to Increase in Your Diet

1. Foods high in insoluble fiber should be increased to about two to three times the current national average intake of fiber. Foods high in fiber include bran, fruits, vegetables, cereals, and fiber supplements.

2. Cruciferous vegetables may have some protective properties against gastrointestinal cancers, a factor quite separate from the influence of their fiber and vitamin content; however, this has not been shown in recent studies. Nonetheless, these vegetables include broccoli, Brussels sprouts, cabbage, cauliflower, collard greens, and kohlrabi and are healthy vegetable choices for other reasons.

3. Foods rich in carotene and vitamin C should be increased since both these nutrients may have some protective value. Good sources include dark-green and yellow vegetables and citrus fruits. Examples are broccoli, spinach, greens, carrots, sweet potatoes, cantaloupe, and oranges.

4. In general, eat more natural foods, whole-grain breads and starches, fruits, vegetables, and meat substitutes such as dried beans and peas (you will have to decrease your intake of fats and meats to allow for these increases).

CHAPTER 17

Preventing Osteoporosis

Osteoporosis is a serious disease which has caused women untold pain and suffering due to bone weakening and resultant bone fractures throughout the centuries. Archaeological evidence reveals that postmenopausal women a millennium ago had the same problems with bone density that today's women face. Of course, women had to make it to the "ripe old age of 40" before the bone thinning process began—and that was unusual in those days. Perhaps the fact that people in general and women in particular are living longer today explains why we are acutely aware of and concerned with this potentially debilitating and even fatal disease.

Osteoporosis is a progressive condition in which there is a significantly reduced amount of total bone mass. This reduced bone mass decreases further with increasing age and causes a lower level of bone strength and an increased chance of bone fracture, especially after menopause. Due to the fact that the American population has a growing number of older adults, the personal and economic costs of this potentially preventable disease have reached staggering proportions.

Twenty million people in the United States are thought to be affected by osteoporosis, and 1 in 4 women over the age of 65 will develop vertebral osteoporosis, resulting in a curvature of the upper spine or Dowager's hump (*Women's Health*, 1985). Additionally, more than 200,000 people fracture their hip each year and as many as 12 to 20 percent of those will die as a result of the injury. Equally important, only one-third of the 200,000 annual hip fracture victims will ever regain normal activity (Notelovitz, 1987). More than 6 billion dollars are spent annually in the United States on hip fractures. Remember, we are working toward a higher quality of life, not just increased years of life. It would be unfortunate to finally make it to those golden years only to have them be "not so golden" due to decreased mobility caused by a bone fracture. This need not happen though, since osteoporosis is a preventable disease if you catch it in the early stages.

CAUSES OF OSTEOPOROSIS

Osteoporosis is a complex disorder caused primarily by advancing age, decreased-estrogen levels, low-calcium intake, poor vitamin D status, and inactivity. In normal bones, there is constant reabsorption or removal of old bone and, at the same time, constant formation of new bone. This give and take of bone metabolism is carefully balanced so that the net result for most young adults is no appreciable change in bone mass. With aging, this balance shifts to the negative side. That is, more bone is being reabsorbed than is being newly formed. It is somewhat like overdrawing your bank account by a few more dollars than you are putting in each day. Even if you are short only by a few dollars a day, the net result after several years can be an astonishing deficit. Likewise, a small loss of bone each day can eventually cause women to lose up to one-half their total bone mass and never realize it.

Women, Advancing Age, and Osteoporosis

Women, as compared to men, are particularly at high risk for the development of osteoporosis. One reason is females typically have less total bone mass. According to Dr. Veronica Ravnikar, director of the menopause unit at Brigham and Women's Hospital in Boston, women achieve peak bone mass at about age 35 (Ravnikar, 1988). *This means that your bones will never be thicker, stronger, or more dense than they were at age 35.* From that point on, women usually experience an escalation of bone loss which is particularly prominent after age 50, the average age at menopause. Further, there is an annual bone loss of about 1 to 3 percent after menopause, with the most rapid loss occurring in the first 3 postmenopausal years. If osteoporosis goes untreated, women will have lost 25 to 50 percent of their total bone mass by age 75.

Estrogen Deficiency and Osteoporosis

Estrogen deficiency appears to be the principal cause of postmenopausal bone loss. With reduced levels of serum estrogen, the rate of bone reabsorption increases while dietary calcium is absorbed in the intestine less efficiently (Heaney et al., 1978), making less calcium available for new bone formation. In the words of Dr. Charles Pak, an osteoporosis expert at the University of Texas Health Science Center in Dallas, Texas, "Estrogen replacement prevents bone loss [in women] but cannot be expected to increase bone mass once demineralization has occurred" (Cooper, 1988). The moral of this story is that *you should begin estrogen therapy as soon as possible after your periods have stopped in order to have the greatest retention of bone*. Most authorities recommend that you wait *no longer than 6 months* after periods cease to begin estrogen supplementation.

Calcium Intake

A lifelong low intake of calcium is another risk factor which cannot be ignored. Dietary patterns formed in the childhood and adolescent years can have a direct bearing on the presence of osteoporosis during the latter years of life. If dietary calcium was inadequate during those formative years, maximal bone mass may never have been reached. Then, when bone loss does occur, there are fewer reserves to draw upon. Also, as previously described in chapter 9, many women avoid dairy products as a way to control their weight and then forget to take a calcium supplement faithfully. *The average American woman receives only 500 mg of dietary calcium per day. A minimum of 1500 mg per day is needed to prevent osteoporosis.*

Inactivity and Osteoporosis

A sedentary lifestyle seems to contribute to the overall progression of bone loss. Specifically, bone reabsorption occurs more quickly in the sedentary postmenopausal woman. And, maximal bone density may have never been reached if she has always exhibited inactivity. We realize that physical activity was not heavily emphasized in the past, so for those of you who are 40 or 50 and over, it may not have been considered "ladylike" to run, jump, and power walk. Well, let us encourage you by saying this: it takes very little exercise to bring you out of that high-risk category. Even 15 minutes of fast walking five times a week would be a tremendous help in maintaining bone mass. Further, some research has suggested that not only can activity slow the bone loss process in postmenopausal women, but it can actually increase the bone mass. In one study involving 50- to 80-year-old women, the cumulative difference in bone mass between the exercising and non-exercising group was 5.7 percent. That is, after a 5-month testing period, the exercising women had an average bone mass which was almost 6 percent greater than the group that had not exercised during that same 5-month period of time. That seems to be a great return for such a nominal investment of time and energy.

Table 17.1.   Risk Factors for Osteoporosis

Factors which apply to you		Factors you can eliminate
_____	Female sex	N/A
_____	Caucasian or Asiatic Race	N/A
_____	Low-calcium intake (current)	_____
_____	Low-calcium intake (past)	N/A
_____	Early menopause or oophorectomy (removal of the ovaries)	N/A
_____	Sedentary lifestyle	_____
_____	Never had children	N/A
_____	Alcohol abuse	_____
_____	High sodium intake	_____
_____	Cigarette smoking	_____
_____	High caffeine intake (coffee, tea, sodas)	_____
_____	High protein intake	_____
_____	High phosphate intake (sodas, processed food)	_____
_____	Secondary causes of bone loss—steroids, malignancy, hyperthyroidism, etc.	N/A

Other Risk Factors

Prevention of a disease often begins with the identification of factors which place an individual at greater than average risk to develop that disease. There are many risk factors associated with osteoporosis, and we have already discussed the major causes which can be changed in your own life. In Table 17.1, we have listed the remaining risk factors as well as those already mentioned in descending order of importance (Silverberg and Lindsey, 1987). Some of these things you can do something about and others you must live with. Check the factors that apply to you and also those that you can change.

THE EFFECTS OF OSTEOPOROSIS

Quite simply, osteoporosis causes bones to break. And once this has occurred, there is a great likelihood that you will break more than one bone and may not ever fully recover. There are two types of osteoporosis—Type I and Type II. _Type I osteoporosis_ has also been called postmenopausal osteoporosis and is the kind we are more concerned with here. It most often occurs in women ages 51 to 65 or within the first two decades after menopause. It may also occur in men of similar age but to a much lesser extent. In this type, there is a markedly accelerated rate of bone loss beyond the expected rate of bone loss due to aging alone. Typically, there is a high incidence of vertebral fractures in this group. Spinal fractures occur when one or more bones in the spinal column collapse from simply carrying the weight of the body or from slight trauma. When this occurs *women can lose height, ultimately as much as six inches in stature*. The lower spine curves inward while the abdomen protrudes outward. There is no possible way for these women to "stand up straight" anymore. The curvature is permanent, and nothing can make it go away once this has happened. The primary cause of postmenopausal osteoporosis is thought to be estrogen deficiency.

Type II osteoporosis is a more generalized bone loss. It is evident in both men and women over the age of 75. The incidence of hip fracture, as well as fractures of the forearm, lower leg, and pelvic bone, is greatly increased in this group. The major cause of this Type II osteoporosis is not thought to be estrogen deficiency but rather, general changes in the bone metabolism associated with aging. Also, decreased levels of the active form of vitamin D in the body after age 75 may play an important role in this type of osteoporosis. Vitamin D supplementation in this group is usually a good idea because many older persons receive less total daily exposure to sunlight. Sunlight is required for your body to synthesize its own active form of vitamin D in the skin.

The real issue is not necessarily which type of osteoporosis is present but rather, the methods by which we can prevent bone fractures from occurring. The term *fracture threshold* is extremely important because it defines the critical stage of bone strength below which these fractures may occur and above which they are less likely (see diagram). Prevention of the first fracture is very important because after the fracture threshold has been passed some restoration of normal bone structure may be required to prevent further fractures. The task of restoration is much more difficult than prevention of bone loss and may even prove impossible (Parfitt, 1987). In most cases, the best you can hope for after significant osteoporotic bone loss has occurred is to maintain bone structure at the existing level.

As a final word in our discussion of the effects of osteoporosis, we want you to know that it is a very secretive disease. *You cannot see it happening to your body*. Generally, your bones do not outwardly appear smaller. You don't feel creaky, weak, or frail due to decreased bone density. Nevertheless, it is silently thinning out your bones from the inside out. Little empty tunnels form where a solid calcium-phosphate

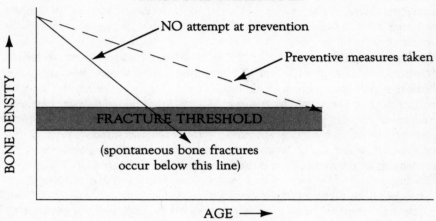

FRACTURE THRESHOLD

The fracture threshold is a particular bone density below which fracturing of the bone occurs easily. Human bone density naturally decreases with age, as shown by the descending solid line. However, if we practice preventive medicine and protect our bones, we can delay or even prevent this disease as we age, as shown by the dotted line.

matrix once existed. And often without warning, your once strong skeletal frame may begin to collapse or insignificant trauma may result in a fracture.

DETECTING OSTEOPOROSIS

As stated earlier, there are very few clinical indicators or tests for osteoporosis. Most patients will become aware of their condition only when they suffer a bone fracture as a result of minimal trauma. Up to 80 percent of crush fractures of the vertebrae occur without any symptoms at all (Silverberg and Lindsey, 1987). It is also possible that a crush fracture could be associated with sudden pain in the area of the fracture, or it may cause mid- or lower-back discomfort over a period of time. Fortunately, this discomfort usually resolves over a period of several weeks. The ultimate result may be a progressive loss of height and a forward curvature of the spine.

Standard blood and urine tests are not particularly helpful in diagnosing osteoporosis. Blood calcium tests measure only the level of calcium circulating in the bloodstream and this amounts to approximately 1 percent of the total body calcium. The rest is in the bones, the portion of calcium with which we are concerned.

X-rays would seem to be a good way of detecting weakening bone structure. But the problem is that *routine x-rays will show no obvious change in the bone structure until at least 25 to 30 percent of the bone mineral content has been lost.*

There are other x-ray methods of analyzing bone mass, each having certain advantages and disadvantages. *Single photon densitometry* is a technique which can be performed in the physician's office. It is relatively inexpensive and involves a low amount of radiation exposure (Mazess, 1984). The problem for this test is that it measures cortical bone (the outside portion of bone), and postmenopausal osteoporosis is primarily a loss of trabecular bone (the inside portion of bone). The *computerized axial tomography (CAT scan)* accurately evaluates trabecular bone (Genant et al., 1982). However, this is much more expensive and involves 10 to 50 times more radiation exposure than the other techniques. *Dual photon densitometry* is a method which measures trabecular bone and the areas considered at greatest risk of fracture, such as the spinal vertebrae and the hip (Ravnikar, 1988). The radiation exposure is low, but the reliability of the results is much less accurate. In fact, measurements may differ by as much as 6 to 8 percent from one test center to another.

As you can see, there is currently no one ideal x-ray or densitometry test to measure bone density. Because of this, densitometry is not favored as a screening technique. In fact, the American College of Physicians has taken the position that bone mineral densitometry should not be recommended for routine screening of osteoporosis. They believe it should be used at this time only for research and in patients receiving costly or toxic treatments. The National Institute of Health also opposes mass screening for osteoporosis with densitometry as not being cost effective and producing questionable results. *With the present methods unacceptable for general screening, it is probably best to assume that all women after menopause are at risk for osteoporosis.*

TREATMENT AND PREVENTION OF OSTEOPOROSIS

Preventing the loss of bone mass is currently the key therapy for osteoporosis. The complications of bone fractures, especially of the hip, have a significant adverse effect on a person's life and in many cases may even prove fatal due to the complications of surgery and recovery. The only proven therapy for osteoporosis is a combination of estrogen/ progesterone supplementation along with increased intakes of dietary and supplemental calcium. With the addition of proper exercise and the elimination of certain adverse risk factors, you will be optimizing your current bone strength while minimizing your risk of disability or death due to an osteoporotic fracture.

Hormone Therapy

There is excellent evidence that estrogen therapy will stabilize bone density and prevent loss of bone. This beneficial effect will remain as long as you continue to take estrogen. However, *therapy should be started as soon after menopause as possible*, as indicated in our previous discussion of the causes of bone loss. Once bone mass has been lost, it is unlikely that new bone mass can be added. However, even when therapy is begun late, it will still help you maintain what bone you currently have and help prevent further loss.

Several hormonal supplements are available, but only a few are commonly used. Postmenopausal bone loss can be prevented by a daily dose of 0.625 mg of conjugated equine estrogen (Premarin) or its equivalent. Transdermal patches are also being used more frequently. They are basically small, clear patches with adhesive backing which attach to your skin. They must be changed twice weekly and are commonly used at the 0.05 mg continuous dosage level. It is not entirely clear how long you will have to take this estrogen, but significant protection from fractures can be achieved in a relatively short amount of time. In fact, you can reduce your risk of hip fracture by as much as 50 percent by using estrogen supplements for only 5 years. *With many women now living well into their 80s, we recommend daily estrogen therapy to prevent osteoporosis until at least age 70.*

There has been considerable discussion in the media as to whether or not estrogen supplementation increases a woman's risk of uterine cancer. We certainly would not want to save ourselves from bone loss only to contract a potentially more deadly and difficult disease. Let's look at the facts and put our minds to rest on this issue. In 1980 there were 2,718 nationwide deaths attributable to endometrial cancer. Of this number, only 10 percent were estrogen users. Thus, if we conclude that the 10 percent contracted endometrial cancer as a direct result of estrogen therapy, then only 271 American women died in 1980 as a result of the therapy. In all likelihood, however, these women probably contracted cancer by chance as at least 10 percent of women or more in the United States are taking hormonal supplements. Also in 1980 there were 150,000 hip fractures and 15,000 related deaths, nationwide. As you can see, the longterm effects of untreated osteoporosis kill many more American women than any endometrial cancers which might result from estrogen usage, even in the worst case scenario.

To further protect you from any possible increase in risk for endometrial cancer, it is advisable to add progesterone to the estrogen therapy. In this way, you can avoid what is called *endometrial hyperplasia*, an abnormal buildup of the lining of the uterus. There is some evidence that progesterone may also have a protective effect on the bones as well. For these reasons, we recommend that all women who are being treated with estrogen and still have their uterus also be treated with 10 mg of progesterone for at least 14 days each month. If the uterus has been removed, then progesterone supplementation need not accompany the estrogen therapy.

Calcium Supplementation

The average dietary calcium intake for adult women in the United States is only 500 milligrams (mg) per day (Heaney et al., 1982). The recommended daily allowance (RDA) of calcium has been determined to be 1000 mg for premenopausal women and 1500 mg for postmenopausal women. It is estimated that two-thirds of the women in America are consuming less than these amounts.

Lifelong, high-calcium intakes reduce the risk of bone fracture and foster optimum bone density at the time of menopause. *After menopause, however, calcium supplementation is in no way an adequate substitute for estrogen therapy.* Calcium is an adjunct to estrogen and highly recommended because most women are consuming less than half the recommended daily requirement for calcium. Another factor is that calcium absorption decreases dramatically after menopause. In fact, a recent study proved that taking as much as 2000 mg of extra elemental calcium per day was not an effective alternative to estrogen therapy in the prevention of postmenopausal bone loss (Riis et al., 1987).

As stated earlier, the calcium requirement for postmenopausal women is 1500 mg per day. This should be obtained at least in part from dietary sources. One 8-ounce cup of milk contains about 300 mg of calcium. There are other good sources of calcium as well (see Table 17.2). But we typically find that most women have difficulty in getting 1500 mg per day from dietary sources. It goes without saying that you must be very selective about your food choices. For example, only low-fat dairy products should be used. Three cups of whole milk contain 480 calories while 3 cups of skim milk contain only 240 calories. The only nutritional difference is the fat content (we don't need it anyway). The protein, calcium, and phosphorus contents found in skim milk are actually a little higher than those found in whole milk; it just doesn't contain the fat and extra calories. Table 17.2 indicates the calcium content of a few foods, but for a full description of low-fat dairy products and other calcium-rich foods, see Table 9.7 in chapter 9.

We usually recommend that our patients take one of two supplements—*calcium carbonate or calcium citrate.* Calcium carbonate is inexpensive and available everywhere but is most effective when used by premenopausal as opposed to postmenopausal women. Name brands are no better than generic brands, and we usually recommend the

Table 17.2. **Principal Nutritional Sources of Calcium**

Source	Quantity	Calcium (mg)
Whole milk	8 oz.	291
Skim milk	8 oz.	302
Cheese	1 oz.	150–340
Cottage cheese	½ cup	77
Ice cream	½ cup	88
Yogurt	1 cup	350–400
Sardines (with bones)	3 oz.	372
Salmon (with bones)	3 oz.	167
Broccoli	1 stalk (5 inches)	100
Collards	½ cup	150

cheapest source you can find in 500 or 600 mg tablets. You should take one or two tablets daily to meet your nutritional requirement.

When buying calcium carbonate or any other calcium supplement, you must always determine the content of *elemental calcium* in the tablet. It can be deceptive. For instance, a high-potency calcium tablet which contains 600 mg of elemental calcium actually contains 1500 mg of calcium carbonate. *Elemental* simply means how much actual calcium you are getting when you subtract all the other things present in that pill. Due to the chemical nature of calcium, you must combine it with something else in order to make it chemically stable enough to put in pill form. One problem with calcium carbonate is that in order for this compound to dissolve in your stomach, acid must also be present. This is usually not a problem for most premenopausal women. However, postmenopausal women do not have as much acid in their stomachs.

Calcium citrate is now being used for persons who require a calcium supplement but who have a less acidic stomach. This supplement is also the recommended choice for anyone having kidney problems or kidney stones. It is better absorbed than calcium carbonate but usually a little more expensive. We recommend calcium citrate (Citracal) for all our patients over the age of 65. Depending on your dietary intake of calcium, women of this age should take 500 to 1000 mg of elemental calcium in the form of calcium citrate daily and fill in the rest of the 1500 mg per day requirement with nutritious, calcium-rich food choices.

Exercise and Osteoporosis

Exercise completes the third arm in our efforts to prevent osteoporosis. Weight-bearing exercise such as walking, jogging, and bicycle riding are proven to increase muscle mass and reduce bone loss. New evidence also reveals that even resistive type exercise (any time you are pulling, pushing, or in some way resisting another opposing force) will also help maintain bone mass. Even more encouraging are some recent studies that indicate bone mass can actually increase with consistent exercise.

Provided your physician agrees that increased exercise is appropriate for you, you can definitely retard bone loss. The American College of Sports Medicine has established these guidelines for people wanting to improve bone health. Weight-bearing exercise (walking, jogging, biking) performed for 30 to 45 minutes 3 to 4 days per week will help maintain your current level of bone mass (Notelovitz et al., 1986).

Additional Therapies

Fluoride intake can stimulate the formation of new bone. However, this newly formed bone has an abnormal bone architecture. Fluoride supplementation also has a high incidence (40 percent) of adverse side effects, including gastric irritation, bleeding and ulceration, vomiting, and inflammation of the joints. Fluoride is not currently approved by the Food and Drug Administration (FDA) for prevention or treatment of osteoporosis. Please note that fluoridation of public water supplies involves such small concentrations that there are no known side effects from this highly successful practice.

Calcitonin is a hormone which acts to directly inhibit ongoing bone loss. Medical tests using an injectable, synthetic calcitonin (Calcimar) have shown it to be effective in stopping bone loss and in some cases actually increasing bone mass. Synthetic calcitonin is available, but only in an injectable form. The injections must be given daily, much like diabetics give themselves insulin. Nausea and skin rashes occur in about 10 percent of those treated. As oral forms of this medication become available and further research is completed, it is possible that calcitonin might become an alternative to estrogen therapy in the treatment of osteoporosis.

Parathyroid hormone (PTH) is another therapy under investigation in the treatment of osteoporosis. Small doses seem to enhance bone formation and appear to be potentially helpful for those women with progressive bone loss. This injectable medication is still undergoing further research.

Vitamin D is essential in the absorption of calcium from the intestine. As we get older, less vitamin D in its active form is available for this task. Therefore a modest vitamin D supplement, such as those found in conjunction with a calcium supplement or that which is found in a daily vitamin/mineral supplement, is adequate. We rarely recommend that anyone take more than 100 percent of the RDA for vitamin D. The back label of your supplement should give the percentage of the RDA for vitamin D in each tablet.

SUMMARY OF TREATMENT OPTIONS FOR OSTEOPOROSIS

For All Women

- Avoid smoking and excessive alcohol intake.
- Avoid a high-sodium (salt) intake. Do not exceed 3 grams of sodium per day.
- Avoid anything more than 2 servings of caffeine per day.
- Do not overeat high-protein foods.
- Limit high-phosphate foods including sodas and processed foods using phosphate preservatives.

For Premenopausal Women

- Try to meet the RDA for dietary calcium each day (1000 mg per day).
- If dietary requirements are not met, consider a 500 to 1000 mg supplement of calcium carbonate daily.
- Exercise regularly, at least 30 minutes, 4 times per week.

For Perimenopausal and Early Postmenopausal Women

- Try to meet the RDA for dietary calcium each day (1500 mg per day).
- If dietary requirements are not met, consider a 500 to 1000 mg supplement of calcium carbonate or calcium citrate daily.
- Exercise regularly, at least 30 minutes 3 to 4 times a week.
- All women should discuss estrogen/progesterone therapy with their physician, especially after missing periods for more than 6 months.

For Older Women (Over 65)

- Try to meet the RDA for dietary calcium each day (1500 mg per day).
- If dietary requirements are not met, consider a 1000 mg supplement of calcium citrate (Citracal) daily.
- Exercise regularly. Even 15 minutes per day is beneficial. More would be better.
- Treat disabilities that may cause falls.
- Correct possible hazards that may cause falls in the home.

CHAPTER 18

Smoking— The Greatest Risk

Cigarette smoking is the single greatest preventable cause of premature death and disability today (Gritz, 1988). Each year 350,000 of our friends and relatives die from the effects of smoking. Smoking is *the* major cause of cancer deaths, accounting for 30 percent of all deaths due to cancer each year. The economic aspects of smoking affect all of us, smoker and nonsmoker alike, in added medical costs, insurance payments, and taxes. The figures are staggering. Current estimates are that smoking-related health-care costs total approximately *65 billion dollars* each year (Gritz, 1988). This expense amounts to about $2.17 for every pack of cigarettes smoked. Considered another way, this amount is more than 50 times what we spend on care for AIDS patients each year.

Many of you are probably thinking one of two things: *"I'm a nonsmoker so all this really doesn't matter to me"* or *"Okay, so I smoke; I already know I should quit so stop bugging me."* The fact is that being around smoke can cause harmful passive effects even if you personally do not smoke. And, most smokers are not aware of the full impact smoking poses on their health.

Let's talk first to the 1 in 4 women who smoke. More women are smoking now than ever before, and it shows. Lung cancer has become the leading cause of cancer deaths for women, and smoking increases your risk of this lethal cancer by more than 10 times. Women suffer more heart attacks and strokes now, and cigarettes are directly responsible for 17 percent of deaths due to cardiovascular disease. Smoking increases your risk of stroke by 300 percent, and if you smoke and have high blood pressure, your risk will be 20 times greater than nonsmokers.

Table 18.1. Direct Effects of Smoking on Your Health

Smoking can cause:

1. Cancer, including lung, larynx, esophageal, oral, bladder, kidney, pancreas, and cervix.
2. Heart attack
3. Stroke
4. High blood pressure
5. Problems with pregnancy
6. Miscarriages and stillborns
7. Low-birthweight babies
8. Peptic ulcers
9. Lung disease (emphysema and chronic bronchitis)
10. Greater and earlier skin wrinkling
11. Early menopause
12. Hygiene problems (stained teeth, fingers, and bad breath)
13. Social and work problems

People who have difficulty breathing are often miserable and their lifespan is significantly shortened. Smoking causes 80 percent of emphysema and chronic bronchitis (Amler and Dull, 1987). Table 18.1 shows some of the many direct effects of smoking.

If smoking harmed only the smoker then perhaps a case could be made to let an informed adult make her own choices and suffer the consequences. Unfortunately, this is not the case. The passive effects of smoking on those around you are both significant and serious. The personal and economic costs to you and your family cannot be fully measured.

PASSIVE EFFECTS OF SMOKING

Passive smoking or involuntary smoking is the inhalation of smoke given off by a burning cigarette. This exposure can occur by just being in the same room with a smoker. *Evidence continues to mount regarding the harmful effects of passive smoking.*

A 1986 report by the Surgeon General entitled *The Health Consequences of Involuntary Smoking* drew three major conclusions (*Health Consequences*, 1986).

1. Involuntary smoking causes disease, including lung cancer, in healthy nonsmokers.

2. The children of parents who smoke have more frequent respiratory infections, more respiratory symptoms, and impaired lung function compared to other children.

3. Separating smokers from nonsmokers within the same area may reduce, but does not eliminate, the exposure of nonsmokers to tobacco smoke.

Nonsmokers and smokers are both exposed to sidestream smoke coming from the burning tip of a cigarette and the smoke exhaled by a smoker. Sidestream smoke contains most of the 50 known cancer-causing agents and other toxic products in tobacco smoke. These agents are not merely present, but they occur at significantly high concentrations (Papier and Stellman, 1987). In fact, formaldehyde and acrolein, two agents in cigarette smoke which cause eye and nasal irritation, are found in sidestream smoke at concentrations 3 times higher than the government limits for occupational exposure.

Recent studies have shown that the risk of all cancers increases significantly with exposure to household smoke. Children exposed to cigarette smoke in the home have a 50 percent greater likelihood of developing cancer later in life (Sandler et al., 1985). A woman exposed to her husband's smoke is at greater risk for lung cancer and heart disease.

Few people would disagree that children should not smoke, yet passive smoking by children occurred in 62 percent of homes surveyed in 1970 (Papier and Stellman, 1987). Not only do children exposed to smoke have more respiratory problems, but they are also more likely to have learning and behavioral problems. These children are more frequently hyperactive and exhibit shorter attention spans. Cigarette

Table 18.2.   Potential Ill Effects of
Passive or Involuntary Smoking

1. Increased risk of cancer
2. Increased risk of heart disease
3. Increased respiratory problems
4. Eye and nose irritation
5. Low-birthweight infants
6. Learning and behavioral problems in children
7. Infantile colic
8. Higher rate of miscarriages and stillborns
9. Aggravation of allergies
10. Headaches, nausea, dizziness
11. Impairment of lung function

smoke exposure may also contribute to infantile colic. It has been known for sometime now that a pregnant woman who smokes can cause her newborn to have a low birthweight and other problems. Now there is evidence that this fetal exposure to smoke may actually predispose the infant to cancer later in life.

The issue of passive smoking is a controversial one with individuals, offices, and sometimes families divided into two camps. *The right to breathe clean air is gaining momentum despite the efforts of the tobacco industry to downplay and criticize the issue.* The more people, both smokers and nonsmokers, who are aware of the facts, the more likely we are to be able to speed the decline in the number of people who smoke.

CALLING IT QUITS

To accomplish anything you must have proper motivation. This basic principle is seen very clearly in a smoker's approach to quitting. Why should you *not* do something that currently gives you pleasure? We would be happy to use almost any motivational device if it helps you quit, but *ultimately each individual must come to grips with the personal dangers of smoking.*

Until you fear the consequences of continued smoking more than you experience pleasure, quitting will be difficult. Heart disease, lung cancer, and other smoking-related illnesses are real and *can* happen to you. You have too much to live for and too much to do to be burdened with a preventable illness. Hopefully, now you truly recognize the danger to yourself in continued smoking.

Success usually requires a plan, a method to achieve the desired goal. Choosing to stop smoking is really no different from any other endeavor in this regard. Decide on a realistic quit date and begin to work on your plan. But by all means, get started!

There are many programs available to help people quit smoking. The reason why there are so many different approaches is that individuals respond differently to different methods. A programed approach in a group setting may be perfect for you. On the other hand, an individualized approach may be better. Don't get discouraged and give up—keep trying; if necessary, take a different approach.

Finally, close followup is important to prevent relapses. Either a group or your doctor can help here. It takes 6 months or more before an ex-smoker is at low risk for relapse. Women often fear they will gain weight if they quit. Studies have shown that 50 percent of ex-smokers will gain weight, but only for a short time and no more than five to eight pounds on average (Gritz, 1988). Increased exercise and good nutritional planning are advised to cope with this potential problem. Think about it—which would you rather have, a little more weight or a little lung cancer?

ARE YOU HOOKED?

"I can quit any time I want; I just like smoking." We have heard this kind of statement hundreds of times in our office when confronting someone with her/his smoking habit and the need to stop. The Philip Morris Tobacco Company publishes a magazine promoting the rights of smokers and smoking. The 1988 summer issue polled readers on various topics. Of those polled, 95.5 percent smoke because they "like it" and only 4.5 percent considered smoking a habit. How do you explain those survey results when a recent Gallup Poll indicated that 77 percent of smokers would like to quit?

The answer can probably be stated in one word—*nicotine*. It is now clear that nicotine is the real reason most people keep smoking and like it in spite of a very real desire to quit and the knowledge that they are actually harming themselves.

Within hours after their last cigarette, smokers may begin to experience withdrawal symptoms. These symptoms may include irritability, anxiety, difficulty concentrating, restlessness, headache, drowsiness, and stomach upset. A Swedish researcher, Karl-Olov Fagerstrom, developed a simple test to evaluate nicotine dependency. This test can help you or someone in your family better understand the relationship between smoking and nicotine dependency (see Table 18.3).

DON'T LET YOUR BABIES GROW UP TO BE SMOKERS

A popular song urges mothers not to let their children grow up to be cowboys. No doubt about it, parents have a great deal of influence over their children both directly and indirectly, for good and for bad. We have discussed at length the harmful long-term effects of cigarette smoking, but unfortunately most kids don't think long-term. Non-smoking parental role models and direct thoughtful information about the risks of smoking may be the best way to help your child not ever start smoking.

Teenagers are five times more likely to smoke if one or both parents or an older sibling smokes (Gritz, 1988). They are heavily influenced by peer pressure and are the targets of intensive advertising by tobacco companies. Statistics show that most smoking begins in junior high

Table 18.3. Nicotine Dependency Test

Circle your answer under column A, B, or C. Then total the individual columns with each answer under A receiving 0 points, B 1 point, and C 2 points. For your final score, add all three column totals.

Questions	Answers		
	A	B	C
How soon after you wake up do you smoke your first cigarette?	After 30 minutes	Within 30 minutes	
Do you find it difficult to refrain from smoking in nonsmoking areas?	No	Yes	
Which is your most satisfying cigarette of the day?	Any other than the first in the morning	The first one in the morning	
How many cigarettes do you smoke in a day?	1–15	16–25	More than 26
Do you smoke more cigarettes during the morning hours or during the rest of the day?	No	Yes	
Do you smoke when you are sick enough to be in bed most of the day?	No	Yes	
Does the cigarette brand you smoke have a low, medium, or high nicotine content?	Low	Medium	High
How often do you inhale the smoke from your cigarette?	Never	Sometimes	Always
TOTALS			

Scoring. Seven points or more indicates high nicotine dependence. Six points or less indicates low to moderate nicotine dependence.

Adapted from K. Fagerstrom, *Addictive Behavior*, 3 (1978), p. 235–241.

school and that 75 percent of first cigarettes are smoked with another teen (Gritz, 1988).

The strongest influence on a teenager to start smoking is the desire for social status. There is a powerful need for acceptance and accelerated maturity. Tobacco advertising presents an idealistic view of the sophisticated, mature, always attractive, athletic, and sexy smoker who is independent and highly acceptable to others. This is a tough act to follow, but there are some ways to counter this potential problem.

Since up to 90 percent of all smokers begin smoking by age 19, with tobacco use beginning for many as early as age 12 (Gritz, 1988), prevention of the onset of regular smoking should be the goal with your children. Teenagers are well aware of the long-term risk of heart and lung disease from smoking, but most of them have difficulty relating to potential breathing problems at age 50 when they are just now 14 years old. Your teen is much more likely to be motivated by the immediate consequences of smoking on exercise and athletic performance; aggravation of bronchitis, asthma, and colds; and the cosmetic implications of smoking.

So one of the best ways to prevent smoking is to make your child aware of the unpleasant things that come with smoking—increased and earlier skin wrinkling as well as the discoloration of teeth, halitosis (bad breath), and unpleasant odor in clothes and hair. Also emphasize the struggle of addiction to nicotine because most teenagers think they can quit anytime. Encourage activities which enhance your teenager's self-image especially social and athletic activities. Finally, promote a healthy lifestyle first and foremost by your own personal actions.

STILL NOT CONVINCED?

Sometimes statistics about smoking and its consequences are difficult to comprehend fully. The magnitude of the problem can easily be underestimated, so let's try to put the figures into perspective.

- Seven times more Americans die from smoking *each year* than were killed in the entire Vietnam war.

- Deaths from tobacco-related disease annually in the United States equal the death toll which would result from the crashes of three jumbo jets (all seats filled) every day of the year, killing all aboard.

Prevention strategy. Don't start smoking; it's dangerous and addicting. Quit if you do. Educate your children to avoid smoking. Support anti-smoking and clean air legislation.

SMOKING CESSATION MATERIALS AND PROGRAMS

Videos

"In Control: A Video Freedom from Smoking Program" is available from your local American Lung Association, $59.

"Larry Hagman's Stop Smoking for Life" is available through Lorimar Home Video, 17942 Cowan, Irvine, California 92714. Call 1–800–323–5275 to order, $14.95.

Self-help

Quitter's Guide—Seven Day Plan to Help You Stop Smoking is available from your local office of the American Cancer Society.

Freedom from Smoking for You and Your Family and "Freedom from Smoking Clinic" are available through a local office of the American Lung Association.

Calling It Quits is available through the American Heart Association, 7320 Greenville Ave., Dallas, Texas 75231.

Smoking, Tobacco and Health: A Fact Book is available through the Office on Smoking and Health, 5600 Fishers Lane, Park Bldg. Room 110, Rockville, Maryland 20857.

Group Programs

"Fresh Start" is a program of the American Cancer Society.

"Freedom from Smoking" is a group program sponsored by the American Lung Association.

CHAPTER 19

Preventing Alcohol Abuse

Alcohol abuse is a major problem—both for those who are alcoholics and for those who have a spouse or family member fighting alcoholism. Indirectly, however, many more of us are affected by the consequences of alcohol abuse, whether it's poor job performance by co-workers or damaged lives and families as a result of traffic fatalities caused by drunk drivers. *Many Americans—70 percent, in fact—drink, but only about 5 to 10 percent of drinkers are or will become alcoholic.* The heavy-drinking 10 percent consume half of all the alcohol drunk in the United States (Milhorn, 1988).

There may be as many as 200,000 alcohol-related deaths annually. Fetal alcohol syndrome occurs in one of every 1000 births and *half of all violent deaths are related to alcohol misuse* (Milhorn, 1988). Obviously the problem of alcohol abuse is widespread, and it is only recently that the significance of the problem among women has been fully realized.

Fewer women drink alcohol than men, and they usually drink less; however, this difference appears to be diminishing. Studies clearly show that women drinking the same amount compared to men are more likely to be impaired both in short-term and in long-term results (*Women's Health*, 1985).

When a woman drinks, she usually gets intoxicated on less alcohol than a man because she has lower total body water and because alcohol is absorbed into the tissues faster in women than in men. Women alcoholics tend to be more severely impaired as compared with their male counterparts, and one study showed that *a female alcoholic lives on the average 15 years less than a nonalcoholic woman* (*Women's Health*, 1985). Gynecological problems also occur more frequently, and sexual dysfunction accompanies alcohol abuse in up to 72 percent of alcoholic women.

WHO IS AN ALCOHOLIC?

An alcoholic can be anyone. The problem in early recognition of the problem is primarily one of denial. The person herself, her family, even her physician may ignore or deny the problem. But *denial will not make this problem magically go away. Alcoholics cannot stop without help; if they could, they would.*

Alcoholism is the continuation of drinking when it would be in the best interest of the individual to stop. Problems related to alcohol abuse may include medical and physical problems, behavioral problems, or social difficulties with job, family, or friends. The disease is chronic and progressive and may take 5 to 20 years to develop (Milhorn, 1988).

Anyone who drinks alcohol is at risk for this disease. The following test is designed to identify people at increased risk for alcohol problems (see Table 19.1). Answer yes or no to all the questions in this table to determine your own risk of alcoholism.

Table 19.1.   Alcoholism Screening Test*

1. Do you feel that you drink more than most other people?
2. Does your spouse, parent, or other near relative ever worry or complain about your drinking?
3. Do you ever feel guilty about your drinking?
4. Do friends or relatives think that you drink more than normal?
5. Are you unable to stop drinking when you want to?
6. Have you ever attended a meeting of Alcoholics Anonymous?
7. Has drinking ever created problems between you and your spouse, parent, or relative?
8. Have you ever gotten into trouble at work because of your drinking?
9. Have you ever neglected your obligations, your family, or your work for two or more days in a row because you were drinking?
10. Have you ever gone to anyone for help about your drinking?
11. Have you ever been in a hospital because of drinking?
12. Have you ever been arrested for drunk driving (DWI)?
13. Have you ever been arrested, even for a few hours, because of other drunken behavior?

Scoring: Yes answers to two of the questions suggests the possibility of alcoholism. *Three or more yes answers indicate a definite problem with alcohol.*

*Based on the Short Michigan Alcoholism Screening Test, *Journal of Studies on Alcohol,* Vol. 36, pp. 117–26, 1975. Copyright by Journal of Studies on Alcohol, Inc., Rutgers Center of Alcohol Studies, New Brunswick, NJ 08903.

Only 3 percent of alcoholics are the skid-row types so often associated with the disease. Of the remaining 97 percent, most are employed, married, and appear to be doing well (Milhorn, 1988). Because of this normal, outward appearance and the incredible denial which accompanies the disease, *alcoholism is vastly under-treated.*

Prevention strategy. Avoid excessive and inappropriate drinking. Be especially careful not to consistently use alcohol as a way of reducing stress. If a close relative is an alcoholic, you may be at special risk for alcoholism.

Screening strategy. All persons who drink alcohol should take the alcoholism screening test.

Treatment strategy. Seek help from: Alcoholics Anonymous, private substance abuse treatment centers, or your personal physician.

CHAPTER 20

Immunizations:
You Still Need Them

Immunization programs have been highly successful in preventing many illnesses, especially children's diseases. However, many adults mistakenly think they no longer require immunization and go unprotected against several potentially serious illnesses. *The Centers for Disease Control estimate that each year there are over 25,000 unnecessary deaths due to vaccine-preventable diseases* (Amler and Dull, 1987).

Adult women should be aware of their need to be immunized against seven diseases. These are (1) tetanus (2) diphtheria (3) influenza (4) pneumococcal infection (5) hepatitis B (6) measles (7) rubella.

Measles and rubella vaccines are primarily for young adult women in their childbearing years. Hepatitis B vaccine is important for certain health-care workers who are exposed to blood products in their work. *There is a definite need for all women to receive immunizations against some or all of the remaining four diseases.*

TETANUS AND DIPHTHERIA

Tetanus is a life-threatening illness which usually occurs after a penetrating wound. The spores of the tetanus bacterium are found everywhere, especially in soil. Tetanus infection is not common, thanks to the vaccination program, but 90 to 100 cases still occur each year in the United States (Forbes, 1988). Many of those infected die from the illness, and most of them (70 percent) have not been immunized.

Diphtheria is another uncommon illness thanks to adequate immunizations, but 200 to 400 cases still occur annually (Forbes, 1988). Unfortunately, less than 40 percent of adults are protected against diphtheria. Tetanus and diphtheria vaccines are combined and given together. They are virtually 100 percent effective and side effects are mild.

Adults should have completed an initial series of three tetanus-diphtheria shots; the first two should be one month apart, and the third a year later. Thereafter, *a booster injection is needed every 10 years for the rest of your life.*

INFLUENZA

The flu or influenza is usually a brief, annoying illness which makes your life miserable for a few days to a week. However, pneumonia is its most common complication, and *each year more than 10,000 people die from the flu in the United States* (Forbes, 1988). During epidemics this number can increase three to four times that figure.

Each year a new vaccine is formulated with the strains of influenza A and B that are expected to be most prevalent in a given flu season. *The vaccine should be received each year in the fall by those at risk.* The vaccine is effective about 2 weeks after it is given and lasts about 6 months.

Women at high risk for influenza are those over 65 and anyone with chronic pulmonary, renal, or heart disease. Anyone with anemia, diabetes, or an altered immune status is also at high risk.

PNEUMOCOCCAL DISEASE

Pneumococcus can cause a variety of severe illnesses including pneumonia, meningitis, and blood infections. *Pneumococcal pneumonia causes 500,000 cases a year and 60 percent of all adult pneumonias.* The risk of dying from this infection is 5 to 10 percent and increases gradually after age 40 (Forbes, 1988).

The vaccine now used is effective against 23 different serotypes of pneumococcus which are responsible for 87 percent of pneumococcal infections (*Women's Health*, 1985). A single injection which is believed effective for life provides 60 to 80 percent protection for people over 60 years old.

The immunization is recommended for all women over 65 and any woman with underlying chronic health problems. Side effects are few and mild and the vaccine can be given anytime, even along with flu vaccine. Unfortunately, despite the clear need for this vaccine, its safety, and Medicare coverage, only about 10 percent of older adults are immunized.

Prevention strategy. For prevention of tetanus and diphtheria, all women need an immunization booster every 10 years. For prevention of influenza, any person with severe chronic illness such as pulmonary, renal, or heart disease, anemia, diabetes, altered immune status should receive vaccine. Also anyone over 65, even those in good health, should be immunized. For prevention of pneumococcal disease, people with chronic illnesses such as those just mentioned need to be immunized— also those who have had their spleen removed or who have received organ transplants and anyone over 65.

Your
Inner
Self

CHAPTER 21

Stress: The Invisible Illness

Stress is an inevitable part of life. There is no way to totally avoid it. Certain amounts of stress can actually be useful and even motivational if kept in check. Small amounts of this "motivational stress" can help you complete a job on time, fulfill a prior commitment, or give the best piano performance of your life. However, when difficult, external factors exceed your ability to cope, stress may cripple you with fear and anxiety, causing severe psychological and physical problems.

There is no single definition of stress. However, most of us can agree that stress refers to those situations and circumstances that affect our lives by causing feelings that range from simple inner tension to anxiety and outright fear. Stress not only causes emotional feelings, but may also lead to uncomfortable physical responses as well.

Two factors which seem particularly important in determining the human response to stress include:

1. *Duration of stress.* Prolonged stress exhausts one's ability to cope and diminishes the level of function.

2. *Timing during the life cycle.* If the event seems appropriate for your particular stage of life, then it will probably be a less stressful event than if it were "off-phase," so to speak.

Let's talk about those two factors for a moment. Have you ever experienced the "when it rains it pours" stress syndrome? Maybe you have been trying to recover from some emotional trauma when another one knocks you flat. We have seen patients (and ourselves) continue to function through some devastating situations only to decompensate when the hot water heater goes out, due to the fact that it was last on a long list of continuous stressors. If you have recently been under a lot of stress, don't add anything else to your life which might enhance the situation. Keep commitments to a minimum. Also, remember that it is easy for *small and insignificant problems to be blown totally out of propor-tion during stressful times.*

Timing during the life cycle can also be a major factor in your response to stress. For example, though breast cancer is a tremendous stress at any age, it seems even more difficult to handle at an early age. If you have breast cancer at age 60, the chances of at least three or more of your friends having the same affliction are very great. At this phase of your life, you don't feel singled out. You have a support group of similar-aged women. If, however, you are 35 years old and have breast cancer, you will probably feel somewhat alone and "out-of-phase" with what you think should be happening to you at this time of life.

This leads us to two additional significant factors which determine our personal response to any given stress situation. The first of these is the meaning we attach to a certain stressor. For instance, if your father died from a heart attack after having an episode of chest pain and you later develop an unexplained chest discomfort, your response to this stress will probably be much greater until your pain is diagnosed. Therefore, *by considering the meaning we place on different issues, we can better predict the nature of our response to different stress factors.*

The second factor that determines our personal response to any given stress is *our own personal coping skills.* In fact, they have a great deal to do with whether we consider something stressful or not. Due to experience, practice, and background some people are able to shoulder tremendous burdens and stress. Others are not so gifted in this area and require more personal support to help them make it through tough times. By understanding your own coping abilities, you can work on improving these skills and recognizing when you need help from friends or a counselor.

WHAT CONSTITUTES STRESS?

Stressful events come from many different areas in our lives and are defined by their emotional and physical effects on the body. These stressors can influence your health directly or can cause emotional turmoil—which in turn causes physical problems. Stress factors can be divided into four groups: biological stressors, physical stressors and hazards, life cycle stressors, and psychosocial stressors.

Biological stressors include injuries, chronic illness, and infections. Don't overlook biological stress in your life as being sporadically (or chronically) one of your major sources of anxiety and depression. In some cases, you can develop an illness as a result of other types of emo-tional stress. Inactivity can also be classified as a biological stressor since the body and muscles need challenge to avoid atrophy. Also, physical exercise is one of the best methods of relieving tension and anxiety.

Physical stressors and hazards can include things such as environmental toxins, crowding, loud noise, poor lighting, isolation, disruption of sleep or sleep deprivation, malnutrition, and excessive physical workloads. Drug abuse of prescription medications, caffeine, nicotine, alcohol, and dietary indiscretions can also cause a stress response, either immediately or after several hours. We rarely consider that too many cigarettes or too many cups of coffee, coupled with a virus cold and inactivity might be the main reason for being unable to cope with small stresses throughout our day.

Life cycle stressors. Many of you are dealing not only with your own stresses but also with the stresses of young children, teenagers, older children, and aging parents. Table 21.1 will help you understand stresses at different phases of life.

Psychosocial stressors are the problems we most often identify with a day-to-day stressful life. Three major types of psychosocial stresses have been suggested:

Table 21.1. Life Cycle Stressors

Early childhood	Adolescence (*continued*)
Prematurity	Hypochondriasis
Malnutrition	Lack of adult acceptance
Separation from caregivers	Young adults
Social deprivation	Marital strains
Parental incompetence/	Parenting
inconsistency	Household economics
Disruption of diurnal rhythm	Work stressors
Lack of parental acceptance	Midlife adults
Preschool years	Decreasing career opportunities
Inadequate parental support	Marital problems
Lack of peer acceptance	Dissatisfaction with role
Authoritarianism	Loss of significant others
Inconsistency	Realization that life/health is finite
Later childhood	Older adults
Lack of peer acceptance	Deteriorating health
Inadequate parental support	Loss of significant others
School pressures	Dependency
Adolescence	Recognition of mortality
Social isolation	Nutritional deficiencies
Peer pressure	Housing problems
Failure to separate from parents	Income deficiencies
Failure to integrate socially	Lack of sexual outlets
Failure to prepare for work	

Reprinted by permission. *The Preventive Approach to Patient Care* by D. Sheridan and I. Winogrond (Elsevier, 1987), p. 356.

1. *Cataclysmic events*—earthquakes, wars, famine, and imprisonment.

2. *Major loss*—death of a loved one, divorce, loss of a job, loss of health, financial loss.

3. *Hassles*—little irritating things such as arguments, losing your purse, getting stuck in traffic, having car trouble, or discord in the workplace.

Which of those types of stress do you think cause people the most trouble? Most of us would answer that question with one of the first two, seemingly more important categories. However, *many psychologists have suggested that the daily hassles we encounter are the major stress contributors.* This is probably true due to the fact that hassles are simply much more common and numerous—especially when you also consider that duration, cumulative effect, and your own ability to cope with these day-to-day situations are major factors.

"Hassle-promoting situations" which are almost universally considered stressful include:

- Lack of participation or control over life or work.
- Lack of information of anticipation of events and possible responses.
- Ambiguity or conflict about one's expected role.
- Overload, related either to absolute demands or personal skills.
- Lack of positive reinforcement.
- Lack of social support.

RECOGNIZING STRESS IN YOUR OWN LIFE

One of the most frequently quoted sources in professional literature is the Social Readjustment Scale developed by Thomas Holmes and Richard Rahe, psychiatrists at the University of Washington School of Medicine in 1967. This important scientific work has withstood the passage of time because it envelopes so many of the age-old sources of stress in the human experience. In short, the test scale rates the stressfulness of various life events from minimal stress (valued at 1) to maximal stress (valued at 100), and then makes a prediction about your level of stress based on the total score.

A copy of this stress test has been presented in Table 21.2. Review

Table 21.2. Social Readjustment Scale

Life Event	Stress Value
Death of a spouse	100
Divorce	73
Marital separation	65
Jail term	63
Death of a close family member	63
Personal injury or illness	53
Marriage	50
Fired from job	47
Marital reconciliation	45
Retirement	45
Change in health of family member	44
Pregnancy	40
Sex difficulties	39
Gain of a new family member	39
Business readjustment	39
Change in financial state	38
Death of a close friend	37
Change to a different line of work	36
Change in number of arguments with spouse	35
Mortgage over $50,000	31
Foreclosure on mortgage or loan	30
Change in responsibilities at work	29
Son or daughter leaving home	29
Trouble with in-laws	29
Outstanding personal achievement	28
Wife begins or stops working	26
Beginning or end of school	26
Change in living conditions	25
Revision of personal habits	24
Trouble with boss	23
Change in work hours or conditions	20
Change in residence	20
Change in schools	20
Change in recreation	19
Change in church activities	19
Change in social activities	18
Mortgage or loan less than $50,000	17
Change in sleeping habits	16
Change in number of family get-togethers	15
Change in eating habits	15
Vacation	13
Christmas	12
Minor violations of the law	11

Reprinted by permission. T. J. Holmes and R. H. Rahe, "The Social Readjustment Rating Scale," *Journal of Psychosomatic Research*, Vol. 11. Copyright 1967, Pergamon Press, Ltd.

the items on the list, and then check off the ones you have personally experienced within the last 12 months. *If your score reaches or exceeds 300, you are overstressed and have a 90 percent chance of becoming ill or having a major accident because of excess stress in your life.* However, even a score of 150 indicates a high level of stress.

STRESS-RELATED SYMPTOMS

Even though stress is not always manifested in a visible way, as are arthritis, heart disease, or even a broken bone, its effects on the human body can be just as great. In Table 21.3, the symptoms of stress on the human body are listed in detail. Circle the ones which you have noticed in your own life. Stress symptoms need to be evaluated by your personal physician to insure that there is no serious underlying medical condition.

Table 21.3. Stress-Related Symptoms

Physical

Head and neck
  Dry throat, mouth, eyes
  Grinding of teeth
  Headache, viselike throbbing
  Lump in throat
  Facial, sinus, jaw, neck pain
  Ringing or noise in ears
Gastrointestinal
  Anorexia
  Belching
  Bloating
  Constipation
  Cramping
  Frequent loose stools
  Gas
  Heartburn/reflux
Respiratory
  Chest tightness
  Fleeting chest pain
  Shortness of breath
  Substernal discomfort
Cardiovascular
  Pounding heart
  Racing heart

Musculoskeletal
  Back pain
  Cramping or painful extremities
  Joint pain
  Weakness
Neurologic
  Dizziness
  Hot or cold spells
  Incoordination
  Shakiness
  Stuttering, stammering
Genitourinary
  Decreased lactation
  Pain on urination
  Erectile dysfunction
  Pelvic pain or discomfort
  Urgency, frequency of urination
  Irregular or no menses
  Painful menses
  Lack of interest in sex

Table 21.3. *(Continued)*

Psychological

Alienation	Impatience
Anger	Inability to express emotions
Anxiety, specific or floating	Job or life dissatisfaction
Cynicism	Loneliness
Dependency	Low self-esteem
Disorientation/unreality	Neurotic behavior
Fatigue	Tension
Frustration	Urge to cry
Hopelessness	Urge to run and/or hide
Hostility	Worrying

Behavioral

Increasing use of	Decreased memory
alcohol	Decreased productivity
caffeine	Emotional lability
pain medication	Fear of strangers
sedatives	Fussiness/whining
stimulants	Impulsiveness
tobacco	Inability to concentrate
other drugs	Inflexibility
Agitation	Insomnia
Apathy	Recurrent conflicts
Blaming	Regression
Bossiness	Risk taking
Changes in eating patterns	Withdrawal
Communication difficulties	Yelling

Reprinted by permission. *The Preventive Approach to Patient Care* by D. Sheridan and I. Winogrond (Elsevier, 1987) p. 364.

Stress and Your Immune System

Besides the symptoms listed in Table 21.3, it now seems clear that one's immune system can also be seriously compromised by excessive stress. Have you ever noticed that severe emotional stress often seems to manifest itself in terms of an actual illness? Sometimes we think of it this way, "I got that cold virus because I was run down." *Run down* usually means tired, fatigued, overworked, and "stressed-out." Many researchers now believe that increased stress can cause decreased immune function. In other words, the very things which help our bodies fight off the onslaught of viruses, bacteria, cancerous cells, and other diseases may be impaired by severe and out-of-control stress.

TREATMENT AND PREVENTION OF STRESS

A healthy, balanced person is one who has a controlled level of incoming stressors, adequate coping skills, and a high level of social support. Anticipating life cycle changes can ease a certain amount of inherent stress. Recognizing the difference between stressors which are controllable and those which are uncontrollable will allow you to focus your coping skills where they can really make a difference.

As with most things in life and certainly matters pertaining to our health, *prevention of a problem is much easier and more desirable than trying to correct a disease which has already occurred.* Prevention of stress is no exception. Once you become overwhelmed with incoming

Table 21.4.   Stress Management Alternatives

Work and Time Management
Delegate tasks; get help.
Revise goals and expectations; clarify your desires.
Obtain more information.
Practice asserting yourself.
Protect your personal rights.
Consider good alternatives.
Be flexible.
Learn to be more efficient and effective.
Learn new skills or enhance old ones.

Lifestyle Options
Get regular aerobic exercise.
Get adequate rest.
Use humor.
Decrease caffeine and nicotine use.
Limit alcohol and sedative use.
Use no drugs (except prescription medications).
Optimize your diet and current state of nutrition.
Try to be within 10 to 20 pounds of your ideal bodyweight.
Develop a support group in your church and community.

Effective Relaxation Techniques
Progressive relaxation (alternate tensing and relaxation of different muscle groups).
The relaxation response (a breathing exercise like Lamaze).
The quieting response (a quiet assessment of whether the stressor is worth the upset).

Adapted from Sheridan and Winogrond, 1987.

stress, it is easy to "fall to pieces" very quickly if appropriate coping methods are not already in place.

By incorporating sound stress-management techniques into your everyday life now, you will be better able to withstand the effects of acute stress when it does occur. Table 21.4 outlines some effective stress-management options. Physical, mental, and spiritual health all contribute to wellness. Maintaining a balance in these areas of life is one of the most important health rules you can follow.

CHAPTER 22

Blue Mondays, Terrible Tuesdays—What's the Matter with Me?

You're feeling down again, kind of blue. There is nothing in particular wrong, but nothing seems right either. Perhaps these feelings and other uncomfortable symptoms have become part of your life and resolution of this problem is nowhere in sight! It's quite possible you are suffering from depression.

Depression is a common and often misunderstood disease. All of us get depressed and feel sad from time to time, but this does not mean we have the disease depression. We may be sad and very unhappy when we experience unpleasant circumstances, and for a limited time, we may feel depressed. However, the disease depression may occur entirely separate from any unpleasant circumstances and does not quickly go away. There are other symptoms which differentiate depression *the disease* from simple feelings of *sadness*. Knowing how to recognize some of the more common symptoms of the disease may allow you to find the help you need to avoid the problems which often accompany this illness.

Table 22.1 is a self-test that will help you rate depression in your life. If you answer "true" to a majority of the statements, you are probably experiencing depression and may need to seek help in overcoming the problem. Remember—help is available, and there is no need to suffer without reason.

About 1 in 5 women will experience a significant depression at some time. Our goal in this chapter is to explain to you what depression really is, when it is serious, and what you can do about it. You can always maintain a better defense when you are well-informed and prepared for evasive action.

Depression can become a major problem for anyone, but it is twice as

244

Table 22.1. A Self-Rating Depression Scale

	True	False
1. I feel like crying more often now than I did a year ago.	☐	☐
2. I feel blue and sad.	☐	☐
3. I feel hopeless and helpless a good part of the time.	☐	☐
4. I have lost a lot of my motivation.	☐	☐
5. I have lost interest in things I once enjoyed.	☐	☐
6. I have had thoughts recently that life is just not worth living.	☐	☐
7. My sleep pattern has changed of late. I either sleep too much or too little.	☐	☐
8. I am losing my appetite.	☐	☐
9. I am too irritable.	☐	☐
10. I am anxious of late.	☐	☐
11. I have less energy than usual.	☐	☐
12. Morning is the worst part of the day.	☐	☐
13. I find myself introspecting a lot.	☐	☐
14. When I look at myself in the mirror, I appear to be sad.	☐	☐
15. My self-concept is not very good.	☐	☐
16. I worry much about the past.	☐	☐
17. I have more physical symptoms (headaches, upset stomach, constipation, rapid heartbeat, etc.) than I did a year ago.	☐	☐
18. I believe people have noticed that I do not function as well at my job as I did in the past.	☐	☐

Totals: True _____ False _____

Reprinted by permission. *Happiness Is a Choice* by Minirth and Meier, Baker Book House, 1978, pp. 28–29.

common in women as it is in men (*Women's Health*, 1985). Estimates of depression range from 10 to 20 percent of the general population (Amler and Dull, 1987), and the costs related to treatment and time lost due to this problem are tremendous. Estimates of direct hospital and medical care expenses plus the economic productivity lost due to depression is greater than 16 billion dollars each year (Stoudemire et al., 1986).

SYMPTOMS OF CLINICAL DEPRESSION

The symptoms of clinical depression fall into five major categories (Minirth and Meier, 1978). They are as follows:

1. Moodiness. This is merely the first stage of depression but is an important one nonetheless. This symptom is usually visible in terms of outward appearance, grooming, facial expressions, personal hygiene and the like—all of which decline with increasing depression.

The depressed person may have a variety of feelings, including sadness, helplessness, and hopelessness. She will almost certainly be unhappy, irritable, and anxious. As the illness progresses, the appearance of sadness and a general lack of regard for personal appearance may occur.

2. Painful thinking. We have all experienced emotionally painful thoughts. However, when these thoughts persist and literally invade your innermost being without relief, there is a serious problem which can ultimately lead to suicidal tendencies. Some of the major characteristics of this type of depression include being blue, gloomy, introspective, pessimistic, self-critical, and inadequate. Other feelings include those of being hopeless, helpless, and unmotivated. Depressed people often have great difficulty concentrating and making decisions. Clearly, the pangs of severe emotional pain can run much more deeply than that of physical pain.

The key issue with painful thinking is *negativism*. Negative thoughts about life, self, the future, and one's environment may continually plague a person's thoughts. Eventually the individual may become literally immobilized with pessimism and a sense of futility.

Inappropriate guilt also plays a major role in depression with the doubt-filled individual who is totally convinced of her own inadequacy and worthlessness. With these overwhelming negative feelings, it is easy to understand why the depressed person loses motivation and hope for the future. If the depression continues, the person may withdraw from others, refusing all efforts of help, and eventually, as the pain of living becomes too great to bear, she may attempt suicide. The seriousness of depression and the need for an accurate diagnosis and proper treatment become alarmingly clear when you consider that as many as 10 percent of severely depressed individuals ultimately commit suicide.

3. Physical symptoms. Having physical problems such as insomnia, headaches, or back pain are much more socially acceptable to most people than admitting to a severe depression. Unfortunately, there seems to be a moral stigma attached to emotional illness which can interfere with treatment. Depression is a medical illness with psychological symptoms. Perhaps there would be less confusion about depression if more people realized that the physical symptoms of a clinical depression occur as a result of biochemical changes in the brain and the rest of the central nervous system.

As many as 50 to 80 percent of all people will at some time experience physical effects from a psychological problem. The symptoms are real, not imagined, and the consequences can be quite serious. It does not take a medical genius to realize that a tearful, sad person who hands you a note reading "I hate myself and want to die" is seriously depressed. However, it is difficult sometimes for both patient and physician to realize that the physical symptoms plaguing that patient are not the real problem, but rather evidence of an underlying depression. Sometimes you've got to read between the lines to get to the root of emotional problems.

Depression may cause a variety of physical symptoms including sleep disturbances, frequent difficulty falling asleep, or being sleepy all the time. A wide range of physical aches and pains such as headaches, abdominal pain, back pain, nausea, or diarrhea may also occur. Fatigue and lack of energy bring many patients to their family doctor who, after many tests, may finally realize that depression is the root of the patient's complaints. (See Table 22.2.)

Poor concentration, difficulty making decisions, and work-related problems are often apparent in depression. There may be a *change in appetite*, either an abnormal increase or a disinterest in food altogether. While a few patients become agitated, many show an abnormal slowing of activity until they become almost immobile. Lastly, suicide attempts mark the ultimate despair, hopelessness, and depth of depression which some people experience.

4. *Anxiety.* Anxiety and depression frequently occur together. However, the anxious person is not always depressed. The major symptoms of anxiety include being irritable, agitated, and unable to sit still. We will discuss anxiety in more detail later, as this is a very common problem in our society.

Table 22.2. Physical Symptoms of Depression

Depressed mood
Lack of interest
Sleep disturbance
Inappropriate guilt or feelings of worthlessness
Fatigue or loss of energy
Lack of concentration and indecision
Appetite alteration
Weight change
Physical slowing and lethargy
Agitation
Decreased sexual drive
Recurrent thoughts of death
Suicide attempts

The presence of five symptoms is suggestive of a depression.

---

5. Delusional thinking. This symptom may occur in severe cases of clinical depression, but it is not always present. Delusional thinking is considered a "psychotic break" with reality. In most cases, a person with this affliction will have thoughts of persecution (i.e., the world is out to get me), inadequacy, and punishment—sometimes complete with hallucinations. With such severe symptoms of depression, hospitalization and appropriate medical treatment are necessary.

There are similar symptoms and problems associated with other depressive illnesses. For example, bipolar illness (or manic-depressive illness) is characterized by mood swings and inappropriate behavior of which the individual is often completely unaware. Bipolar illness has a definite link to heredity.

Several medical problems are also associated with depression. Thyroid disease can often cause psychological changes, one of which is depression. Recently a patient who initially had all the classic symptoms of depression shortly thereafter developed symptoms of hyperthyroidism. The patient's depression cleared completely as soon as the thyroid was controlled. As you can see, a complete evaluation by your family doctor is very important, even when the problem is depression.

CONSEQUENCES OF DEPRESSION

Depression often leads to withdrawal from friends, family, work, and ultimately from life itself. This withdrawal may result in separation, divorce, and significant parent-child conflict. Depression frequently extends into a person's professional life and may result in unemployment and further loss of self-esteem.

Financial difficulties can certainly increase the already tremendous stress on the individual. As the pressure mounts, *the person may try to self-treat her depression with alcohol and/or drug abuse.* Depressed people frequently push away and avoid those who try to help them even while they paradoxically cry out for help.

As you can see, depression—which can begin as mild, uncomfortable feelings of doubt, lowered self-esteem, and stress—feeds on itself from one point to another resulting in a downward spiral of negative thoughts and actions. If not self-limiting, somehow intervention must take place before the consequences of depression become too great and the emotional burden of the individual becomes too heavy to bear. *Hope for recovery from depression lies in early identification and proper intervention on behalf of those at increased risk.*

In Tables 22.3 and 22.4, some of the risk factors associated with depression and suicide are listed. Do any of them apply to you?

Table 22.3.   Risk Factors for Depression

1. Female
2. Family history of mood disorders in biologic relatives
3. Lower socioeconomic status
4. Separated or divorced
5. Stressful life events (death of a parent, loss of job)
6. Absence of intimate, confiding relationships
7. Chronic or acute medical illness (stroke, renal disease, cancer)
8. Child of a mentally ill or chemically dependent parent
9. History of childhood abuse
10. Co-existing psychiatric disorders
11. Bad marriage
12. Chemical or alcohol dependency

Table 22.4.   Those at Risk for Suicide

1. Individuals with intense emotional pain, as seen in depression.
2. Individuals with intense hopeless feelings.
3. Single white males over forty-five years of age.
4. Individuals with a prior history of a suicide attempt, and individuals who have warned others of their suicidal intentions. Of any ten people who commit suicide, eight have given definite warning.
5. Individuals with severe health problems.
6. Individuals who have experienced a significant loss of some kind—death of a spouse, loss of a job, etc.
7. Individuals who have made a specific suicide plan. The process builds as follows: Fleeting thoughts of suicide are followed by a serious consideration of suicide, which is followed by an actual attempt.
8. Individuals with chronic self-destructive behavior (such as alcoholism).
9. Individuals with an intense need to achieve.
10. Individuals with an excess of disturbing life events within the last six months.

Reprinted by permission. *Happiness Is a Choice* by Minirth and Meier, Baker Book House, 1978, p. 33.

TREATMENT FOR DEPRESSION

Women are indeed frequently troubled with depression. In many cases, your personal physician can provide the care needed. However, a psychiatrist should see difficult cases, suicidal patients, or those requiring hospitalization.

Unless the depressed person is of potential harm to herself or others, no help can be given until she recognizes and confronts her problems. Unfortunately, there is still, in our society, a commonly held view that mental illness, including depression, is a sign of moral or spiritual weakness. This stigma has prevented many people from receiving the care they so desperately needed.

Today we understand much more about depression and its treatment than ever before. In fact, with a combination of psychotherapeutic counseling and the proper use of antidepressant medication, most depression can be rapidly controlled. In most cases, after several months of therapy, the medication may be gradually reduced and ultimately discontinued.

Misconceptions abound regarding the treatment of depression and the medications which are used. Psychotherapy is not lying on a couch and telling a stranger everything inside your head. It is simply the guidance of a well-trained professional, helping restore reality and objectivity to a confused and depressed individual who is going through a time of crisis.

The medications used in the treatment of depression are safe, effective, and nonaddicting. However, it is important not to stop medications too abruptly or too soon because the depression may return. Occasionally, adverse side effects may occur. If this happens, medications can be changed. In most cases, the risks of treatment are low and the rewards of regaining a healthy outlook on life are great.

Depression is common among women and potentially very serious. But, fortunately, depression is always treatable; and in most cases with time and appropriate treatment, it is curable.

SUMMARY

Clinical depression is a complex disorder which cannot be ignored. It can range from merely having a sad appearance to a complete psychotic break with reality. Although most clinical depressions do not reach these extreme stages, much pain and suffering are present even in the initial stages. If the symptoms of depression ever become disabling, either biologically or socially, a depressive illness is present.

Most experts agree that almost anyone can be cured of this condition with quality, professional psychotherapy and the appropriate use of antidepressant medication. Unfortunately, the obstacles to treatment are often the individuals themselves who are reluctant to seek psychological counseling.

In the words of Frank Minirth, M.D., and Paul Meier, M.D., (1978), "As a last resort, you swallow your middle-class pride (upper-class people love to see psychiatrists) and see a psychiatrist. He gives you an antidepressant and weekly psychotherapy. He puts you in touch with your anger, he gets you to verbalize it and resolve it. Three to six months later you get off antidepressants and feel great even without them."

CHAPTER 23

Anxiety—
Why Am I Afraid?

Anxiety is the unwanted, painful emotional baggage that many people carry with them for much of their life. Most of us experience some inner discomfort when faced with difficult circumstances. It is the amplification of these feelings to the point of excessive or unrealistic anxiety and worry about some facet of life which characterizes anxiety disorders (DSM-III-R, 1987).

Anxiety can be highly unpleasant and self-perpetuating. A vicious cycle often begins with the physical symptoms of anxiety which in time create worry about the person's physical health and this adds to the already overloaded emotions of the anxious person. *Recognition and treatment are necessary to control this self-defeating cycle and restore control and calm to a person's life.*

The characteristic which separates anxiety from fear is the inability to identify the source of the anxiety. With fear you can recognize a known source of danger. Anxious people sense danger and are truly fearful, but the real source of their fears cannot be identified. Fear and anxiety are very much alike, and if examined superficially, they seem the same. It is natural to be afraid of a large snarling dog, but what about a woman who suddenly has to leave the theater for some unexplained reason or the individual who lies awake night after night, afraid to shut her eyes?

It has been said that we live in the *Age of Anxiety*. Proposed causes for such pervasive anxiety range from the decline of the nuclear family to the threat of nuclear war. Donald Goodwin has suggested in his book *Anxiety* that *perhaps the real reason for increased problems of anxiety in our society is that we have less to fear.*

When we are truly afraid, there is no time for anxiety. Those of us living in North America are perhaps more secure than any other

252

people in history. Certainly the typical family living in the eighteenth century, struggling daily for existence, food, and shelter, faced fear on a more identifiable and personal level. Half of their children usually would die by age 10 and most marriages lasted only 15 years, not due to divorce but to separation by death. Each uneventful day was almost a miracle. Perhaps anxiety is the price we pay for a safer but more complicated society, and an improved but often impersonal civilization.

EFFECTS OF ANXIETY

Most people do not seek medical help outright for anxiety. Instead, they go to the doctor with a multitude of physical complaints, some specific and some extremely vague, but all a direct result of their anxious emotional state. These symptoms (see Table 23.1) are the response of the body to a perceived threat and the subsequent arousal of the sympathetic nervous system. This is the system which prepares you for *fight or flight* when under attack.

The problem with anxiety is that unlike a snarling dog which will either attack or eventually turn away, anxiety just hovers and blankets the individual with dread. Dr. James Dobson uses the term *"routine panic"* to explain the continual stress many of us experience and accept as part of our normal life. The problem here is that anxiety doesn't let up. And when our body stays on continual alert, eventually it begins to fatigue and break down from stress. It is at this point that physical symptoms begin to surface.

Panic attacks are full-blown episodes of extreme anxiety which can come on suddenly and with little warning. Usually, the anxiety symptoms

Table 23.1. Symptoms of Anxiety

Motor tension
    shakiness, jitteriness, trembling, muscle aches, easy fatigue, inability to relax, eyelid twitch, restlessness, weakness

Autonomic nervous system hyperactivity
    sweating, heart-racing, palpitations, dry mouth, dizziness, light-headedness, tingling hands and feet, frequent urination, diarrhea, upset stomach, lump in the throat, hot or cold spells, rapid breathing and a sense of suffocation

Apprehension
    anxiety, fear, worry, anticipation of bad things to come

Vigilance
    hyperalertness, trouble concentrating, insomnia, impatience, irritability, being on edge

with these episodes are very severe, and the person is extremely fearful, even to the point of fearing for her life.

One of the first casualties of anxiety is the sex drive. This is due to a principle of psychology known as the law of reciprocal inhibition. Basically, this refers to the fact that you cannot experience two opposite emotions at the same time. *It is pretty hard to feel afraid and sexy at the same time.*

Even though an anxious person knows in most cases that she is not in real danger, there is a heightened awareness and tension to the body. The physical and mental faculties are placed on continual alert. Sometimes the normal routine is disrupted by this vigilance, but in most cases people just uncomfortably get by.

TREATMENT OF ANXIETY

It is important, first of all, for your physician to be sure that anxiety is your only problem. There are some medical disorders such as thyroid disease and drug or alcohol problems which can produce anxiety symptoms. In many cases, the diagnosis of anxiety is clear to everyone except the person with the problem. The anxious individual knows she feels nervous and upset, but is afraid her pounding heart and sense of dread are a sign of heart disease. A careful physical exam and reassurance that her physical body is functioning properly can be the first step toward control of anxiety.

It is often hard for some people to accept anxiety as a "real" disease. Where are the abnormal laboratory tests and physical findings? This problem often sends the anxious person in quest of a "real" diagnosis from one physician to another. Unfortunately, some doctors give the impression and some patients get the idea that they are being rejected because "it's all in their head."

Anxiety, however, is a *real* problem that causes *real* pain, suffering, and disability. It is a disease that deserves sound medical management with emphasis on prevention and alleviation of disabling symptoms. Sigmond Freud, who himself had an unnatural fear of trains, believed that the cure for anxiety lay in confronting your fears and continuing to do so until they disappeared. However, Freud was like most people facing uncomfortable feelings—he avoided trains as much as possible.

Psychotherapy and Counseling

Successful treatment for anxiety involves supportive psychotherapy, usually in the form of reassurance and counseling, and sometimes medication. It may be reassuring to a person to hear that she doesn't have cancer or heart disease as she supposed, but that simple reassurance may not completely take away the overwhelming anxiety. Behavioral treatments are often used in anxiety disorders, especially phobias. A good example is the treatment of someone who is deathly afraid of flying. Gradual work on just going to an airport, then sitting in an airplane, and finally actually taking a flight can allow a person to overcome or control this phobia.

Medications

Antianxiety medication. Appropriate use of *antianxiety medication,* carefully monitored and controlled, is often needed to restore normal functioning. Taken regularly for a period of time and then gradually reduced in dosage and frequency seems to be the most effective treatment strategy. Occasional low-dose use may be needed from time to time as certain situations dictate. These medications must be used properly as they have a potential for abuse and even addiction with long-term use.

Beta-blockers. These medications are often used in hypertension but also can help control the physical symptoms of anxiety such as heart palpitation and muscle tremor.

Antidepressant medication. Depression can often accompany anxiety and antidepressants may be of use. As we noted before, the relationship of anxiety and depression is often like the question of Which came first, the chicken or the egg? Antidepressants may be useful in anxiety disorders even when depression is not present, especially for control of panic attacks. They have the added advantage of not being addictive.

Physical Exercise

As we have mentioned frequently, vigorous *aerobic exercise* can play a vital role in many areas of your health. Regular exercise has proven significant in reducing high levels of anxiety and preventing anxiety from building. During an anxiety attack, *rebreathing into a paper sack* can relieve the uncomfortable symptoms of hyperventilation. Rebreathing can help slow breathing, eliminate dizziness, lightheadedness, and prevent fainting.

Every living person faces fear and can relate to the feelings it causes. Some of us will confront anxiety with its unidentifiable feeling of dread and distress. For most people, these anxiety episodes will be short-lived and mild. Unfortunately, many people try to self-medicate themselves to control their anxiety by the inappropriate use of drugs or alcohol. The risk of addiction under these circumstances is great. If you are experiencing daily anxiety which is impairing your life, treatment to prevent further injury to yourself is highly recommended.

CHAPTER 24

Mid-Life Transition—
Crisis or Opportunity?

With any situation in life requiring transition and change, comes the possibility of crisis and the opportunity for improvement. The mid-life crisis we hear so much about is simply the natural transition from one life stage to another gone awry. Somehow, in crisis, the smooth process of transition jumps the track and becomes a runaway situation with no end in sight. Women in crisis want to get off the track; they want to start over—but how?

It is important to understand the transition that is taking place and the ways you can approach the changes. In every stage of life, for growth to occur, one must move from the safety and security of familiar, comforting old situations to an unfamiliar and often threatening new stage. It is natural to want to cling to the old and comfortable ways, but change is inevitable and without growth, we stagnate. The transition we are talking about is one of those broad, sweeping movements in life which occurs at various predetermined intervals. As you enter your 40s and 50s, change is all around you. Your family is growing up or is grown. Perhaps you and your husband are a couple again for the first time in a long while. Your body is changing physically, and your attitudes toward life may even be different. Mid-life transition with its elements of social, physical, intellectual, and spiritual change is not unlike other transition stages you have already been through. Consider your evolution from a young girl to a budding adolescent or from a newlywed to a mother of young children. These times of change seldom happen suddenly, and fortunately, we usually have time to prepare for and understand them.

256

METHODS OF TRANSITION

Your method of transition could be termed your "style of living." We all have an individual style based on our cumulative life experiences, but there are several basic techniques of transition. Identify yours, understand and work with its strengths, but try to avoid its weaknesses.

Slow and Steady

Nobody is going to rush you. You are careful and considerate, usually not a risk-taker, but you will stay the course and accomplish what you set your mind on. Like the tortoise and the hare, slow and steady will usually win the race. By taking the long view and following a careful plan, you will have little difficulty making the transition in midlife.

Life, unfortunately, does not always follow a carefully mapped-out plan. Not all women experience slow, steady change. Sometimes change comes suddenly and without warning. This inability to be flexible in the face of sudden, unexpected change—whether physical, financial, or personal—could be your weak point. Test your ability to be flexible, and always consider alternative plans to the ones you have laid out.

Reluctant

Perhaps you are reticent to leave your world of children and home-centered activity. Possibly you have achieved or may be nearing the apex of your career with little opportunity for further advancement. Whatever your life has been until now, it has obviously been satisfying because you are so reluctant to move on.

An extreme view of the reluctant method is one we call the "*Kicking and Screaming*" type. Nobody is going to change you, not for any reason—no way! Just as your strength can be the deep satisfaction you feel with your life circumstances, your weakness may be hanging onto that which can no longer be. Whether it is children, a job, physical attributes, or whatever, desperate clinging to that which is in transition can lead only to frustration and life dissatisfaction.

Opportunist

You are ready for what lies ahead. Each day opens new vistas, new relationships, new opportunity. With the mid-life transition comes advancement, and each new experience leads to another. Perhaps you have planned for this stage of life and now all the years of effort and planning are about to pay off.

For those of you with this style of living, more power to you. Don't let the rest of us stand in your way! But just a word of caution: don't let enthusiasm take the place of common sense. We once took care of a very unhappy woman who, with her husband, had planned and saved for years to take to the highways of America when they reached retirement. At last they made it; they sold their home, bought a trailer, and said goodbye to their old routine. Six months later and thousands of miles from home on the way to nowhere in particular, they were both unhappy and homesick. The moral: *Enjoy life, but have a good plan and take the time to be sure of where you are headed.*

ARE YOU AT RISK FOR A MID-LIFE CRISIS?

Every person making the mid-life transition is at risk. *Remember, mid-life crisis is simply the normal transition gone haywire.* Fortunately, crisis is not going to overwhelm every woman, although change, whether we like it or not, will occur. Jim and Sally Conway in their book, *Women in Mid-Life Crisis,* have identified eight major factors which produce stress or crisis in mid-life women:

Risk Factors for Mid-Life Crisis

1. Our present-day cultural view of women.

2. An unhappy marital situation or lack of a marriage.

3. Your husband's own mid-life crisis.

4. Demands from children and their growing independence.

5. Career priorities related to other life priorities.

6. Accumulation of tragic losses such as death, illness, or aging.

7. Urgency from inner clocks to accomplish life's dreams.

8. The need for time to review the past and plan for the future.

Perhaps it is helpful to assess your own personal situation as you consider the issues of mid-life. Most of us, when asked how we are, generally reply "Doing fine," "I'm O.K.," or "No problem." Is that the truth? No doubt, the inquirer was just making polite conversation and would be astonished if you answered "No, I'm not fine, and let me tell you what's wrong!" But perhaps you privately need to consider the question a bit more closely.

Table 24.1. Life Satisfaction Evaluation

_____ 1. As I grow older, life seems better than I thought it would be.

_____ 2. I have gotten more breaks in life than most people I know.

_____ 3. This is the greatest time of my life.

_____ 4. I am just as happy as when I was younger.

_____ 5. These are the best years of my life.

_____ 6. Most of the things I do are interesting and varied.

_____ 7. The things I do are as interesting to me as they ever were.

_____ 8. As I look back on my life, I am pretty well satisfied.

_____ 9. I have made plans for things that I will be doing a month or a year from now.

_____ 10. When I consider my life, I got most of the important things I wanted.

_____ 11. Compared to other people, I seldom get down in the dumps.

_____ 12. I have gotten pretty much what I wanted out of life.

_____ 13. In spite of what people say, the lot of the average person is getting better, not worse.

Ratings: 0–12 Low life satisfaction
13–21 Moderate life satisfaction
22–26 High life satisfaction

If you have low satisfaction consider yourself *at risk* for dealing with stress, change, and mid-life crisis.

Adapted from information in *The Preventive Approach to Patient Care* by D. Sheridan and I. Winogrond, 1987.

ARE YOU SATISFIED WITH LIFE?

By using Table 24.1 do a self-evaluation of your personal life satisfaction. If you agree with the statements, score 2 points. If you are uncertain about a statement, score 1. If you disagree with the statements, score zero.

DO YOU HAVE PROBLEMS WITH SELF-ESTEEM?

Self-esteem is often at the core of how we deal with life. Healthy self-esteem allows us to weather the storms of change and self-doubt which can overcome anyone. Low self-esteem is often the root of depression and anxiety and renders the individual incapable of adjusting

Table 24.2.   Self-Esteem Evaluation

1. I feel that I am a person of real worth, at least equal with others.
2. I feel that I have a number of good qualities.
3. All things considered, I feel that I am a success.
4. I can do things as well as most people.
5. I feel that I have a lot to be proud of.
6. I take a positive attitude with myself.
7. All in all, I am satisfied with myself.
8. I have good respect for myself.
9. Most of the time I feel capable and useful.
10. I usually think I am a good and worthy person.

Five negative responses will often indicate a lack of self-esteem and may reflect problems in personal and family roles that interface with well-being.

Adapted from information in *The Preventive Approach to Patient Care* by D. Sheridan and I. Winogrond, 1987.

to mid-life changes such as the loss of a job, illness, physical changes, marital difficulties, or problems with children. Take the self-esteem test (Table 24.2) and evaluate your current status.

SOME ANSWERS

How did you rate yourself on the two tests? We hope that you hold yourself in high esteem. Your worth as an individual should never be underestimated. Midlife presents questions of worth, values, and purpose for most people. And just because you are questioning doesn't mean you are ungrateful or confused. On the contrary, questions often signal a movement from one stage to another, just one more step in the lifelong process known as personal growth.

If you have reached this time in your life and recognize a serious lack of personal satisfaction and perhaps poor self-esteem, let's look at some general principles which may help you work through these issues.

1. *Change is inevitable.* There is really no use fighting it and struggling in vain to maintain the status quo. Accept this fact and save your energy for other issues that you can change.

2. *Take time.* You need time to assess your current situation, time for yourself, time to set new goals. Try not to allow events to rob you of the valuable time necessary to achieve your personal goals.

3. *Establish priorities and set goals.* For most of us, one day we

wake up and wonder where the years went. The reason is fairly simple. How time flies when you're on *the young-family conveyer belt or racing up the career ladder*. One cycle begins with your first baby and deposits you somewhere in the future where your obligations and life are not dictated by diapers, carpools, piano lessons, and the school year. And, if you haven't been doing this, then perhaps you've been spending your time in rush-hour traffic, airports, business meetings, or just trying to find the bottom of the in-basket. Or perhaps you've even been trying to do both at once. A reassessment of life priorities and personal goals is probably long overdue. Failure to establish clear goals which lead to the future may leave you stagnated in midlife, possibly frustrated and unhappy, and unsure why you feel that way.

4. *Take action.* Goals without action are invalid and meaningless. Depending on the goal, you might consider returning to work, resuming your education, or becoming more involved in community or church activities. The possibilities are, in most cases, limited only by your own imagination and may be short- or long-term in nature.

This is a point where self-esteem plays a very important role. Low self-esteem may inhibit both your dreams and your goal-setting, possibly preventing you from acting on your dreams. It is important to discover your strengths and to concentrate on those areas when you have a problem with low self-esteem.

5. *Seek advice and encouragement.* Seek out people who really believe in you and lift you up. Avoid those who are negative and seem to discourage your efforts. Professional counseling can help you clarify your goals and establish your strengths and weaknesses.

Sometimes mid-life transitions can be painful, but they are always challenging. *You must overcome the inertia of the routine and set aside for a moment the clanging bells of all the urgent demands which face you daily.* Do whatever it takes, plan now, set new goals, take action!

SUMMARY

Our emotional inner self, perhaps as no other facet of life, has the potential to make or break the concept of mid-life as Prime Time. Prime time—the best, the most productive, the optimal period of our life—will be a sham, even with good health, if we are discouraged, defeated, and burdened with low self-esteem.

It has been written that "No other decade is more intriguing, complex, interesting, and unsettled. Its characteristics are change, flux, crisis, growth, and intense challenges. Other than childhood, no period has a greater impact on the balance of our lives, for at no other time is anxiety coupled with so great a possibility for fulfillment" (Davitz and Davitz, 1976).

Summing It Up

CHAPTER 25

The Bottom Line—
A Summary of
Good Health Habits

In today's world we have a new set of health problems which were once reserved for only the wealthiest of Earth's inhabitants. In terms of the American food supply, we have progressed from the horn of plenty right through to the barrel of excess.

Simultaneous to this increased intake of concentrated calories is a decrease in the amount of calories we expend through physical activities. Let's face it—we have a time-saving, energy-sparing device for almost everything humans need (and then some). And yet, within the old American work ethic, we refuse to acknowledge that we just might need some "artificial" exercise (i.e., jogging, walking, swimming) because that would be a sure sign that we are not working hard enough. Of course, most of that work is now done in a chair, behind a desk, pushing a pencil. Our fingers are in great shape!

The main things to remember as you reorient your thinking about your health are these:

1. Go slow. Change one thing at a time. Make a lifelong commitment to good health.

2. Have a positive attitude about all the good things you are doing for your health. You will live longer. More importantly, you will live better.

3. Expect setbacks. They will always come. Get right back on course as soon as possible, but with no guilt.

4. Start today. There will never be a better time. Whatever your age, you are at the perfect age to begin this program.

5. Expect it to be fun. Look for results almost immediately.

The following list of health goals can bring about some wonderful changes in your life. Remember these goals are not based on the "all or none" principle. They have a cumulative effect on your health. Therefore, don't be discouraged if you cannot do everything now, or ever. But, remember this, the more goals you accomplish, the greater the returns on the best life insurance policy you have ever had—good health.

We recommend the following health goals for every woman:

1. Eat a healthy diet according to the following guidelines:

   - Limit total fat intake to 30 percent of total calorie intake.
   - Lose weight if necessary.
   - Consume 25 grams fiber/day.
   - Consume 3 servings of calcium rich foods/day.
   - Read food labels carefully—be an informed shopper.
   - Don't eat high-cholesterol foods.
   - Limit caffeine to 2–3 servings/day.
   - Choose natural foods without additives when possible.
   - Eat plenty of fresh vegetables.
   - Take calcium supplements.

2. Include aerobic exercise 3 times per week for 45 minutes.

3. Don't smoke.

4. Limit alcohol to one drink per day if you choose to drink; none if you are at high-risk for breast cancer.

5. Practice breast self-examination monthly.

6. Get a baseline mammogram and repeat the mammogram at least once before age 45.

7. Get a baseline electrocardiogram (EKG).

8. Consider a maximal exercise stress test before beginning a vigorous exercise program if you are at high risk for heart disease.

9. Have your eyes checked at least every 5 years.

10. Avoid excessive sun exposure, and use SPF 15 or greater sunscreen.

11. Have a tetanus/diphtheria booster every 10 years.

12. Get a metabolic blood screen, including a cholesterol profile and complete blood count every 5 years if normal and more often if there is a problem.

13. Have a urinalysis every other year.

14. Identify and correct any risk factors for heart disease, cancer, hypertension, and diabetes.

15. Have an annual physical exam, including blood pressure check, heart and lung exam, breast exam, pelvic exam and Pap smear, skin cancer check, rectal exam and check of stool for blood.

After age 45 continue the preceding recommendations and add the following:

1. Get a mammogram twice in the next 5 years.

2. Begin glaucoma screening every other year.

3. Have a hearing assessment every 5 years.

4. Be prepared to start estrogen replacement within 12 months of menopause.

After age 50 continue both of the above lists and add the following:

1. Now have a mammogram done every year.

2. Get an EKG every 5 years.

3. Have a flexible sigmoidoscopy every 3 years after two normal exams 1 year apart.

4. Discuss hormone replacement therapy with your doctor if you have not already started it.

5. Review, at least annually, all medications that you take.

After age 65 continue the previous recommendations and add the following:

1. Get an annual flu vaccination.

2. Get a pneumonia vaccination (one time only).

3. Change your calcium to calcium citrate (Citracal) if you are not already taking it.

Table 25.1. A Checklist for Your Personal Health Maintenance Plan

Age	35	36	37	38	39	40	41	42	43	44	45	46	47	48	49	50	51	52	53	54	55	56	57	58	59	60	61	62	63	64	65	66	67	68	69	70	71	72	73
Blood Pressure	√	√	√	√	√	√	√	√	√	√	√	√	√	√	√	√	√	√	√	√	√	√	√	√	√	√	√	√	√	√	√	√	√	√	√	√	√	√	√
Hearing Exam						√										√					√					√					√					√		√	
Vision Check	√					√					√					√					√					√					√					√			
Glaucoma Screen								√			√			√			√			√			√			√			√			√			√			√	
Breast Exam	√	√	√	√	√	√	√	√	√	√	√	√	√	√	√	√	√	√	√	√	√	√	√	√	√	√	√	√	√	√	√	√	√	√	√	√	√	√	√
Mammography	√					√		√		√		√		√		√	√	√	√	√	√	√	√	√	√	√	√	√	√	√	√	√	√	√	√	√	√	√	√
Pap Smear	√	√	√	√	√	√	√	√	√	√	√	√	√	√	√	√		√		√		√		√		√		√		√		√		√		√		√	
Metabolic Screen	√					√					√					√					√					√					√					√			
Urinalysis		√		√		√		√		√		√		√		√		√		√		√		√		√		√		√		√		√		√		√	
Complete Blood Count	√					√										√										√										√			
Tetanus Booster						√										√										√										√			
Stool Check						√	√	√	√	√	√	√	√	√	√	√	√	√	√	√	√	√	√	√	√	√	√	√	√	√	√	√	√	√	√	√	√	√	√
Digital Rectal Exam						√	√	√	√	√	√	√	√	√	√	√	√	√	√	√	√	√	√	√	√	√	√	√	√	√	√	√	√	√	√	√	√	√	√
Sigmoidoscopy																				√			√			√			√			√			√			√	
EKG						√					√					√					√					√					√					√			
Flu Vaccine																														√	√	√	√	√	√	√	√	√	√
Pneumovax																															√								

"√" marks indicate optimal intervals for specific disease-screening tests. Compare your current level of health maintenance with these goals and correct any deficiencies.

APPENDIX 1

Information Resources

Aging parents	—Children of Aging Parents 2761 Trenton Road Levittown, PA 19056
Alcohol abuse	—Alcoholics Anonymous P.O. Box 459 Grand Central Station New York, NY 10163
	—Al-Anon Family Groups P.O. Box 182 Madison Square Station New York, NY 10159
	—National Council on Alcoholism 733 Third Ave. New York, NY 10017
Alzheimer's disease	—Alzheimer's Association National Headquarters 70 East Lake Street Chicago, IL 60601–5997
	—Alzheimer's Disease and Related Disorders 360 N. Michigan Ave. Chicago, IL 60601
Arthritis	—National Arthritis Foundation Room 1101 3400 Peachtree Road, N.E. Atlanta, GA 30327
	—American Lupus Society 23751 Madison Street Torrance, CA 90505

Breast cancer	—Reach to Recovery 19 W. 56th St. New York, NY 10019
Cancer	—American Cancer Society 777 Third Ave. New York, NY 10017
Dental care	—American Dental Association 211 East Chicago Ave. Chicago, IL 60611
Diethylstilbesterol (DES)	—Office of Cancer Communications National Cancer Institute Bldg. 31, Room 10A-18 9000 Rockville Pike Bethesda, MD 20205
Drug abuse	—National Clearinghouse on Drug Abuse P.O. Box 416 Kensington, MD 20795
Health	—Council on Family Health 633 Third Ave. New York, NY 10017
	—National Foundation for Women's Health 3300 Heury Ave. Philadelphia, PA 19129
	—Grey Panthers Health Task Force 3700 Chestnut St. Philadelphia, PA 19104
Heart disease	—American Heart Association 7320 Greenville Ave. Dallas, TX 75231
Herpes	—Herpes Resource Center P.O. Box 100 Palo Alto, CA 94302
High blood pressure	—High Blood Pressure Information Center 120/80 NIH Bethesda, MD 20205
Lung disease	—American Lung Association 1740 Broadway New York, NY 10019
Mental health	—National Mental Health Association 1800 N. Kent Street Arlington, VA 22209

Nutrition	—The American Dietetic Association 430 North Michigan Ave. Chicago, IL 60611
Retirement	—American Association of Retired Persons (AARP) 1909 K St., NW Washington, DC 20049
Sexually transmitted disease	—Technical Information Services Center for Prevention Services Centers for Disease Control Atlanta, GA 30333
Single parents	—Parents Without Partners 7910 Woodmont Ave. Bethesda, MD 20014
Smoking	—American Cancer Society 777 Third Ave. New York, NY 10017
	—American Heart Association 7320 Greenville Ave. Dallas, TX 72531
Sterilization	—Association for Voluntary Sterilization 122 E. 42nd St. New York, NY 10168
Urine incontinence	—The Simon Foundation P.O. Box 835 KC Wilmette, IL 60091
	—HIP, Help for Incontinent People P.O. Box 544 Union, SC 29379

APPENDIX 2

Nutrient Content of Selected Foods

This list is here for you to make nutritional comparisons between general types of foods. It is not exhaustive but is included primarily so that you may make a comparison of fat content of different meats, dairy products, and other potentially high-fat food.

Food, Amount	Calories (kcal)	Fat (g)	Protein (g)	Carbo-hydrate (g)	Choles-terol (mg)
Meat, Fish, and Eggs					
ground beef, X-lean cooked, 3 oz.	185	10	23	0	72
ground beef, regular cooked, 3 oz.	235	17	20	0	75
round roast or steak, lean, cooked, 3 oz.	165	7	25	0	68
ribs or rib roast, fat and lean, cooked, 3 oz.	375	33	17	0	75
liver, beef, cooked, 3 oz.	195	9	22	0	407
liver, chicken, cooked 3 oz.	185	9	21	0	633
pork loin, roasted, lean, 3 oz.	225	12	25	0	76
lean ham, cooked, 3 oz.	195	13	22	0	76
chicken, light meat, cooked, no skin, 3 oz.	142	4	27	0	72

Food, Amount	Calories (kcal)	Fat (g)	Protein (g)	Carbo-hydrate (g)	Choles-terol (mg)
chicken, dark meat, cooked, no skin, 3 oz.	151	6	24	0	78
turkey, light meat, cooked, no skin, 3 oz.	151	3	28	0	58
turkey, dark meat, cooked, no skin, 3 oz.	174	7	26	0	72
halibut, cod, flounder (others), cooked, 3 oz.	120	1	24	0	52
shrimp, steamed, shelled, 3 oz.	100	2	23	0	175
crab, meat only, cooked, 3 oz.	90	2	22	0	86
oysters, shucked, cooked, 3 oz.	120	2	23	0	54
egg, whole, large	80	6	7	0	274
egg, yolk	70	6	3	0	274
egg, white	10	0	4	0	0
Milk, Yogurt, and Cheeses					
milk, whole, 8 oz.	160	8	8	12	33
milk, 2% low-fat, 8 oz.	120	5	8	12	18
milk, 1% low-fat, 8 oz.	105	2	8	12	10
milk, skim, 8 oz.	90	1	9	12	5
yogurt, nonfat, plain, 8 oz.	90	1	9	12	5
yogurt, fruit-flavored, 8 oz.	230	2	8	47	5
cottage cheese, creamed, ½ cup	120	5	15	4	17
cottage cheese, low-fat, ½ cup	90	2	15	4	5
natural cheddar cheese, (Swiss, jack, munster, etc.), 1 oz.	115	9	7	1	30
mozzarella, part-skimmed milk, 1 oz.	80	6	5	1	17
sour cream, 1 Tbsp.	26	3	0	1	5
Borden Lite-line cheese slices, 1 slice	35	1	5	1	7

Food, Amount	Calories (kcal)	Fat (g)	Protein (g)	Carbo-hydrate (g)	Choles-terol (mg)
Fats and Oils					
beef fat, 1 Tbsp.	126	13	0	0	14
chicken fat, 1 Tbsp.	126	13	0	0	11
butter, 1 Tbsp.	107	11	0	0	31
corn oil (or other vegetable oil), 1 Tbsp.	126	14	0	0	0
margarine, stick or tub, 1 Tbsp.	108	11	0	0	0
diet margarine, 1 Tbsp.	50	6	0	0	0
shortening, vegetable	124	13	0	0	0
mayonnaise, 1 Tbsp.	100	11	0	0	8
mayonnaise-type salad dressing, 1 Tbsp.	60	5	0	0	4
Thousand Island, regular, 1 Tbsp.	70	6	0	0	4
Italian, regular, 1 Tbsp.	77	7	0	0	0
Nuts and Seeds					
peanuts, dry roasted, salted, 2 Tbsp.	170	14	9	5	0
walnuts, chopped 12 Tbsp.	98	9	2	2	0
pecans, 12 halves, 2 Tbsp. chopped	104	9	2	2	0
peanut butter, 2 Tbsp.	175	14	8	6	0

Nutrient Calculator

Food Eaten	Amount				
TOTALS					
GOALS					

Instructions: Use the last four columns of this table to calculate your nutrient intake of any four items (i.e., calories, fat, calcium, protein, sodium, etc.). You will find information concerning the nutrient content of foods on package labels, and in reference books which specialize in the nutritional content of foods, as well as Appendix 2 of this book.

Blue-Ribbon Recipes

The following recipes are merely a representation of the health-conscious food dishes you can prepare at home. The sky is the absolute limit when it comes to health-oriented cookery. Take your old favorites and conform them to new eating standards. Experiment with new foods and new recipes; and be prepared for a few failures amidst the new delicacies coming your way.

There are many good cookbooks on the market which promote prudent eating habits. We highly recommend that you choose the one that suits you and your family the best. Then develop your own recipe file with only the *creme de la creme* "healthy" recipes. The following recipes are from our own family file and have been tried and proven many times over. Each serves a specific purpose in both our health program and eating satisfaction. We hope you will enjoy them as much as we do.

—— **Baked Orange Roughy** ——

(or any other mild, filleted white fish)

20 oz. orange roughy fillets, raw
 2 Tbsp. diet margarine
 3 Tbsp. freshly squeezed lemon juice
 2 Tbsp. Ranch Salad Dressing Mix, dry and unprepared
⅓ cup Italian Bread Crumbs (Progresso Italian style preferred)
    parsley flakes, pepper, PAM or other vegetable oil spray

Spray a metal baking dish with PAM nonstick spray. Place fillets in pan. Sprinkle with 2 Tbsp. lemon juice, spices, dry salad dressing mix, and bread crumbs. Dot with margarine. Bake at 350° for 20 minutes in a preheated oven or until flaky when pierced with a fork. *Do not* cover while cooking. Sprinkle with remaining lemon juice when done.

Nutritional Information: Baked, boiled, or poached fish is probably your very best meat choice. Try to include it at least two times per week. Even if you have never cooked fish, *this recipe is foolproof.* It is also quick and easy, and it will impress the entire family. Consumption of fish and fish oils is thought to lower serum cholesterol and triglyceride levels.

Number of servings	4
Size of serving	4 oz.
Calories per serving	180
Grams of fat per serving	3.5

Exchanges per serving: 4 meat, ½ fat

—— Blackened Orange Roughy ——
(or any other mild, filleted white fish)

20 oz. orange roughy fillets, raw
    PAM buttery-flavored spray
1½ Tbsp. butter (or oil)
    McCormick's blackened redfish mix (or something similar in another brand)
2 fresh lemons

Sprinkle fillets with seasoning mix. Spray a heavy skillet (such as copper lined with stainless) with PAM and place on range-top over medium heat. Melt butter in pan. Place fillets in hot skillet and cook 3 to 5 minutes on each side until fish is flaky. Turn off pan, sprinkle with fresh lemon juice. Serve immediately with more lemon juice, brown-rice pilaf, and a vegetable. Delicious!

Nutritional Information: Again—fish is your best nutritional meat choice. This recipe does not have to be charred as is often the case when prepared in a restaurant. The spice mix, which contains pepper, can provide the same appearance without the burning. (Burned foods may be carcinogenic, anyway). The slight use of real butter in this recipe should not matter since so little is actually present in one serving. However, if an elevated serum cholesterol is a problem for you, use oil instead.

Number of servings	4
Size of servings	4 oz.
Calories per serving	190
Grams of fat per serving	3.7

Exchanges per serving: 4 meat, ½ fat

── One-Dish Chicken Dinner ──

    4 chicken breasts, no skin, boiled, boned, and diced
    2 cups cooked brown rice, no butter
  16 oz. chopped frozen broccoli, thawed but not cooked
    1 can cream of mushroom soup
    4 oz. processed cheese (such as Velveeta or Old English)
  ⅓ cup Parmesan cheese
  ⅓ cup bread crumbs (Progresso Italian style preferred)
    3 Tbsp. fresh chopped parsley

Combine soup and cheese in saucepan. Heat until mixed and smooth. Combine thawed broccoli with cooked rice and soup mixture and gently fold together. Place in a 9″ × 12″ casserole pan. Cover with diced chicken, cheese, and crumbs. Bake at 350° for 30 minutes. Serve hot with a salad.

Nutritional information: Poultry is always a good selection as long as the skin and fat have been removed. If you are using a traditional chicken and rice recipe, always remove the skin before cooking so that it is not absorbed by the rice. We use broccoli in our own kitchen at every opportunity. If there is one "super vegetable," it has to be this one. If you are watching your salt intake, then use the low sodium counterparts for the soup and cheese—they are available. One-dish dinners are a good idea because people tend to eat more if they are presented with several different choices. Also, this recipe is a good choice when you want to take food to a friend; it contains an entire meal in one dish and can be frozen (uncooked) for several weeks or months.

Number of servings	4
Size of servings	¼ of recipe
Calories per serving	365
Grams of fat per serving	15

Exchanges per serving: 3 meat, 1 starch, 1 fat, 1 vegetable

Note: This casserole is a true one-dish dinner. It is high in fiber, relatively low in fat and contains starch, protein, a dairy product, and a highly nutritious vegetable.

—— Beef Lover's Smothered Steak ——

4 4-oz. cubed steaks or pieces of round steak, all visible fat trimmed
      (cubed steak is tenderized round steak)
1 pkg. Lipton's Onion Soup Mix, dry (or low-sodium alternative)
1 (medium) onion, sliced and rings separated
½ (medium) bell pepper, sliced
2 Tbsp. skim milk
2 Tbsp. flour

Place heavy-duty foil on a jellyroll pan (cookie sheet with a 1″ side). Dip steak in milk and then flour and place in pan on the foil. Sprinkle with remaining ingredients. Cover with foil and crimp the edges. Bake at 325° for 90 minutes.

Nutritional Information: When choosing beef, you must concentrate on the leanest cuts, such as round steak, and then learn how to tenderize them during the cooking process. Though this recipe is a little high in sodium (because of the soup mix), it is a quick, low-fat way of serving beef. By using other spices instead of the soup mix, this recipe can be changed into either Italian-style (cover with spaghetti sauce) or Spanish-style steak (cover with chili powder, garlic, and onions). As you will see in Appendix 1, having lean round steak (no fat) is not very different from having the dark meat of chicken (no skin) in terms of fat and cholesterol content.

Number of servings	4
Size of servings	3½ to 4 oz.
Calories per serving	320
Grams of fat per serving	12

Exchanges per serving: 3½ meat

—— Baked Lasagne ——

½ lb. ground round beef, browned (or ground turkey)
4 zucchini squash, washed and sliced (not peeled)
⅓ onion, chopped, softened in microwave
½ bell pepper, chopped, softened in microwave
1 cup commercial, thick spaghetti sauce
1 6-oz. can tomato paste
6 oz. water
    spices—oregano, basil, Italian seasoning, and pepper (to taste)

12 oz. ricotta cheese, made from skim milk
¼ cup skim milk
2 egg whites, raw
1 Tbsp. Italian seasoning mix
1 cup grated mozzarella cheese
¼ cup Parmesan cheese
8 oz. lasagne noodles, cooked

Mix the first eight ingredients in a large bowl or pan. Mix the ricotta cheese, skim milk, egg whites, and Italian seasoning. Mix until creamy smooth and spreadable. Spray a large baking dish with nonstick vegetable oil, and place one layer of cooked noodles on the bottom. Then cover with a layer of meat sauce, ricotta cheese mixture, and mozzarella cheese sprinkled over the top. Layer with noodles, meat, and cheese mixtures. Top with the grated Parmesan cheese. Bake at 350° for 50 to 65 minutes. Let this recipe stand for 10 minutes after taking out of the oven before cutting and serving.

Nutritional Information: Italian food is usually a good choice if you control the amount you are eating. Homemade recipes will always be lower in sodium as well. Mozzarella cheese is one of the lower-fat, natural cheeses. This recipe could be made with or without the beef or the zucchini to produce a different taste. Whole-wheat lasagne noodles are also a nice variation on this recipe.

Number of servings	8
Size of serving	⅛ of recipe
Calories per serving	300
Grams of fat per serving	11

Exchanges per serving: 2 starch, 2 meat, 1 fat, 1 vegetable

—— Southwestern Vegetarian Chili ——

- ½ lb. pinto beans, uncooked
- ½ lb. kidney beans, uncooked
- 1 (large) onion, chopped
- 1 (large) green bell pepper, chopped
- 1 (large) red bell pepper, chopped
- 3 to 4 (large) tomatoes, chopped
- 3 to 6 Tbsp. Masa Harina
- 1 pkg. commercial chili mix
- 12 oz. beer (optional—the alcohol boils away leaving flavor only)
  cumin, celantro, garlic, chili powder, salt, pepper

Soak the beans in water at least 2 hours and as long as overnight. Cook beans in 1½ quarts of water until soft. Add chopped onion, pepper, tomato, beer, and prepackaged chili mix. Simmer uncovered at least one hour. Stir occasionally. Add extra spices if desired. Mix Masa Harina (or substitute white cornmeal) with ½ cup water to make a paste. Stir in gradually to avoid lumping. If 3 Tbsp. of Masa does not thicken the chili enough, then you may add more. Serve with low-cholesterol corn-bread (made with egg whites) and salad for a complete meal.

Nutritional Information: Beans provide fiber, protein, and calories all in the same non-fat package. Use them frequently in place of meat. Remember to combine any legume (beans) with a grain product such as rice or corn to make a complete protein source for that meal.

Number of servings	12 (approx.)
Size of servings	1 to 1½ cup
Calories per serving	250
Grams of fat	1

Exchanges per serving: 2 meat, 1 bread, 1 vegetable

Note: Precooked ground turkey or ground beef (extra lean) may be added to this recipe.

—— The Italian Super Sub ——

1 loaf French bread (Choose one that is rather flat and about 16"
   long.)
4 oz. finely sliced turkey breast
2 oz. finely sliced mozzarella cheese
4 thin slices of sharp cheddar cheese
¼ cup Kraft Zesty Italian salad dressing
1 cup finely shredded lettuce
2 (medium) tomatoes, thinly sliced
2 thin slices purple onion, separated into rings (optional)
   pepper to taste

Slice the bread in half, lengthwise, and place both halves on a cookie sheet. Spread the Italian dressing evenly over both halves. Layer meat and then cheeses on both halves (cheese should be on top). Broil until bubbly. Add vegetables to bottom half. Then place top half of the loaf containing meat and melted cheese on the other half to form a giant submarine sandwich. Place four decorative toothpicks in the loaf and cut into four evenly-sized pieces. This is a real hit at any party. Use a larger loaf (or more loaves) for larger crowds.

Nutritional Information: French bread may have white flour but it is also very low in fat and usually in salt content. The Italian dressing is only 6 calories per tablespoon as opposed to 100 calories per tablespoon for regular mayo or 80 calories per tablespoon for regular Italian dressing.

Number of servings	4
Size of serving	¼ of sandwich
Calories per serving	340 (depending on bread density)
Grams of fat per serving	7

Exchanges per serving: 3 starch, 2 meat, 1 vegetable

—— The Incredible Low-Cal Rueben ——

2 slices whole-wheat low-cal bread (or 2 slices of rye bread)
1 oz. shredded deli ham
1 slice Borden's Lite-line Swiss Cheese
2 tsp. diet margarine
2 tsp. low-cal Thousand Island
2 Tbsp. German Sauerkraut, drained and dried

Preheat a heavy nonstick skillet. Spread diet margarine on one side of each of the bread slices. Spread the other side with Thousand Island. Add the ham, cheese, and sauerkraut in sandwich style. Place the sandwich (with margarine side out) in a medium hot skillet. Brown each side. Serve with a hot soup or a chilled salad for a great lunch.

Nutritional Information: Sandwiches are in! Bread is no longer on the "No-No" list set up in the 1960s and '70s when we were protein-crazed and carbohydrate was a dirty word. Sandwiches are always a good choice when you do not use mayonnaise or high-fat meats and cheeses. Although 100 percent whole-grain breads (without additives) will always be the best choice, the newer low-calorie breads can make sandwiches very low in total calories. This basic recipe could be used for several other types of sandwiches including: grilled cheese, tuna salad, chicken salad, grilled turkey and cheese, ham and cheese on rye, vegetable and cheese, or many others.

Number of servings	1
Size of serving	1 sandwich
Calories per serving	225 (lite bread)
	325 (regular bread)
Grams of fat per serving	9

Exchanges per serving: 1 starch, 2 fat, 1 meat (lite bread)
2 starch, 2 fat, 1 meat (regular bread)

Note: By comparison, a regular Rueben sandwich may have as many as 600 to 700 calories and is loaded with fat.

Note: To reduce the sodium content, rinse the ham in cool tap water and pat dry on paper towels. This procedure will wash away much of the sodium used for food preservation.

—— Brown Rice Pilaf ——

1 cup long-grain brown rice
1 chicken bouillon cube
2 cups water
1 Tbsp. dried parsley
1 Tbsp. diet margarine
10 oz. mixed vegetables, frozen
1/4 cup red bell pepper, chopped (optional)
    salt, pepper, basil, garlic powder to taste

Bring water, bouillon, spices, and margarine to a rolling boil. Add rice and cook on low heat for 20 minutes. Then add vegetables and cook until everything is tender (usually 15 to 20 more minutes).

Nutritional Information: Brown rice should be a staple food for all of us. It provides wonderful nutrition, body fuel, fiber, and great taste in one package. Try it in other recipes.

Number of servings	6
Size of servings	heaping 1/2 cup
Calories per serving	100
Grams of fat per serving	.8

Exchanges per servings: 1 starch, 1/2 vegetable

Note: Any other type rice may also be used for this recipe. There are quick cooking varieties of brown rice. White rice may also be used, but you will miss the flavor, fiber, and nutrients of brown rice.

—— Stuffed Baked Potatoes ——

4 (medium) baking potatoes, baked
2 Tbsp. diet margarine
1 tsp. Molly McButter, sour cream flavored
2 Tbsp. green onion tips, chopped
2 Tbsp. low-fat plain yogurt
2 Tbsp. skim milk
1 oz. sharp cheddar cheese, grated
    salt, pepper, garlic powder, parsley flakes

Bake potatoes in 350° oven. Cut ⅓ of the potato off (cut lengthwise to make a boat). Scoop out inside of the potato, leaving the skin and a ¼ inch rim of potato intact. Place the potato pulp in a mixing bowl with all other ingredients except cheese. Mash ingredients together with a potato masher and restuff the mixture back into the potato shells. Top with cheese. Bake at 350° for 25 minutes. These may be made ahead of time and refrigerated for two days.

Nutritional Information: Potatoes provide energy, fiber, and nutrients. The trick is to find low-cal recipes which are palatable but not saturated with high-fat ingredients. Plain yogurt gives the sour cream taste in this recipe. The *sharp* cheddar cheese is used because it has a stronger flavor and can therefore be used in smaller quantities while providing that great taste of cheese.

Number of servings	4
Size of servings	1 potato
Calories per serving	150
Grams of fat per serving	4

Exchanges per serving: 1½ starch, 1 fat

—— **Skinny French Fries** ——

2 large Idaho potatoes, unpeeled, cut in strips
  PAM, buttery-flavored spray
  seasoned salt, pepper, or cajun seasoning mix

Wash and prepare the potatoes. Dry the surface of strips by placing them on paper towels. Spray a nonstick cookie sheet with PAM spray. Then spray the potatoes with the PAM and sprinkle with the seasoning of your choice (cajun spiced fries are great if you can find that particular seasoning mix). Bake at 350° for 30 to 35 minutes until tender and golden brown. Turn occasionally with a spatula.

Nutritional Information: You and your entire family are going to love this recipe! These fries are suitable for anyone including persons with elevated cholesterol or those who need to lose weight. Unpeeled potatoes provide fiber, starch, and many other valuable nutrients. They can be a staple in your diet as long as you keep the portion sizes reasonable.

Number of servings	4
Size of servings	equivalent to ½ large potato
Calories per serving	120
Grams of fat per serving	2

Exchanges per serving: 1½ starch, 1 fat

—— Broccoli and Cauliflower Parmesan ——

1 10-oz. pkg. frozen broccoli florets, thawed
1 10-oz. pkg. frozen cauliflower florets, thawed
2 oz. sharp cheddar cheese
3 Tbsp. grated Parmesan cheese
2 Tbsp. bread crumbs
1 Tbsp. diet margarine
   garlic salt, pepper, parsley, dry Italian seasoning mix to taste

Spray a 1 to 1½ quart casserole dish with a nonstick spray. Arrange one layer of thawed broccoli and cauliflower in the bottom of the dish. Sprinkle with half of the remaining ingredients. Add another layer of vegetables and top with the rest of the cheeses and spices. Cover and bake at 350° for 30 minutes or until the cheese bubbles.

Nutritional Information: This is a wonderful side dish for any plain meat. Note that both broccoli and cauliflower are both very high in many vitamins and minerals and were at one time considered anti-cancer foods. This is a good way to introduce people to these vegetables if they do not enjoy them steamed. Using sharp cheddar cheese instead of mild may help you use less of this high-fat food because it has such a strong flavor.

Number of servings	4
Size of servings	¼ of recipe
Calories per serving	120
Grams of fat per serving	4.5

Exchanges per serving: 2 vegetables, 1 fat, ½ meat

—— Unbelievable Oat-Bran Muffins ——

Dry ingredients
1½ cup Oat-Bran Flour (This is oat-bran flour milled very finely; oat
     bran may be used.)
1½ cup Quick Oats
  1 cup all-purpose flour
  ¼ cup sugar
  ⅓ cup wheat bran
  2 tsp. baking soda
  1 tsp. salt
  2 tsp. cinnamon

Wet ingredients
  4 egg whites, raw
 16 oz. canned crushed pineapple in own juice (fruit and juice used)
  2 cups mashed bananas
  ½ cup vegetable oil
  ¼ cup honey
  1 Tbsp. vanilla extract

Mix the dry ingredients together. In a separate bowl, mix wet ingredients. Combine the wet and dry mixtures, and mix gently. Spray muffin pan with nonstick, vegetable oil such as PAM and bake at 350° for 20 to 25 minutes.

Nutrition Information: This is the recipe you've been waiting for. It is high in pectin fibers (approximately 4 grams per muffin) which help lower serum cholesterol levels, and it contains no cholesterol or saturated fats. Note that egg whites have been used in lieu of whole eggs and corn oil instead of shortening.

Number of servings	30
Size of servings	1 muffin
Calories per serving	110
Grams of fat per serving	3

Exchanges per serving: 1 bread, 1 fat

Note: Kids of all ages love these—little ones and big ones. To make these look like cupcakes, bake them in a paper muffin liner sprayed with a nonstick vegetable oil.

—— Wheat-Bran Muffins ——

Note: Food manufacturers have really caught onto wheat-bran muffins. Recipes abound on the back of cereal and wheat bran boxes found in any grocery store.

For that reason we have not included a recipe for this one. You can easily find your own personal favorite. Just look for one that is not overly sweet. Also, try to find one which is made from a pure bran product or one of the very high-fiber cereals such as Fiber One, as opposed to the medium high-fiber cereals like Bran Flakes. Using pure wheat bran is your best choice.

—— Pumpkin Bread (or Cake) ——

- ¼ cup vegetable oil
- ¾ cup brown sugar
- ½ cup honey
- 1 16-oz. can pumpkin
- ⅔ cup water
- 4 egg whites
- 3⅓ cup unbleached or all-purpose flour
- 2 tsp. soda
- 1 tsp. salt
- ½ tsp. baking powder
- 1 tsp. cinnamon
- 1 tsp. ground cloves
- 1 tsp. pumpkin pie spice
- ⅓ cup coarsely chopped walnuts
- ½ cup golden raisins

Heat oven to 350°. Spray two 9 × 5 × 3 inch loaf pans or a Bundt pan (this makes an especially nice-looking cake) well with a nonstick vegetable oil. In a large bowl, cream the oil and sugar. Stir in the honey, pumpkin, water, and eggs until fully mixed. Then blend in dry ingredients until mixed (be careful to evenly distribute the baking soda and powder). Stir in nuts and raisins. Pour into pans and bake for about 45 to 65 minutes, depending on the size of your pans or until a wooden pick inserted in the center comes out clean.

Nutritional Information: Vegetables such as pumpkin, sweet potatoes, winter squashes, and carrots are extremely high in vitamin A.

Remember that this is one of the vitamins that help protect you against certain forms of cancer. This particular recipe is a favorite any time it is served. You can use it as a party bread (serve with a mixture of ricotta cheese and crushed pineapple as a topping). Or it can be used as a dessert (one slice from a Bundt cake pan topped with 2 tablespoons of whipped cream).

(for plain bread, no topping)

Number of servings	32
Serving size	1/32 of recipe
Calories per serving	115
Grams of fat per serving	3

Exchanges per serving: 1 starch, 1 fat (does not include topping)

—— Quick Angel Food Shortcake ——

3/4 inch slice angel food cake, homemade or commercial
1/4 cup sliced fresh or frozen strawberries
1/4 cup vanilla ice milk

Place the slice of angel food cake in the middle of a dessert saucer. Then mound 1/4 cup low-fat ice cream on top and pour sliced strawberries on top of that. Add a sprig of fresh mint on the side for garnish. (Note: the strawberries can be sliced into a bowl with a small amount of sugar or Nutrasweet; then add a little water to form its own syrup.)

Nutritional Information: Angel food cake contains no fat or cholesterol. This is very unusual for any dessert. Take advantage of this and use angel food cake in other recipes as well.

Number of servings	as many as needed (make individually)
Size of serving	as listed above
Calories per serving	150
Grams of fat per serving	2

Exchanges per serving: 1 1/2 starch, 1/2 fruit

—— Oatmeal and Molasses Cookies ——

½ cup all-purpose flour
1 tsp. baking soda
½ tsp. salt
½ tsp. ground cloves, ginger, and cinnamon (each)
½ cup sugar
⅓ cup oil or butter
2 egg whites
⅓ cup dark molasses or honey
1½ cup Quick Oats

Mix all ingredients in the order listed. Bake at 375° for 8 to 10 minutes. Makes 3 dozen 2-inch cookies.

Nutritional Information: While this may look like a traditional cookie recipe, notice that the total amount of fat and sugar have been reduced. Also, there are no egg yolks in this recipe, and if you use oil instead of butter, it is cholesterol-free. Oatmeal cookies (with or without raisins or other fruit) are among the best cookie choices in terms of overall nutritional value.

Number of servings	18
Size of servings	2 cookies
Calories per serving	124
Grams of fat per serving	4.8

Exchanges per serving: 1 starch, 1½ fat

—— Chips and Dip ——

16 oz. low-fat cottage cheese
2 Tbsp. lemon juice
½ pkg. dry Ranch Dressing Mix (or other flavoring mix)

Place cottage cheese and lemon juice in a food processor and blend until smooth (non-fat yogurt may be added for a more tart taste). Add Ranch Dressing Mix to processor and pulse until blended. Serve with any of the chip alternatives listed in the grocery shopping list, including Skinny Munchies, pretzels, or Craklesnax crackers. Or, this is also an excellent vegetable dip.

Nutritional Information: Don't scoff! Cottage-cheese dip can and does taste great, and you can eat it every day if you like. This dip is also high in protein and calcium.

Number of servings	8
Size of servings	¼ cup
Calories per serving	45
Grams of fat per serving	.5

Exchanges per serving: ½ milk or ½ meat

Add the chips

¼ cup dip plus 1 oz. Skinny Munchies

Calories per serving	165
Grams of fat per serving	4.5

Exchanges per serving: 1 starch, 1 meat, 1 fat

Note: If you eat 1 oz. of potato chips with ¼ cup sour cream dip, the figures would be:

Calories per serving	272
Grams of fat per serving	20.5

The real difference is the percent of calories coming from fat. In this case it is 68 percent fat as opposed to our low-fat alternative above which is 24 percent fat. Remember, fat turns into fat and promotes heart disease and cancer!

BIBLIOGRAPHY

American Cancer Society, Texas Division, Inc. *How to Examine Your Breasts* (May, 1988).

American Diabetic Association and American Dietetic Association. *Exchange Lists for Meal Planning* (1986).

American Dietetic Association. *Handbook of Clinical Dietetics*. New Haven: Yale University Press, 1981.

Alford, B. and M. Bogle. *Nutrition During the Life Cycle*. Englewood Cliffs, NJ: Prentice-Hall, Inc., 1982.

Amler, R. W. and H. B. Dull. *Closing the Gap: The Burden of Unnecessary Illness*. New York: Oxford University Press, 1987.

Barbo, D. M. *Medical Clinics of North America* 71 (1987): 11–22.

Begoun, P. *Blue Eyeshadow Should Still Be Illegal*. Seattle: Beginning Press, 1988.

Bell, J., et al. *Obstetrics and Gynecology* 64 (1984): 699–702.

Bente, R., T. Karsten, and C. Christiansen. *New England Journal of Medicine* 316 (1987): 173–177.

Berkeley Wellness Letter. University of California, October, 1988.

Bonita, R. and R. Scagg. *British Medical Journal* 293 (1986): 6–8.

Bush, T. L., et al. *Journal of the American Medical Association* 249 (1983): 903–906.

Byers, T. *Postgraduate Medicine* 84 (1988): 275–281.

Cade, R. and D. Marrs. *American Journal of Medicine* 77 (1984): 785–790.

Conway, J. and S. Conway. *Women in Mid-life Crisis*. Wheaton, IL: Tyndale House Publishers, 1985.

Cooper, K. Third Annual Wellness Conference; Women's Health: Issues and Insights, Dallas, TX, 1988.

Creasey, W. *Diet and Cancer*. Philadelphia: Lea and Febiger, 1985.

Daniell, H. W. *Archives of Internal Medicine* 136 (1976): 298–304.

Davitz, J. and L. Davitz. *Making It from Forty to Fifty*. New York: Random House, 1976.

Diagnostic and Statistical Manual of Mental Disorders (DSM). American Psychiatric Association, Washington, DC, 1987.

Drinkwater, B., K. Nilson, and C. Chestnut. *New England Journal of Medicine* 311 (1984): 277–281.

Eddy, D., et al. *Journal of the American Medical Association* 259 (1988): 1512–1524.

Eichner, E. *American Family Physician* 37 (1988): 217–221.

Ettinger, B. *American Journal of Obstetrics and Gynecology* 156 (1987): 1298–1303.

Fagerstrom, K. *Addictive Behavior* 3 (1978): 235-241.

Fenske, N. and C. Conrad. *American Family Physician* 37 (1988).

Forbes, R. *Postgraduate Medicine* 84 (1988): 217-221.

Genant, H., C. Cann, and B. Ettinger. *Annals of Internal Medicine* 97 (1982): 679-705.

Goodwin, D. *Anxiety*. New York: Oxford University Press, 1986.

Grant, J. *Handbook of Total Parenteral Nutrition*. Philadelphia: WB Saunders, 1980.

Gritz, E. *Cancer Journal for Physicians* 38 (1988): 194-212.

Grodin, J., P. Siiteri, and P. MacDonald. *Journal of Clinical Endocrinology and Metabolism* 36 (1973): 207-214.

Grundy, S. and P. Greenblad. *Circulation* 75 (1987): 1340A-1362A.

Hartung, G. and J. Forey. *Journal of the American Medical Association* 249 (1983): 747-750.

Hatcher, R. and F. Guest et al. *Contraceptive Technology*. New York: Irvington, 1986.

Haynes, S. and M. Feinleib. *Second Conference on the Epidemiology of Aging*, no. 80-969. Washington: NIH Publications, July 1980.

Health and Public Policy Committee, American College of Physicians, *Annals of Internal Medicine* 107 (1987): 932-936.

Health Consequences of Involuntary Smoking: A Report of the Surgeon General. Department of Health and Human Services (CDC) 87-8398 (1986).

Heaney, R., R. Recker, and P. Saville. *Journal of Laboratory and Clinical Medicine* 92 (1978): 953-963.

Heaney, R., J. Gallagher, and C. Johnston. *American Journal of Clinical Nutrition* 36 (1982): 986-1013.

Hennekens, C. H. *Cancer* 53(4) (1984): 1020-1024.

Holmes, T. J. and R. H. Rahe. *Journal of Psychosomatic Research* 11 (1967).

Huppert, L. *Medical Clinics of North America* 71 (1987): 23-39.

Iddenden, D. *Medical Clinics of North America* 71 (1987): 87-94.

Imai, A. *Hypertension* 8 (1986): 223-228.

Javitz, J. and L. Javitz. *Making It from Forty to Fifty*. New York: Random House, 1976.

Johnson, S. *Clinical Obstetrics and Gynecology* 30 (1987): 367.

Karafin, L. and M. Coll. *Medical Clinics of North America* 71 (1987): 111-121.

Kennedy, R., C. Baum, and M. Forbes. *Obstetrics and Gynecology* 65 (1985): 441.

Lazar, A. and P. Lazar. *The Female Patient* 13 (1988).

Leaf, D. *Postgraduate Medicine* 84 (1988): 75-81.

Levy, R. *American Journal of Medicine* 80 (1986): 18-22.

Lindsay, R. *American Journal of Obstetrics and Gynecology* 156 (1987): 1347-1351.

Lippman, S. *Texas Medicine* 84 (1988): 48-53.

McCarron, D. and C. Morris. *Annals of Internal Medicine* 103 (1985): 825-831.

Mazess, R. *Dalborg Stiftsrbogtrykkeri* (1984): 57-63.

Milhorn, H. *American Family Physician* 37 (1988): 175-183.

Minirth, F. and P. Meier. *Happiness Is a Choice*. Grand Rapids: Baker Book House, 1978.

Mishell, D. *Menopause: Philosophy and Pharmacology*. Chicago: Year Book Medical Publishers, 1987.

National Academy of Sciences/National Research Council. *Recommended Dietary Allowances*. 9th rev. ed. 1980.

National Cancer Institute. *American Family Physician*. May 1984.

Notelovitz, M., C. Fields, and K. Caramelli. *American Journal of Obstetrics and Gynecology* 154 (1986): 1009.

Notelovitz, M. *Clinical Obstetrics and Gynecology* 30 (1987).

Odom, M. and B. Carr. *Comprehensive Therapy* 13 (1987): 58–63.

Paffenbarger, R., et al. *New England Journal of Medicine* 314 (1986): 605–613.

Papier, C. and S. Stellman. *Women and Cancer* 11 (1987): 267–277.

Parfitt, A. *Clinical Obstetrics and Gynecology* 30 (1987).

Piver, M. *The Female Patient* 13 (1988): 22–32.

Ravnikar, V. *Modern Medicine* 56 (1988): 54–69.

Riis, B., K. Thomsen, and C. Christiansen. *New England Journal of Medicine* 316 (1987): 173–177.

Rippe, J., et al. *Journal of the American Medical Association* 259 (1988): 2720–2724.

Rubin, P. *Clinical Oncology*. 6th ed. American Cancer Society, 1983.

Rubin, S. *Medical Clinics of North America* 71 (1987): 59–69.

Rutgers Center of Alcohol Studies. *Journal of Studies on Alcohol* 36 (1975): 124.

Rutherford, G., et al. *Western Journal of Medicine* 147 (1987): 104–108.

Sandler, D., A. Wilcox, and R. Everson. *Lancet* 1 (February 9, 1985): 312–315.

Saville, P. *Journal of Bone and Joint Surgery* 47 (1965): 492–499.

Schatzkin, A., et al. *New England Journal of Medicine* 316 (1987): 1169–1173.

Shangold, M. and G. Mirkin. *The Complete Sports Medicine Book for Women*. New York: Simon and Schuster, 1985.

Sheridan, D. and I. Winogrond. *The Preventive Approach to Patient Care*. New York: Elsevier, 1987.

Silverberg, S. and R. Lindsey. *Medical Clinics of North America* 71 (1987): 41–57.

Sneed, S. and J. McIlhaney. *PMS: What It Is and What You Can Do About It*. Grand Rapids: Baker Book House, 1988.

Speroff, L., et al. *Clinical Gynecologic Endocrinology and Infertility*. 3rd ed. Baltimore: Williams and Wilkins, 1983.

Stoudemire, A., et al. *General Hospital Psychiatry* 8 (1986): 387–394.

Sullivan, J., et al. *Annals of Internal Medicine* 108 (1988): 358–363.

Utian, W. *Menopause in Modern Perspective*. New York: Appleton-Century-Crofts, 1980.

Washington, A., R. Johnson, and L. Sanders. *Journal of the American Medical Association* 257 (1987): 2070–2072.

Women's Health. Report of the Public Health Service Task Force on Women's Health Issues. Vol. 3. U.S. Dept. Health and Human Services, 1985.

Whitehead, M. and D. Fraser. *American Journal of Obstetrics and Gynecology* 156 (1987): 1313–1322.

Williams, S. *Essentials of Nutrition and Diet Therapy*. 4th ed. St. Louis: Mosby College Publishing, 1988.

INDEX